SPANISH VIGNETTES

AN OFFBEAT LOOK INTO SPAIN'S CULTURE, SOCIETY & HISTORY

BY NORMAN BERDICHEVSKY

SANTANA BOOKS

First published in 2004

Designed by Chris Fajardo

Spanish Vignettes
is published by Ediciones Santana S.L.,
Apartado 422, 29640 Fuengirola (Málaga).
Phone 952 485 838. Fax 952 485 367.
Email: info@santanabooks.com
www.santanabooks.com

Printed in Spain by Graficas San Pancracio S.L.
Depósito Legal: MA-1.731/2004
ISBN 84-89954-40-2

DEDICATION & ACKNOWLEDGMENT

I owe my original enchantment and fascination with Spain, its language and culture to my teachers at Stuyvesant High School and CCNY, 1957-62. I remember how proud I was to be awarded a high school certificate for proficiency in Spanish upon graduation and the feeling this gave me that even without travelling, new worlds had been opened up for my exploration.

Those interests lay dormant for many years until circumstances led me to long-term residence here, proving that nothing is ever taught in vain. Knowledge of Spanish enabled me immediately to appreciate a charming and welcoming environment that for many of my English-speaking friends and acquaintances in Spain was still too new and obscured by the dark veil of the language barrier. This encouraged me to unveil our lovely Spanish hostess to all those who made the best decision of their lives to come and live in Spain but still don't realize how much they are missing.

I owe a great deal to my friend, Mr. Peter Sandiford, the former Director of the British Council in Madrid, who generously volunteered his time to proofread the manuscript and offer many helpful suggestions that have made this a better book. My thanks also go to Antonio Díaz Grau of the local Santiago de la Ribera municipal library for his assistance, and once again to my wife Raquel for her counsel, proof-reading and essential computer skills.

I dedicate this book to the memory of a close childhood friend, the late Ralph Zakar, former Captain in the New York City Police Department and a recipient of its highest decoration for valour; The Medal of Honour. Ralph will be sorely missed by all those who knew him and were honoured to call him friend. His untimely death prevented him from visiting the lands of his ancestors in Greece and Spain. He was delighted to learn that the name "Zakar" was mentioned in a comprehensive list of Sepharadi names that appeared in a recently published book in Spain (*"El Lobby Judío - Poder y Mitos de los Actuales Hebreos Españoles"*; by Alfonso Torres, *La Esfera de los Libros*, Madrid. 2002).

His infectious laugh and love of debate will remain with me always.

CONTENTS

ECONOMY

FESTIVALS & PAGEANTS

THE FOUR OFFICIAL SPANISH LANGUAGES

ILLUSTRATIONS

INTRODUCTION

Spain has become more than just a major tourist attraction for millions of foreign visitors. It is now home to well over half a million north Europeans and in many coastal areas one hears more English, German, Swedish, Norwegian or Dutch than Spanish.

Many among those who live in Spain all year round have acquired only the most rudimentary Spanish and realize that they are generally excluded from participation in the rich social, cultural and political life of the country. Even for those who are past the language barrier, there is a considerable gap to overcome in becoming familiar with the culture, politics, history, arts, traditions, cuisine and folklore of their adopted country.

This book is NOT an encyclopaedia or textbook on Spanish culture. It presents 34 topics of interest for those who feel the need to relate to what they see and hear on radio and television and to what they overhear of the conversations of their Spanish neighbours.

It is an inside look at the same type of subjects involving society, politics, history, foreign affairs, art, music, food and drink, sports and the holidays about which they feel most likely to engage in discussion and be familiar with in their countries of origin.

EDITOR'S NOTE: Place names in Spain are given according to their Castilian Spanish spelling (i.e. Cataluña rather than the Catalan *Catalunya* or the English Catalonia; Sevilla instead of Seville, etc.). The same applies to Spanish and Catalan personal names; Dalí instead of Dali, etc. Foreign place names are spelt as they are in English (Lisbon, and not Lisboa).

En un lugar de la Mancha, de cuyo nombre no quiero acordarme...

SPORTS AND ENTERTAINMENT

Spain's Great Football Rivalry

A sked to select the greatest football rivalries in the UK, few British fan(atic)s would disagree that for an intra-city London battle, it would be Arsenal vs. Tottenham. On a higher level of regional strife with ethnic or religious overtones, it must be Celtic vs. Rangers and on a "national level" it has to be England vs. Scotland. Imagine now all three combined into one and you would still not reach the epic confrontation of historic rivalry fuelled by mythology and passion that exists each time Real Madrid plays FC Barcelona (nicknamed affectionately as *Barça*).

The Regional Rivalry

One cannot understand the passions aroused without a familiarity with the political history of Spain and the sense of loss and displacement felt by many Catalans going all the way back to the historic fifteenth century merger of the Kingdom of Aragon-Cataluña with Castilla. Catalan nationalists are convinced that Castilla usurped Cataluña's dominant position as the leading region in the Iberian peninsular as a result of Columbus's voyages and the expansion of Spain overseas in the Americas and the Philippines, shifting the centre of commercial prosperity away from the Mediterranean.

It was not until 1713, following an uprising brutally suppressed by the central government in Madrid, that local Cataluñan autonomy and administration were ended, and official use of Catalan were superseded by Castilian Spanish. No other part of Spain later identified so strongly with the anti-monarchist and Republican cause as Cataluña. The region has always had a more commercial, industrial, liberal and radical character than Castilla, and has been influenced by French and Italian ideas and fashions that are expressed in an appreciation of elegant styles in art and architecture.

The Castilian heart of the Spanish state most accurately reflects the values of Medieval Christianity and devout Catholicism – the haughty pride and exaggerated sense of honour and disdain for manual labour exemplified by the quest of Don Quixote to achieve the status of a knight errant and create a just world, but one in which everyone knows his place. The opposite pole is represented by Cataluña, a region whose people are characterised by commercial astuteness, ambition, risk-taking, international trade, sobriety, and literacy. These values were often held in contempt by the wealthy Castilian land-owning class. The Catholic Church in Castilla and Falangist propaganda during the Spanish Civil War regarded Catalan separatism as an indication of the "Judeo-Catalan Conspiracy" to destroy Spain. Support for a republic, socialism and a reassertion of the Catalan language made relations with Madrid always difficult.

The language issue became a central tenant of the movement for Catalan autonomy or independence. The language was suppressed under Franco who prohibited its use in education, the press, and theatre and even encouraged campaigns to prevent people from speaking Catalan in public. These included putting stickers up in telephone booths urging callers to conduct their conversation in Castilian, and who were insulted by the exhortation in common use by Francoist officials to "Speak Christian!" – as if they were natives of an underdeveloped, remote and primitive country.

The insult has been historically paid back by the public assertions of some Catalan nationalists that Castilian Spanish has already seen the last of its glory days and is now spoken badly, mostly by illiterates from the third world. Such views are often expressed publicly. This intense emotional baggage was transferred to the field of sport at the end of the nineteenth century.

The Teams' Founding

The blue and burgundy-red colours of *Barça* were first worn on Christmas eve 1899. The first players were predominantly English and Swiss residents of the city, many of them prominent businessmen who missed the recreational pastime of their home country – and for quite a few years, local residents referred to the team as *los ingleses*! Real Madrid with its uniform of virginal white was founded in 1902. Its white colour was a symbol of "purity" and may have been purposely chosen even at that early date to make the strongest possible contrast with the Barcelona team.

The Real Madrid hymn declares that:

> *De las glorias deportivas*
> *que campean por España*
> *va el Madrid con su bandera*
> *limpia y blanca que no empaña*

> "Of the glories of sport
> that fight on behalf of Spain,
> Comes Madrid with its clean and white flag
> that is never tarnished"

To be as contrary as possible, Barcelona praises the vivid colours of its own team:

> *Tot el camp*
> *'s un clam*
> *som la gent blaugrana,*
> *tant se val d'on venim,*
> *si del sud o del nord,*
> *ara estem d'acord, estem d'acord,*
> *una bandera ens agermana.*
> *blau grana al vent,*
> *un crit valent,*
> *tenim un nom,*
> *el sap tothom:*
> *¡BARÇA !... ¡BARÇA!... ¡ BARÇA!*

> "The entire camp
> is one clan,
> this blue-red people.
> Wherever they may come from,
> whether the south or the north,
> they all agree, they all are of one accord,

the Scarlet-Blue makes all of us brothers.
The Scarlet-blue is borne by the wind,
it makes a valiant cry.
It has a name
that everyone knows...
BARÇA!... BARÇA!... BARÇA!

At the end of the nineteenth century, there was already tension in the air between the two rival regions and cities. Few Catalans identified with the remnants of the Spanish empire in Cuba and the Philippines, which the monarchy tried in vain to maintain, resulting in a war with the United States in 1898. From its inception, Real Madrid (Royal Madrid) by its very name was identified with the monarchy as well as Castilla, and regarded as the darlings of the establishment.

Nationwide support

Not until the 1920s did the matches between Real Madrid and F.C. *Barça* become THE sporting event of the year, eclipsing whoever won the national cup title. Both Madrid and Barcelona continued to attract new migrants from rural areas of Spain, whose easiest and most secure way of winning acceptance to a new life in the big city was to immediately become a rabid fan of the local club.

What is truly amazing is that the rivalry has become national in scope. No matter where one lives in Spain, there are local social clubs of team supporters known as *peñas* for both Real Madrid and *Barça*. Catalan nationalism and separatism were regarded as the greatest internal threat to the dictatorial regime of Primo de Rivera, who had assumed power in 1923. The steps taken then seem tame compared to the later repression carried out by General Franco at the end of the Civil War, but they immediately signalled to all *Barça* supporters that sport could not be separated from politics.

Political Overtones

The use of the Catalan flag was prohibited and the club's files of members had to be submitted for police inspection. Castilian Spanish was made obligatory for use in all the club's announcements, both written and spoken. Until World War I, the club had largely been controlled by wealthy businessmen unwilling to rock the boat, but in the 1930s, during the depression, control was wrested away by those who identified with *Accio Catalá*, a left wing nationalist movement that broke with the past suspicions regarding sport as cheap mass entertainment or old Marxist ideology, identifying it as just another "opiate of the people" like religion.

A campaign initiated by the Catalan journalist Josep Sunyol made the newspaper *La Rambla* the club's mouthpiece. No one better expressed the sense of mission of the club that transcended football, and became the origin of the slogan that *Barça* "is more than a club". He wrote that, "To speak of sport is to speak of race, enthusiasm, and the optimistic struggle of youth. To speak of citizenship is to speak of Catalan civilisation, liberalism, democracy and spiritual endeavour".

The ferocity of the Civil War (1936-39) left a bitter legacy that endured for two generations and has only recently abated. Atrocities that shame the world of sport were committed by both sides. Sunyol became President of FC Barcelona and the club's first real martyr. He was executed without trial by Franco's soldiers during the Civil War.

On the other side, Catalan anarchist fans of *Barça* seized and executed the retired 90-year-old General Joaquin Milans del Bosch in an act of "revenge" for his "crime" of 11 years earlier. The general had been ordered by dictator Primo de Rivera to close the *Barça* stadium in 1925, following whistling by local fans that drowned out the playing of the Spanish national anthem. The club was also forced to pay a fine and its activities were suspended for six months. During the Civil War, the *Barça* team was sent abroad to play and raise funds for the Republic in the United States and Latin America. Many players did not return.

Following the Civil War

By the end of the war, there was a fear that *Barça* might not even be reconstituted under pro-Franco management. The traditional rivalry had now become an opportunity to settle old scores and demonstrate that Catalan separatist hopes were dashed forever. The most notorious incident of intimidation occurred in the 1941 return match played in Madrid's famous Bernabeu stadium after *Barça* had defeated Real Madrid 3-0 in their first encounter at home. The Madrid crowd was so hostile that both players and referee feared for their lives. The police on hand also ensured that *Barça* was sufficiently intimidated and the result was an 11-1 defeat!

In 1943, following further violent clashes between the rival fans, the government demanded that both club presidents stand down. In Madrid, the legendary player Santiago Bernabeu took over and held the post until his death in 1978. The 90,000-capacity Real Madrid stadium now bears his name.

In the years that followed, government agents regularly cooperated with the leadership of Real Madrid to ensure that any foreign stars contemplating signing a contract with *Barça* encountered "visa problems". In the 1950s and 60s, Spanish television covered every important match played by Real Madrid, while almost totally ignoring FC Barcelona – thereby encouraging fans from all over the country to identify with the team favoured by the regime.

The post-Franco era

Towards the end of Franco's life, and with the advent of a new democratic regime, the rivalry has been contested on a "level playing field". One of the most famous incidents in the mixed history of sport and politics was the first match played between the two rival clubs immediately following the death of General Franco in December, 1975.

The police could not prevent thousands of fans from taking the forbidden Catalan flag with them into the Barcelona stadium and hoisting it in a massive demonstration of repressed patriotism when *Barça* scored its first goal in the match. The demonstration of defiance against the entire period of Franco rule was repeated even more loudly when the team scored the winning goal in the final minutes of play to win a 2-1 victory.

In 1957, Barcelona became home to the world famous Camp Nou stadium, an architectural wonder with a seating capacity of over 100,000, – and filled to capacity for every match with Real Madrid. The inauguration of the stadium was also an occasion for open demonstrations of Catalan nationalism. The stadium has an adjoining museum devoted to the history of the club. In 2000, it attracted 1,156,000 visitors surpassing even the Picasso museum and making it the most popular tourist attraction in all of Cataluña!

Passions sometime still run amok. Extreme *Barça* fans who are spoiling for a fight and follow the club into the heartland of arch-rival Real Madrid or wherever the club plays a particularly notable opponent, unashamedly call themselves *cules* (asses) and *boixos nois* (our boys). Players who have switched teams have received death threats. The popular star Luis Figo has received many. He is Portuguese and was a top player for *Barça* until lured by more money to play for Real Madrid. Figo could hardly be accused of treason since he is always at his patriotic best only in Portuguese national colours playing against the united Spanish national team.

FC Barcelona, in spite of all its devotion and patriotism and its 108,000 dues-paying club members (the largest fan club in the world according to the official website) is now like any other professional sports team, run as a multi-million euro business. The best players are bought on the basis of their skill and not for any local sentimental patriotism. Whereas in the 1920s, almost the entire starting team were Catalans, there is only a single native-born Catalan on the roster of the starting team today.

Police still have their hands full when each match approaches and follow young enthusiasts who go out of their way to be provocative, especially when they travel with the team on an away game at the rival stadium and city to show their bravery. I think most foreigners would prefer 90 minutes alone in the bullring.

Bullfighting – an essential part of the Spanish identity?

Public opinion polls in Spanish magazines and newspapers a few years ago showed that well over half of Spaniards have "no interest or enthusiasm" for bullfighting. Nevertheless, whatever the criticism against Spain from abroad may be, most people here instinctively protect what they have come to regard as an essential part of their national identity.

The skills of the Spanish *matador* have been a rich source of folklore, inspiring great works of music (the opera *Carmen*, for example), novels and short stories (Hemingway's *Death in the Afternoon*), sculpture, paintings, costumes and poster art. *Aficionados* regard bullfighting more as an art than a mere form of sport or entertainment.

Prehistoric origins

The origins of bullfighting are mysterious, predating the domestication of animals. The traditional Spanish bullfight, the *corrida*, is the outcome of a long development that began with the fascination of the prehistoric caveman with the hunt for wild bison. Many cave paintings in Spain testify to the hunting of these animals, that were held in awe due to their savage nature and tasty meat.

Most features of the bull – its blood, crescent shaped horns and sexual organ – were all signs of divinity in the ancient world. In early

Mediterranean religions, gods were pictured as part man, part bull (*minotaurs*). These were especially prevalent on the Greek islands and in Akkadia-Sumeria (modern Iraq). Ancient cylinder seals show legendary heroes wrestling the "Bull of Heaven" that wore a special belt for wrestlers to grab.

One of the most famous pre-historic monuments in Spain is the massive collection of stone bull statues in Avila province that clearly indicate the bull's importance in early Iberian mythology. A Minoan bronze figure and a palace painting from Crete depict a young man leaping over the horns of a bull and landing on its back. Apparently this was some ritual sport – a kind of pole-vault and somersault, defying the awesome power of the bull.

Roman and Arab times

The Roman arena occasionally featured bulls in spectacles, but there is no evidence to point to any mortal combat between men on foot and the bulls. The first written evidence in any ceremonial bullfight dates back to the 1135 coronation of Alfonso VI of Castilla. However, bullfighting and bull hunting were most likely practised in Visigothic and Moorish times. In Cataluña, Galicia and the Canary Islands, where Arab domination was short-lived, bullfighting never developed quite the same popularity as in Castilla and Andalucía.

The close association of nobility with mounted bullfights has become part of the Spanish language of today, with the word for gentleman (*caballero*) directly recalling the horse (*caballo*), which was central to the lifestyle of the Spanish aristocracy. Many old paintings show mounted riders attacking bulls with long lances, often accompanied by dogs.

The *matador* on foot

The transition from mounted bullfighting *(rejoneos)*, which is still accorded a more central role in the typical Portuguese bullfight, to the now classical Spanish style of the *matador* on foot with his cape and sword, took many centuries to evolve.

The Spanish church, at various times, was vehemently opposed to the spectacle of a man in mortal combat with a beast. It saw bullfighting as an obvious reminder of the pagan days of the Roman Empire. Even Queen Isabel tried to end it, encouraging Cardinal Torquemada to issue a treatise against the practice in 1489.

However, to her surprise and disgust, the Vatican itself staged a bullfight in 1493 in celebration of the fall of Granada to the Christian

23

monarchs of Spain. Apparently, succeeding Popes had second thoughts and Pope Pius V issued a ban on bullfighting not long afterwards, and this was repeated by Pope Sixto V in 1583, when it became apparent that the original one had had little effect. Carlos V, the first Hapsburg king to be elected Holy Roman Emperor, arrived in Spain in 1516. Among the numerous ceremonies of welcome were displays of bull wrestling. In spite of the papal bans, it had become evident that the spectacle was a very popular form of mass entertainment in Spain.

It was not until the Bourbon Dynasty ascended to the throne of Spain in the eighteenth century that the nobles were directed to refrain from their "ostentatious displays" of mounted bullfights. These spectacles were deemed to be incompatible with their obligations to the throne. The lowly foot servants then took the initiative of demonstrating their own skills and it is from this change in the *corrida* format that the modern tradition of *matadors* has developed.

This new spectacle won great popularity. Kings and entrepreneurs alike built circular bullrings and the traditional *pasodoble* or march-rhythm music and the colourful costumes gradually developed into the traditional *corrida* that has endured until today.

Bullfighting as popular entertainment

At first, the royal edicts limited the proceeds of any spectacle in the bullring to charity but, by the end of the Napoleonic Wars, bullfighting had clearly become established as a money-making operation, which grew in popularity.

Many tourists are surprised to discover that there are other competitive spectator events in bullrings that are practised by totally unarmed young men, recalling how the prehistoric hunters must have realised how agility and cunning could outwit the brute strength of the bull.

Such competitive exhibitions or *Recortes* are exercises in "getting the hell out of the way" that require deft manoeuvring, dodging, jumping or scrambling over a fence. The winner is chosen by a panel of judges and receives a prize that can at best be described as ludicrous when the threat of serious injury or even death is always present.

Other well-known events involving bulls include the famous Pamplona bull running in July, reported on in detail by Hemingway. This event usually causes serious injuries to a number of participants. It is hard for many foreigners, especially Brits, to avoid reacting with other than the immediate comment of "...the idiots got what they deserved." Nevertheless, for many young Spanish men there is no better way to demonstrate their courage and manliness. Ancient history has endured right into the twenty-first century!

There is also a *Comic Corrida* featuring clowns and midgets. In fact, it seems that only a striptease done to the accompaniment of the *pasodoble* is missing from the programme. Today, top professional Spanish bullfighters earn fabulous incomes. Unlike in the past, when bullfighters came almost exclusively from the poorest class, present day *matadors* are held in high social regard, practically on a par with top models and movie stars.

In 1991, a law was passed in the Spanish Parliament that defined bullfighting as a "cultural tradition". There is even a special Spanish term – *Tauromaquia* – that could roughly be translated as "The Art and Science of Bullfighting" and covers all the cultural and artistic aspects of what is regarded as much more than a sport. The names and nicknames of famous *matadors* such as Antonio Ordóñez, "Manolete" (Manuel Rodríguez) and "Joselito" (José Miguel Arroyo) are universally recognized by Spaniards, both young and old.

Equally, a significant amount of revenue today comes from tourist interest in bullfighting. Outside Spain, bullfights take place regularly in Southern France and Portugal, and the Spaniards also brought the spectacle to Latin America, where it took deep root in Mexico, as well as being popular in Colombia, Venezuela and Peru. In the remainder of Latin America, most notably in Argentina, bullfighting had become so closely accepted as part of the heritage of Spanish colonial rule that it became fashionable and patriotic to discourage it.

Bullfighting during the revolutionary zeal of the Republic

A similar attempt to "adapt" bullfighting and rid it of its image as an ultra-conservative expression of Spanish culture occurred following the victory of the "Popular Front" in the 1936 elections, and in the following year of euphoric Left-Wing revolutionary fervour in many parts of the Republic, especially in Cataluña, to radically change every aspect of society.

In the bullring, this took the form of abandoning the ultra-traditional dress code of the *matadors*. They were required to wear "civilian clothes". Workers' overalls were particularly favoured to give the sport a "proletarian" flavour – as was the communist clenched fist salute instead of a formal bow. This passing fad disappeared with the increased intensity of fighting during the Civil War, and the mobilisation of most *matadors*. No attempt has been made since to alter the ritual of the *corrida* in any way.

The campaign of the anti-bullfighting camp

The anti-bullfighting campaign in Spain has made special appeals to the Catholic Church and directly to the Vatican to no avail. Their posters and postcards are humorous and often bitingly satirical. Their principal slogan is *Ni arte Ni cultura* (Neither Art nor Culture). They have conclusively documented the injuries to the animal's respiratory system as well as muscle and bone structure and explained how the many thrusts and insertions of the spears by the picadors immobilize the animal's muscular coordination.

This is a clear sign that there is a growing fear in Spain that eventually the European Union will make a move to ban the sport and that it is therefore critical to enlist greater support of the institution as a part of Spain's national culture.

There are also signs of growing antagonism over the issue between foreign residents and Spaniards. The Alfaz del Pi (Alicante, Spain) city hall banned a festival scheduled for the celebration of its patron saint's day at the beginning of November 1999 that included a *corrida*. Foreigners in the area outnumber native Spaniards. The result was a financial loss, causing charges of "interference".

Opponents of the *corrida* were incensed when the ban on entry to children under 14 years of age, in force since 1928, was recently lifted, despite opposition from the *Defensor del Pueblo* (Ombudsman). The ban, however, has been maintained in Cataluña. This is clearly an issue that will not go away.

Opposition to bullfighting has been strongest in Cataluña, where it is a major political issue. As an integral part of the struggle to highlight the separate identity of Cataluña, and following the collection of close to a quarter of a million signatures on a petition, the Barcelona city council approved a ban on bullfighting in April, 2004.

Supporters of the *corrida* maintain this is purely a political ploy by those Catalan nationalists who regard the bullfight – along with gypsy and flamenco traditions – as misrepresenting what are purely Castilian habits and traits that have been accepted abroad as if they were synonymous with all of Spain and Spanish culture. Clearly the opera Carmen has had a major part to play in this. In any case, the ban has yet to take effect, as it requires the approval of the regional government of all of Cataluña.

Defenders and opponents

The *corrida* season begins in February in the Madrid suburb of Valdemorillo, located in the Guadarrama mountains, and lasts until September. More than two million tickets are purchased by the *aficionados* for the thousand or so annual *corridas*. This compares with well over ten million tickets sold annually for first and second division Spanish football matches.

By any account this is impressive, all the more so since many observers predicted that bullfighting was on its way out and that its decline would be accelerated by the disappearance of the authoritative, traditionalist Franco regime; but this obviously has not been the case.

Some sociologists believe that the renewed popularity of the *corrida* is in large measure a reaction to the forces of the European Community that have tended to greatly reduce national differences. It is also a business providing seasonal or part-time employment to almost 150,000 workers, and generating an income of close to £500 million.

Supporters of the *corrida* have attacked opponents as hypocritical and point out that fox hunting in Britain, a sport for the rural gentry, has endured and continues to represent many of the finest traditions of a wealthy county set that still prides itself on the skills of horsemanship and an aristocratic lineage that goes back to the Middle Ages.

In spite of repeated attempts to ban it, the foxhunting lobby in Britain remains strong enough to oppose until now an outright prohibition. As with bullfighting, supporters of this tradition maintain that it is an indispensable part of their way of life and does not interfere with other people's rights.

Nor is it true as one might imagine that bullfighting is a political issue dividing Left and Right. Many foreign observers believe that the Socialists must be opposed to it just as the Labour Party is opposed to fox hunting in Britain. This is not the case. Leading members of the *PSOE* (Spanish Socialist Party), including former Prime Ministers such as Felipe González, have come from the heartland of Andalucía, the most traditional bullfighting region, and are "*aficionados*".

Measures have been taken to end some abuses that animal rights activists, perhaps realising their campaign to end bullfighting entirely is not realistic, have insisted upon as a bare minimum. These include age requirements to prevent bulls less than four years old from participating, and careful medical examinations to ensure that the bulls' horns have not been shaved to upset their balance.

On the side of the *matadors*, the discovery of penicillin in 1928 by the

27

Scottish doctor Alexander Fleming has been the greatest single factor in reducing fatalities. It is for this reason that practically every Spanish town has a street named *Calle Dr. Fleming*. There is a large statue of the good doctor in the Plaza outside Madrid's main bullring, and he visited Spain more than once as an honoured guest of the bullfighting community.

Bullfighting has even given the English language one of its most picturesque expressions, "The Moment of Truth" *(La hora de la verdad)*, the decisive moment when the *matador* takes aim to deliver what should be the death blow. It will continue to be an important part of the Spanish scene for many years to come. ●

Pelota, the fastest ball game in the world

S ince most English speakers in Spain don't live in the Basque country and usually don't flip channels to watch Spanish language television, they are likely to miss out on what has to be the most exciting and certainly the fastest ball game in the world – *pelota*, also known as *Jai-alai*.

Outside the Basque country, the game is also popular at the northern end of the Costa Blanca, although here, too, many of the players are Basque. Americans who have spent vacation time in Florida are much more likely to have seen a game of *Jai-alai*, and many of them have become sworn fans.

If you played handball as a teenager against a single wall in the schoolyard, you have only the most rudimentary idea of the Spanish version. Those memories are light years behind the game the Basques invented and have perfected wherever they are – in Spain, France, Florida, the Philippines, Argentina, Peru, Corsica, Mexico or Cuba.

The game is very much a part of Basque identity and every village worthy of its name has at least its own church, a cemetery and a *frontón*, the building that houses the *pelota* court. These are the symbols of the Basque people. The church stands for the devotion of the Basques to the Catholic faith, a cemetery symbolizes respect for their ancestors who have lived in the rugged ridges and mountain valleys of the western Pyrenees and adjacent rocky coasts, and the fronton indicates the love of an exuberant sporting life.

Origins, development and the *Cesta*

Handball played against a single wall goes back to the ancient Greeks, who called it *pilos* and played it outdoors on rough ground as a form of exercise. The Romans called it *pilatta*, and it was later played with practically no change at some of the royal courts under French and English kings in the fourteenth and fifteenth centuries.

It is, however, the Basque version of the game we know as *pelota vasca* that is a unique national sport. *Jai-alai* is, of course, the Basque term for the game. It means "merry festival" or "happy game" and originated in the Basque country as part of the celebrations revolving around religious festivals.

The Basques originally played *pelota* with their bare hands, then with leather gloves, wooden paddles and primitive rackets. The curved woven basket known as a *cesta*, that is able to propel the ball much faster, came into use in the mid-1800's. According to the sport's folklore, a young French Basque who couldn't afford an expensive leather glove tried hurling the ball with a curved basket that he found in his mother's kitchen – and the idea caught on.

The *cesta* changed much of the game due to the higher speed and skill required to both catch and throw the ball. *Pelota* players often develop their playing arm (always the right), so that it becomes several inches longer than the other, due to the tremendous force exerted. Good players often use both arms, just as tennis players do in backhand shots. Each player (known as a *pelotari*) has his individual *cesta* tailored to his specifications.

The game was played on stone courtyards and against church walls and it is still played this way in many Basque villages today. Another major innovation was the use of rubber balls, a development that made the sport even faster. Several players have been timed in hurling the ball with a *cesta* at speeds over 180 miles per hour!

It is not only the speed of the ball that makes the game exciting and an incredible test of eye and hand coordination. The part of the *cesta* where the ball enters is only a fraction move than 3 inches wide, and the ball's diameter is almost 2 1/2 inches, which leaves just 1/2 inch or less for error on either side. This is a very narrow margin, especially when the ball is curving or wobbling and usually has quite a lot of spin on it,   which is difficult for the audience to see until the ball bounces or hits the wall.

If you are a "lefty", forget about playing the game. Due to the centuries-old tradition, all players are required to wear the *cesta* on their right hand. This prevents needless accidents because the sidewall is on the left side of the court and it would be dangerous and almost impossible for players to throw with their left hand. In the professional game, four players have been killed either by being struck with the ball or the *cesta*.

The game and Basque Nationalism

Today, matches of both *pelota* (without the *cesta*) and *Jai-alai* (with the *cesta*) are shown regularly on several local Spanish television stations in the Basque country and Valencia. An indication of the intensity many Basques feel towards the game as a symbol of their identity occurred in San Sebastian during the "minute of silence" in memory of the victims of the atrocious terrorist attack that occurred in Madrid on 11 March 2004, which at first was thought to have been perpetrated by ETA (the illegal Basque separatist organization). Not all the fans were silent and there were occasional cries of "The Police are Assassins!" Others came to the match with signs bearing the names of ETA members who had died in confrontations with the police.

At the last world championship of *pelota* in Cuba, the Basque team was allowed to march independently from the Spanish team and even allowed to carry the *ikurriña* (Basque flag). When the Spanish government subsequently forbade them to do such a thing again at an international sporting event, a special tournament called *Kultur Gizakera* was created that allowed the Basque team to act as if they represented an independent country in a separate "world championship" of Basque *pelota. Kultur Gizakera*, defined as cultural and non-political, was the initiative of the sculptor Jorge Oteiza, and has gained the support of noted personalities from the Basque region in the arts and sports world.

The game has been used by a prominent film director, himself a Basque, as a metaphor for the conflict between Basque nationalism and loyalty to a united Spain. *La Pelota Vasca: la Piel Contra la Piedra* (Basque Ball: Leather Against Stone), is the most controversial Spanish film (later turned into a book) for a generation.

Its director, Julio Medem, grew up in San Sebastian and moved to Madrid in 1997, hoping to escape the suffocating political atmosphere imposed by Basque nationalism. However, he soon became emotionally involved and wounded by the anti-Basque attitude of the Spanish mass media and decided to devote his skill to producing a movie that would tell both sides of the story. The result is a documentary that is a powerful statement of the director's views. It is a metaphor of the game with fast paced "returns of the ball," representing claims and counter-claims.

The film is a dialogue (or a "conversation between the deaf" according to some critics) between antagonists: the ball becomes a point of union between the two sides. It presents some 100 people from all walks of life and political viewpoints to talk about 30 years of bloodshed and the growing confrontation between the centrist government of former Prime Minister, José María Aznar, and the nationalists of the *PNV* who run the Basque regional government.

Culture Minister Pilar del Castillo has declared that Medem had placed ETA and the Spanish state on the same moral level and claimed that the film resembled the work of German film director Leni Riefenstahl, who portrayed the Nazi Party rallies in Nuremberg in the 1930s. It also leaves a clear, albeit subjective and, for many, controversial message: that only a referendum among Basques can resolve the region's problems. Most Spaniards would disagree.

The game in the U.S.

The sport was seen for the first time in the United States at the 1904 St. Louis World's Fair and, as a special concession to Spain (host of the 1992 Olympic Games in Barcelona), the game was featured as an Olympic sport for the first time. There are five courts in Florida and two more in Connecticut and Rhode Island. America's first permanent *jai-alai frontón* was built in 1924 near Hialeah race track.

The court, legal serve and winning the game

The court itself is called a *cancha*. A standard court in Spain is 178 feet and 8 inches long, 34 feet high to the red foul line and 35 feet wide to the metal/wood apron (15'6" apron). The *cancha* is a three-sided court with one side open to the public, protected by a chain-link fence. A rear wall and left-side wall come into play on rebounds. In the one- and two-man-on-a-side version, the ball is returned to the front wall either directly or on a rebound. In the doubles match, the frontcourt player is known as the *delantero*, and the man in the backcourt is called the *zaguero*.

In the three- and four-man-on-a-side version, the ball is returned by one side to the opposing team's side of the court across a net as in tennis. The game is won by scoring points against your opponent each time he fails to return the ball on a fly or a bounce. The serve, as in tennis, is the opening tactic in which the ball must clear a short-fall line but not land out of bounds or too far by landing past a long-fall line. The serve allows maximum speed and spin. If the server fails to achieve a legal serve, he loses a point.

Can you imagine hitting a ball with your hand and propelling it much faster than a tennis ball? There are three walls, one in front, one behind and one on your left. This creates infinite possibilities of sending the ball bouncing off both of them at awkward angles and greatly increases the agility and speed requirements necessary to return the ball on a fly or just a single bounce.

It also explains why three judges are necessary to judge balls that go out of bounds. Interference is called when a player is blocked from making a play for the ball by his opponent, unless in the judge's opinion he had no chance of reaching it. Juggling of the ball is not considered a foul except where a player holds the ball in the basket more than is considered "natural", a call to be decided by the judges.

The Shots

A *bote pronto* is a ball that is picked up off the court floor on a short hop. This is one of the most difficult catches in *jai-alai*. A *remate* refers to any type of kill shot. A *rebote* is a return of the ball from the back wall with either the forehand or backhand. A *carambola* (carom) is a shot where the ball hits the front wall near the corner, then the side wall and returns to the outside. This shot is very difficult to return because of the tremendous amount of spin put on the ball. A *cortada* (not to be confused with *a cortado* which is an espresso coffee with a dash of milk) is a forehand shot that is thrown low with a sidearm motion. The ball hits just above the red cushion and then cuts toward the sidewall.

An *arrimada* is a ball that hugs the side wall, making it difficult to catch and a *chula* – a "killer" off the back wall. An overhand shot thrown with a great amount of wrist action that results in the ball taking an extremely high bounce is a *picada*. Finally there is a slow "change of pace" called the *Chic-chac* where the shot is thrown very softly and drops with a small bounce to catch the opponent off-guard. This is a minimum of basic vocabulary for the most common shots although there are at least a half dozen more refined ones.

Betting – or the *quiniela*

Today's round-robin game with betting is referred to as *quiniela*. It uses the "spectacular seven" scoring system that was introduced in the 1970's to speed up the game and add excitement for punters. Most games last from eight to 14 minutes and each player runs at least a mile per game, according to studies made with a pedometer. As a fan, you will have to watch out for a stiff neck from the rapid back and forth movements necessary to follow the ball. Another element of excitement is that a match is played round-robin style, usually by eight players or teams.

The game begins when player number one serves the ball to player number two. The winner of the point stays on the court to meet the next player in rotation. Losers go to the end of the line and must wait another turn on the court. The first player to score seven points wins. The next highest scores are "place" (second) and "show" (third).

My most memorable experience the first time I visited Florida was watching a match at a fronton in Miami. The fans were mostly made up of Cuban-Americans and elderly Jewish pensiners. They provided as much entertainment as the players. Their wild cheering and animated betting made me feel part of the game. The same is true of the game in Spain. Playoffs are required when the two leading players have the same score. The format of the game allows for variations in betting just as in horse racing with win, show and place.

The uniform

True to tradition, all players wear a *faja*, a fringed, red sash together with white shoes and trousers and numbered shirts indicating post positions. A helmet known as the *casco* is now mandatory in many games with the *cesta*. Frontcourt players wear yellow helmets and backcourt players wear red ones. Until 1967, players went without helmets or, in Spain and France, wore the traditional berets (*boinas* in Spanish and Basque). For the game played without a *cesta*, the players wear heavy tape wrapped around each finger.

The Two Team Six- and Eight-Man Games

A complex variant of the game is played with two teams of three men or four men on each side. They are separated by a tennis net, and there is an additional high embankment with four steps at the sidewall, but only located on the side of the team returning the serve. The object of this added multiplayer embankment is to intensify the strategy of judging who is to return the ball among the three players, and adding extra angles and bounces to the game. Players must serve off the sidewall embankment and then hit the back wall. The return may be made on two bounces and this variety adds a colossal amount of rapid judgement in playing a carom shot or even jumping up on the embankment steps to return the ball.

The four-man-on-a-side game is played on a *cancha* without the stepped embankment. The serve is lobbed across the centre net to hit a sidewall and land in a rectangle marked off on one side of the opposing court. Both the six and eight man games place tremendous emphasis on position play and deciding which player is to return the ball. In the eight-man version there are more stockily-built players, since speed on one's feet is not so important as hand, arm and shoulder strength and eye coordination. Spectators in the six-man game sit on part of the central embankment and in a gallery behind the back wall or in door like recesses alongside of the court.

Foreign fascination with the game

Since so many movie stars vacation in southern Florida, it was inevitable that many of them encountered *Jai-alai* and were captivated by a sport that they had never before experienced. Fans visiting one of the Miami frontons could be sure to spot such celebrities as Bennie Goodman, Debbie Reynolds, Sophie Tucker, Martha Raye, Polly Bergen, Jack Parr and Vincent Price. Senator and later President Harry S. Truman was a keen fan whenever he was in Florida and so was Eleanor Roosevelt.

Hollywood star Paul Newman went one step further and actually played *Jai-alai* at the Bridgeport *frontón* near his home in Westport, Connecticut. The great American baseball superstar Babe Ruth loved the game and every time the New York Yankees went to Florida for spring training the "Babe" had to be dissuaded by the Yankee manager from playing the game himself. Ernest Hemingway, who immortalized bullfighting for the American public, rated *Jai-alai* as his favourite entertainment, claiming that "it contained constant excitement and manly effort taken to the utmost limits, and that it is fast, attractive and joyful." ●

Gypsies, Flamenco and fortune telling

For anyone who is familiar with the opera *Carmen*, there is a picture of Spain intimately linked with the nomadic, free-spirited Gypsies *(Gitanos)*. They are portrayed as outcasts on the margin of law, order and respectability, who believe in superstitions, fortune-telling and are able to cast spells. Much to the resentment of almost all Spaniards, the "Carmen-Gypsy" image of the country persists in neighbouring France, where the adage "Africa begins across the Pyrenees" originated (Alexandre Dumas).

What is the truth behind this image? Who are the Spanish Gypsies and what is their situation in Spanish society today? Did they invent flamenco? Are they intimately involved with crime and prostitution? Can you distinguish them from ordinary Spaniards? Their name in Spanish, *gitano*, derives from the Spanish term for Egypt, in the mistaken belief that that country was their original homeland. They refer to themselves, however, as *Roma*, and the same name is applied to their language. How many gypsies are there in Spain? The Spanish census is not a big help, and estimates range as high as between half a million and 750,000 (from 1.2 to 1.7 percent of the total population).

It is generally known that gypsies were of the warrior caste who, to escape from encroaching Muslim rule and prejudice, migrated out of

India (the Punjab in the Northeast) into Europe around the eleventh century. There are records of their arrival in Spain in 1425 in Zaragoza, the capital of Aragón. They apparently also entered Spain by sea via Barcelona in 1447, and by crossing over the Pyrenees in smaller groups from France.

Obviously, their life style made them suspect and prime targets for the Inquisition. They immediately feigned Christianity to avoid being expelled from a Spain that, by the beginning of the sixteenth century, only recognized the authority of the Catholic Church. When the Gypsies arrived, the Muslims and Jews were still present in the Peninsula and, following the expulsion of these two religious communities, the Gypsies were motivated to appear as loyal Christians and thus avoid a similar fate.

The authorities by one means or another tried to drive them out of Spain for 300 years. Laws required gypsies to marry non-gypsies, and they were denied their language and rituals as well as being excluded from public office and from membership in the different trades and crafts. Even gypsy dress and clothing were banned and an ordinance in 1560 declared it illegal for more than two gypsies to travel together on the roads.

However, the authorities were not unduly troubled by the gypsies who were absent from the towns and who provided some important services to the rural population by way of their skills, such as woodcarving and iron working. They also offered a bit of entertainment to the village population in what was otherwise a quite dreary existence. Although as early as 1499, during the reign of Ferdinand and Isabella, decrees were issued requiring the gypsies to settle down permanently and attach themselves to a "local feudal lord", they were largely ignored.

Geographic concentration

The great majority have long been settled in Andalucía, and their residence there, combined with its longer lasting Arab heritage, has made it what many observers have regarded as "typically Spanish", a designation many other Spaniards would deny applies to them or the regions where they live. Andalucía, with its population of seven million people, extends over the region's eight provinces with their capital cities of Huelva, Sevilla, Málaga, Almería, Cádiz, Córdoba, Granada, and Jaén. It has been the poorest part of Spain for centuries and has been characterized by rural poverty, landlessness, a rigid class structure and emigration to industrial cities and to other parts of Europe.

Language, appearance and occupations

Although all Spanish Gypsies are bilingual in Castilian Spanish and *Roma*, most who have been educated in Spanish schools make no use of the written form of *Roma* but employ it only as a means of oral communication. The Gypsy language is known both as *Roma* throughout Europe and *Caló* in Spain. It is derived from Sanskrit but greatly influenced by Spanish. Quite a few *Caló* words have entered Andalucian-Castilian-Spanish slang, but are unknown elsewhere in Spain. Gypsies may be a shade or two darker than other Spaniards and a bit shorter but otherwise are physically indistinguishable, and all have Spanish names.

Since General Franco's death in 1975, successive Spanish governments have followed a more sympathetic policy, especially regarding social welfare services. Since 1983, it has operated a special program of compensatory education to promote educational rights for the disadvantaged, including gypsy communities. Traditionally, they have worked as blacksmiths, horse traders, musicians, singers and dancers (especially of *flamenco* music) fortune-tellers and bullfighters.

In the past, many had no alternative except to beg and steal, especially the group known as the *húngaros*, who apparently arrived in Spain via a migration through Central Europe and Hungary. They are usually poorer than the older-settled *gitanos* and have lived an exclusively nomadic lifestyle, usually in tents or shacks *(casitas)* on the outskirts of the larger cities. Many Spanish *gitanos* have traditionally denied the *húngaros* the status of being in their same ethnic group, but the authorities and outsiders still tend to regard them all as "just gypsies".

Flamenco music and dance

Flamenco originated among the gypsies. Today's *flamenco* music, song and dance have been cultivated and polished by them. The theme of all *flamenco* music and the lyrics of all the songs speak of suffering, hunger, prison and death. It became a popular form of *café* entertainment in Andalucía during the latter part of the nineteenth century, in much the same way as "Blues", which began as a folk expression of the people's suffering, became transformed into an art and entertainment form.

The *flamenco* dance is a distinct part of gypsy culture that was shared by the simple landless peasants of Andalucía. The male singers employ a deep and hoarse voice, stylised body movements and complicated falsettos that warble or wail with undulations to the accompaniment of the guitar. There are four *flamenco* styles:

Flamenco jondo or grande – *flamenco jondo* or "great *flamenco*" is a dance that is serious and melancholy. It is the most emotional and difficult to interpret.

Intermediate flamenco – somewhat less intense and difficult.

Flamenco chico (small) is the opposite of the *flamenco grande*. It is a vivacious dance that is at the same time frivolous, exuberant or sensual and tender, and is usually about a happy or enchanting subject, performed at weddings and other joyful occasions.

All three of the above traditional types were typically performed with the participation of an intimate audience who beat time by clapping. The songs were composed by the artists or simple villagers. Like jazz, neither words nor the music were originally written down but passed on by word of mouth and imitation. Much of this tradition was diffused from its homeland in Andalucía by migrants searching for jobs in Madrid, Barcelona and the other great urban centres during the 1950s and 60s, much as jazz spread from New Orleans and the south to the midwest and east and west coasts of the United States before World War I.

Flamenco popular – popular *flamenco* is a commercial variant combining all three traditional ones. It is less personal and is performed in front of a large audience. The dancer concentrates on technique rather than personality and emotions. The object is simply to perform and entertain the audience, and the songs are written by professionals.

During the Franco dictatorship, *flamenco* was a form of tolerated protest by the poor and the oppressed. Its austerity held a morbid fascination for those who despaired of any meaningful change. In the post-Franco years of prosperity and economic boom, much of the appeal has been lost, although its popularity among tourists, who regard it as a remnant of the "traditional Spain" they have come to see, continues unabated.

Social problems

In spite of economic and social progress made by individuals among the younger generation, some of whom have entered the professions, many *gitanos* continue to live in poorer neighborhoods in the larger towns and leave school early. Many work in family-run businesses and are needed to supplement the family's income. As with other "deprived" minorities, there are charges of discrimination and a lack of "role models" for the younger generation, but the close-knit gypsy family is still reluctant to integrate within the larger society and lose its identity.

Fortune-telling and Tarot cards

The prevalence of superstitions, talismans used to ward off the "evil eye" and the ability to predict the future, are elements of gypsy culture that have added their weight to a long-standing and paradoxical Spanish regard, or perhaps a respect, born out of fear for the outcast peoples – the Jews, Arabs, Basques and Gypsies.

The suspicion that such outcast peoples were in league with the devil contributed both to a fear of their power to do evil but also an admiration that such people living outside the Church and "respectable" society had some special insight into the forces of nature or providence. No matter how scorned by the Church, these beliefs made fortune-tellers and "witches" sought after by the common people.

The gypsy religion has some striking similarities with Judaism. Gypsies are monotheistic and believe in one supreme male deity called *Del*. Perhaps this name and its similarity with *El* or *Elohim* (Hebrew for God) reinforced the connection. Gypsies practise circumcision and did not make graven images of their god. Moreover, like the medieval Jews, they have a profound belief in numerology and adhere to strict anti-cruelty laws. Good luck charms, amulets, and talismans are common. Unlike the Jews, the Gypsies have had an unshakeable and fundamental belief in the existence of vampires, spirits, and ghosts.

The importance of numerology, talismans, the belief in Jewish skills in medicine and the astrological system underlying the mystical Jewish Kabbala are important elements in divining the future by means of the Tarot cards. Both the Jews and Gypsies had a much wider world-view and, unlike the Spanish peasants, had travelled widely and were even familiar with foreign languages and climes. This only reinforced the view that they had knowledge beyond the reach of ordinary Spanish villagers.

Gypsy women are renowned for their fortune-telling skills. There are quite obvious reasons why fortune telling has always appealed to them. It is a relatively simple way of earning money that does not require even literacy or any formal education. It gives them an aura of mystery and power and fortune-tellers are able to learn important information from their clients that may benefit the community regarding the authorities or political and economic opportunities. It was also a form of insurance so that whenever a prediction of fortune was realized, the client would be indebted to the fortune-teller.

This can be frequently seen on television, where for the most part the predictions are favourable and the response of the listeners (almost always women) is *¡No me digas!* meaning "No kidding!" or "Don't tell me" or "You don't say!" Much of the time, the "secrets" revealed are psychologically reassuring to the client, such as "Your dead mother is watching over you from Heaven". Callers pay a rate based on their telephone time – at about 1.30 euros an hour. This works out substantially cheaper than going to a "professional" at her home location.

Much of the advice is phrased in general terms and reflects the sharp ability of the fortune tellers to sense what the client would like to hear without going too far out on a limb. Herbal folk remedies are freely offered since they have worked in the past. If a woman wants to know whether or not to end a relationship, the initial advice is "Be patient" – but if the client immediately responds in a voice indicating she is already very impatient, the advice is to "move on" and "you will find a new love".

If a prediction is made that a new relationship will mean another girl in the family, and it turns out the woman already has two daughters and doesn't want a third, the fortune-teller will quickly point out that the new lover or husband-to-be will probably bring his own daughter into the new relationship.

It is my guess that nowhere else in the western world are Tarot cards as popular as in Spain. Tarot card readers advertise in the newspapers and by signs posted in apartment and shop windows in every Spanish town. Turn on Spanish television anywhere in the country at any time of the day until the late evening and you will find several stations featuring women (apparently men are incapable of divining the cards) spreading out the Tarot deck on a table covered with an elaborate cloth and speaking to callers who have problems with their love life, families, children, neighbours, business or career.

In the background is a photograph or painting of mystical symbols or sites such as Stonehenge. The tablecloths contain the signs of the zodiac and many feature the letters of the Hebrew alphabet! In spite of the strong strain of *Judaeophobia* and anti-Gypsy prejudices in a large part of the Spanish population, there is this fascination with the Tarot deck and the occult linked with Jewish and/or Egyptian (i.e."Gypsy") antiquity.

The similarity of the words *Torah* (The entire body of Jewish law, lore and learning and sacred literature) and *Tarot* only increased the relationship. This is also alluded to in the novel *The Golem* (1915) by Gustav Meyrink, in which the character of Rabbi Hillel comments that the Book of Tarot contains all the teachings of the mystical Jewish writings of the Kabbala. The 21 major cards of the Tarot deck correspond closely with the 22 primal letters of the Hebrew alphabet.

The "Clubs" and "Gypsy blood"

The national lottery and gambling in general are a Spanish craze and not an isolated gypsy phenomenon, and the same is true regarding legal and illegal prostitution. However, a large part of both the native Spanish and foreign resident population links these and all "illicit" or "shady" activities with the stereotype of Carmen.

Gypsies have become synonymous with unbridled passion and even the considerable number of East European and Russian prostitutes working in Spanish "clubs" (euphemism for brothels) pretend that they have "gypsy blood" to increase their sex and market appeal. Even many native Spanish prostitutes pretend they have "gypsy blood" no matter how blond or Nordic-looking they may be.

Quite a few Spanish songs mention that a lovely girl is flashing her "gypsy smile" *(sonrisa gitana)*, a gesture that may be interpreted as charming, bewitching, mischievous, sexy, provocative, shy or ingenuous (or all of these). In the Spanish *zarzuela* (light opera, see vignette 21) called *El Huésped del Sevillano* (The Guest of the Man from Seville), there is a Jewish girl, Raquel, the daughter of *maese (master)* Andrés, a *converso* (convert from Judaism) and sword-smith in Toledo. Her lover sings an ode to her as a woman… with a *"Gypsy profile and pagan body"*!

Apparently, no Christian girl could have a body to match! Here too, Gypsy and Jewish women are confused and appear interchangeable as symbols of sensuality, sex and lust in the Middle Ages (recall the Jewish heroine Rebecca in the Sir Walter Scott novel *Ivanhoe* and her counterpart, another *Raquel la Fermosa*, the Beautiful Raquel, the real-life Jewish mistress of Castilian King Alfonso VIII). One well-known, very sexy and attractive Spanish porno actress, who is currently a star, wears a Star of David on a necklace in all her films, even though she is not Jewish.

The Lottery

The passion for gambling was the only vice permitted and even encouraged under the Franco regime, for the reason that it is a state controlled institution that brings in massive revenues and is simply a form of disguised taxation. John Hooper, author of the excellent introduction to modern Spain *The New Spaniards*, in his chapter entitled "High Stakes" declares: "There seems little doubt that the Spanish are among the world's most inveterate gamblers" (p.186), and cites statistics that estimate the total losses of Spain's gamblers at more than £5 billion (in 1991), a figure which has probably doubled since then.

The Gypsies share the same passion and belief as most other Spaniards (with the notable exception of the Catalans) that "fate", "destiny" and their "lucky star" would one day ensure fabulous wealth without the necessity of another day's hard work. The average Spaniard may also be excused for thinking that if a poor gypsy can win the top lottery prize (as has happened on more than one occasion), then this is God's sure sign that even the lowest and most miserable wretch can be lifted up in the lap of luxury – so "Why not me?" ●

En un lugar de la Mancha, de cuyo nombre no quiero acordarme...

SOCIETY
AND RELIGION

45

How Catholic is Spain today?

O f all the pre-1975 images of Spain, the longest, most entrenched and most accepted abroad, notably in the English-speaking Protestant countries, was that of a reactionary, deeply repressive Catholic Church hostile towards any other religion, including all the other variants of Christianity, women's rights, abortion, homosexuality, divorce, and any open expression of eroticism or sexuality.

Spain traditionally had a very high birth rate, massive unemployment and a constant flow of emigrants seeking a better life abroad. The Church had been an ally of the Franco regime. It has always maintained an image as the faithful protector of Catholic doctrines (Trinity, the Eucharist, and Incarnation) against "heresies" dating back to the "Arianism" of the "barbarian invasions" (see vignette 14) and the Protestant Reformation.

In a famous Civil War radio broadcast to the defenders of the Alcázar of Toledo, a fortress successfully defended by the Nationalist forces, Cardinal Gomá y Tomas called on the defenders to resist "the bastard soul of the sons of Moscow and the shadowy societies manipulated by Semitic internationalism" (a reference to the Soviet Union and an oblique suggestion that the degenerate Western democracies had been corrupted by the Jews).

On the day General Franco and his Nationalist forces entered Madrid, ending the Spanish Civil War, Pope Pius XII sent him a telegram of congratulations which read "Lifting up our hearts to the Lord, we rejoice with your excellency in the victory so greatly to be desired, of Catholic Spain".

The Black Legend

This view of the Church was linked with an older shared image (common to most British people and Americans) of a reactionary Spain as perpetrator of the Inquisition, intolerance and the expulsion of Jews

47

and Muslims. The perception was of a country out of step with the rest of Europe in the achievement of widespread literacy and human rights and, among all the European nations and Protestant churches, the cruellest of all in its settlement of the New World, its destruction of the flourishing civilizations in Mexico and Peru and in its treatment of the native Indians.

In contrast, many Spaniards believed that their country and way of life had been maligned unfairly by the "invention" of the Protestant powers who had fostered a "black legend" *(leyenda negra)* against their country and Church.

To this must be added the unquestioned loyalty and privileged position of the Church in the regime of General Franco, enjoying a state monopoly. For almost four decades, from the end of the bloody Civil War in 1939 to Franco's death in 1975, the Spanish Catholic church had supported the regime in every way and stood for opposition to the liberal and democratic trends elsewhere in Western Europe as well as consumerism and secularism. Tourists to Spain as late as the 1960s can recall the Spanish police patrolling the beaches to ensure that no immodest exposure of the female form occurred by wearing the indecent bikini swimsuit.

The Church in Spain today – a shadow of the past

Perhaps the biggest surprise to North Europeans, Brits and Americans on visiting Spain now is the shock of encountering today's reality with their images of the past. What followed Franco has left the Catholic Church in a daze. Today, baptismal records claim that 94 percent of Spaniards are Catholic, although opinion polls show that only 80 percent of the native-born population identify themselves as Catholics. Even more revealing are figures for attendance at Mass. Only 18 percent of Spaniards go at least once a month but about 50 percent NEVER go. At the same time, there is a major shortage of priests and it continues to grow worse.

More incredible to many foreigners in the coastal resort areas is the presence of brothels openly advertising their wares along the highways, hardcore pornography available on local television (without subscription charges), semi-nude and nude bathing on many beaches, and not just legal divorce as an indication of women's rights but the presence of many women in all branches of the services, in the police and Spanish armed forces. Moreover, the Spanish birth rate has fallen to one of the lowest in the world.

The rigid suppression of other doctrines in the past also applied to the Freemasons, who were regarded with great hostility under the monarchy and the Franco regime. It was the opinion of many Catholic "scholars" that the international organization was a "front" or "cover" for Protestant and Jewish missionary efforts to subvert the Catholic Church. Even today, with more than 25 years of unlimited freedom of religion, the number of adherents of other religious denominations is quite small (perhaps 250,000 active Muslims, 60,000 active Protestants and 25,000 Jews).

The growth of secularism

It took a concerted effort to ensure that any specific reference to Catholicism being the majority religion of Spaniards was included in the new Spanish Constitution of 1978, adopted three years after Franco's death. Even this reference was quite bland and did not commit the State to adhere to any Catholic doctrine. It also worked out an arrangement whereby the State would end its direct subsidies to the Church.

Whatever the formal legalistic language of the Constitution, there is no doubt that with each passing year since the adoption of the 1978 Constitution, secularism has made major inroads into society. This is clearly reflected in the views of the young. It may well be that proportion of religious people with a firm personal belief in God among the 20-35 year-old age group is even less (only 42 percent) than in the United States or Canada. However, many surveys show that Spaniards over the age of 65 retain the traditional outlooks of the Church from their youth.

It is undeniable that since then secularism has made great strides. In a survey of Catholic practice, the weekly magazine *Epoca* (April 9-15, 2004), reported the results of several major surveys indicating a decline in Catholic habits. A Spanish minister under the Aznar government, Ana Palacio, even declared that Spain had successfully copied the "European model of relegating religion to the private sphere". Divorce is universally accepted today.

The church's position on celibacy has undoubtedly played a major role in the decision to abandon holy vows on the part of thousands of priests and nuns who are not being replaced. Over the past decade, most of the priests who have left holy orders have married, and their number is estimated at close to 8,000.

In addition, a few priests have even openly declared themselves to be "gay," presenting another challenge to Catholic doctrine. What comes as a shock to many foreigners brought up with the old "black legends" of Spain as an ultra-reactionary Catholic society is the extent that anti-clericalism and hatred of the Church have played a major role in the past.

The Church at the close of the nineteenth century

The Spanish inquisition initially came to an end only in 1813, but was reconstituted following the Napoleonic wars and only finally abolished in the 1830s. In 1851, a Concordat was concluded to forestall any hint of liberalism. The State declared that the Roman Catholic Religion was the only religion in Spain and all other religious services were strictly forbidden.

The Church maintained the closest supervision over both private schools and universities through its bishops. Their task was to make sure that all education was in absolute harmony with Catholic doctrine. According to clauses in the Concordat, the State promised to aid the bishops in suppressing any attempt to pervert believers and in preventing the circulation or publication of harmful papers or books.

Except for the short-lived, 11-month, first Spanish Republic in 1878, the Catholic Church continued to enjoy a monopoly unparalleled in any other Western nation. Following the constitution that restored the monarchy, other forms of religious worship were permitted, but only on the condition that they were not publicly visible and did not advertise via the press or public notices. No other religious denomination was allowed to possess property or publish books. Nevertheless, the Church was outraged at the change.

During the latter part of the nineteenth century, the Vatican's relentless battle against Liberalism was largely successful. Elsewhere in Europe, the power of the Catholic Church was greatly curtailed, especially in France, as a reaction to the Dreyfus scandal, culminating in 1905 with the separation of the state and church.

In Spain, people remained at the mercy of the Catholic Church, and all laws of a civil, social, economic or political nature were made to conform with the teachings and principles of the Church. The Catholic Church reigned in the schools, the Press, the courts, the Government, and the Army. It was sustained by an observant, obdurate and powerful hierarchy, wealthy religious Orders, the great landlords and the Monarchy.

The Church's influence was everywhere and imbued the nation with its spirit of reaction to hinder the efforts of all those labelled as Liberals who tried to bring in new ideas, reforms or weaken the power of the established order. Rome and the ultra-Catholics in Spain became mortal enemies of even the slightest trend towards Liberalism.

Prelude to Civil War

Secondary schools controlled by the Church and almost all State schools taught pupils that if they associated with Liberals they would go to hell. The Church Catechism was republished and distributed in schools as late as 1927. It declared that the State must be subject to the Church as the body to the soul, as the temporal to the eternal. It enumerated the errors of Liberalism, namely liberty of conscience, of education, of propaganda, of meetings, of speech, of the Press, stating categorically that it is heretical to believe in such principles.

The Catholic Church also controlled an immense portion of the country's wealth. From 1874 until the fall of the Monarchy (1931), it steadily gained in riches and influence. On the death of King Alfonso XII, the Queen Regent, in return for the "Pope's Protection", donated vast sums to the Church and to Catholic schools and colleges.

The Spanish Hierarchy, the Queen and French Catholics, upset at the spread of secularism in France, worked hand in hand in a supreme effort to stamp out "Liberal Atheism." A wave of clericalism swept Spain that was crowded with more convents, colleges, and religious foundations than ever before. The Church was tied to the most reactionary elements, in league against any cultural, economic, social, or political innovations.

The powerful anti-clerical tradition in Spain

In spite of the immense power of the Church in Spain, many among the poor, when given a choice free from coercion, rejected their formal affiliation. The Catholic Church continued to lose adherents at an alarming scale. By 1910 more than two-thirds of the population were no longer practising Catholics. Civil marriages and funerals had become common. On the fall of the Monarchy in 1931, scepticism and hostility towards the Catholic Church had reached the point of explosion.

At this time, it is estimated that only five per cent of the villagers of rural Central Spain and Andalucía attended Mass. In many villages, the priest said Mass alone. Some parishes registered that as many as 25 per cent of the children born were not baptized, and more than 40 per cent of the elderly died without the sacraments.

The Catholic Church had unsuccessfully tried to organize the working classes but in reality they had already lost the battle. Many restless Catholics had already rejected the Catholic Church. The most anti-clerical were the rural landless poor and the urban working classes, among whom Anarcho-Syndicalism and Socialism/Communism spread like wildfire.

In their attempt to preserve the status quo, the Church persisted for more than 50 years opposing all elements aspiring to bring about change. From 1890 until the outbreak of the First World War, there were wholesale arrests, thousands were imprisoned, hundreds were shot, and methods of torture used in former times against heretics were employed against political prisoners. The dictatorship of Primo de Rivera in the early 1920s was unable to halt the anti-monarchist and anti-Church sentiments of large sections of the population.

The first President of the Republic, Azaña, declared that Spain had "ceased to be a Catholic country." The Monarchy was abolished; a Republic was declared in 1931; The *Cortes* (parliament) disestablished and disendowed the immense power and wealth of the Catholic Church. It expelled the Jesuits, forbade monks and nuns to tamper with trade and, above all, education, in which the Catholic Church had had a monopoly. Marriage was secularised. Divorce was introduced, and freedom of speech, of the Press, and religious tolerance were proclaimed everywhere. The Popular Front uniting the liberal and more radical socialist, anarchist and communist movements, obtained a majority in the 1936 elections. Its campaign openly attacked the Spanish Catholic Church and the Vatican.

By the outbreak of the Civil War, popular hatred of the Church had reached feverish levels. Churches were sacked and burned and priests and nuns assaulted. The hierarchy of the Catholic Church desperately welcomed the uprising led by General Franco to "restore order, the monarchy and the privileged position of the Church", even to the extent of using the "Moors", Muslim troops from the Army of Africa in Spain, to suppress the anti-Catholic outbreaks of many workers and peasants. The Church claims that several thousand of its priests and nuns were murdered and became martyrs for the faith during the events leading up to and during the Civil War, and the Pope has canonized some of them.

Buñuel and Spanish anti-clericalism in the cinema

Luis Buñuel, Spain's most successful and well-known film producer, was born in 1900. He studied first with Jesuits before enrolling in the University of Madrid, where he met Salvador Dalí and Federico Garcia Lorca. He went on to study film in Paris during the 1920's and was associated with "avant-garde" trends. He worked under the experimental filmmaker Jean Epstein, and in 1928 collaborated with Dalí in the film *Un Chien Andalou*, which became a surrealist classic. It provoked a scandal, but Buñuel went on to make *L'Age d'Or* in 1930.

This led to a break with Dalí, who was convinced that it expressed Buñuel's anti-Catholicism stance. After *L'Age d'Or*, Buñuel gave further expression to his views in the documentary Land Without Bread (1932). The film portrayed what Buñuel saw as the contrast between the poverty, disease, and wretchedness of the Spanish people and the wealthy, powerful and corrupt world of the Spanish Catholic Church.

He worked for Paramount in Paris and supervised co-productions for Warner Brothers in Spain but had to flee the country during the Spanish Civil War. While in the United States, he became director of documentaries at the Museum of Modern Art in New York. Buñuel worked for major Hollywood studios again as well as the U.S. government, supervising Spanish-language versions of films for MGM, making documentaries for the U.S. Army, and dubbing for Warner Brothers.

He moved to Mexico and produced several films there that brought him international acclaim. It was with his Mexican films that Buñuel developed the style of surrealist humour and social melancholy that characterised his work. He returned to France in 1955 and eventually to Spain where he made *Viridiana* in 1961.

Although his script was initially approved by the censors, the film was banned upon release, due to its anti-clerical message, especially through the use of a sarcastic image of "The Last Supper". *Viridiana* achieved international recognition but made him a *persona non grata* in Franco's Spain. The contemporary Spanish film director, Pedro Almódovar, has also been critical or sarcastic of the Church in some of his films.

A comeback ?

Pope John Paul II has helped to re-establish the Church's moral authority by his stand on the issues of abortion, contraception and much more significantly for youth, his position on the issues of Basque terrorism and his opposition to the conservative government of Jose Maria Aznar on the war in Iraq.

A majority sided with the Pope and against Prime Minister José María Aznar on this last issue and revealed a streak of anti-Americanism in the Spanish public, especially among young people. Aznar was among the Bush administration's staunchest allies. Although Iraq did not come up when John Paul and Aznar met, the Pope used some form of the word "peace" 13 times in his two speeches that day, leaving no doubt about his views.

He has also used the phrase "exasperated nationalism," in referring to ETA and terrorism as a political weapon. This was also a clear rebuff to some Basque bishops who had taken a line of formally condemning terrorism but expressing some form of sympathy for the plight of the Basque people and the goals of Basque nationalists.

Others are not so enthused about the Pope's political statement and note how his canonisations of many of the "Church's martyrs" from the Civil War are unwelcome attempts to involve the Church again in internal politics and charge the Republic as a guilty accomplice in their deaths.

Although historically the Spanish clergy was among the most conservative within the Church, it is much more varied today and has a more diverse political colour. Since the end of the Civil War it has not had to contend with its traditional enemies among the Masons, Anarchists, and doctrinaire Marxists. Part of the younger clergy became active in trying to facilitate the end of the Franco regime and a democratic transition in cooperation with both middle and working class opposition.

Spain is still a country with a "religious landscape" that is quite apparent to anyone with an eye for churches, monasteries, nunneries, cemeteries and convents. There are more than ten thousand monks and nuns in the country although their number is declining by the day. In the heady days of the Republic, many Left Wing activists dreamt of expelling them all.

The clerics come from an enormous variety of Catholic orders – Jesuits, Dominicans, Franciscans, Carmelites, Marists and you name it. If you have a hankering to experience the Middle Ages, it is easy to do so – just book a night or two in one of these religious institutions that offer guest rooms and experience the daily routine of "sanctification" through prayer, work, devotion, penitence and a routine without any of the conveniences of the last few centuries.

In the Basque country, many priests sided with the Republic, became radicalised and were much persecuted at the end of the Civil War. The Church is anxious to integrate within the rest of society as a moral force and still has a controlling interest in various schools and mass media. It has hopes to recover some of its lost influence but is resigned to the loss of its monopoly and dominant position in Spanish society.

Many commentators and observers believe that in the last decade there has been a resurgence of "observance" or at least a desire on the part of many Spaniards, including those who vote for the political Left and the young, to outwardly accept certain Catholic "traditions" – such as baptism, marriage in Church, and the importance of a religious education, particularly when these coincide with the so-called "progressive" views of Pope John Paul II on foreign policy issues and aid to the poor and developing countries. In this last regard, there is surprisingly a somewhat shared anti-capitalist outlook between Marxists of every shade and a large part of Catholic opinion. ●

Spain's Muslims today… in the shadow of Bin-Laden?

The Islamic civilization of medieval Al-Andalus endured in various parts of the Iberian peninsular from a few decades to 700 years. It has left its mark and provided Spain, and to a lesser degree Portugal, with an illustrious past that marked the history, language, architecture, art, music, food, place names and society of the country long after the last Muslim had departed.

Due to a troubled history, Spanish involvement in the affairs of Morocco and the religious fervour generated by the Re-conquest, the Crusades and the Counter-reformation, a problematic legacy has been inherited by many Spaniards who maintain a kind of love-hate relationship with their past and with their Muslim neighbours to the South.

From the eighth century to the present day, stereotypes have dominated Spanish attitudes and relations with the Arab states and Muslim civilization no less than with Israel, Judaism and the Jewish Diaspora. Since the 1970s, Islam has re-emerged as a major factor in Spanish society and since then the continual flow of cheap migrant labour and illegal immigration from Morocco has caused the rapid growth of the Muslim community.

From the time of the expulsion of the last "Moors", the term *moros* has been used in Spain and applied indiscriminately to everything connected with Islam. Due to Spain's involvement in Morocco, a large Army of Africa was created. In the 1930s, it was commanded by General Francisco Franco, and its troops came to play a major part in the suppression of a revolt by anarchist miners and other workers in the northern province of Asturias in 1934, and then in the uprising to overthrow the Republic that culminated in the Civil War (1936-39).

In spite of General Franco's frequent use of the theme of "rescuing" Spain´s Christian heritage from "barbarism", the use of Muslim troops brought with him from Morocco earned him a reputation for brutality. They were hated and feared by ordinary Spaniards wherever they fought.

Contemporary Muslim society in Spain: 1939 to 1966

Due to Spain's increased involvement with Morocco, dating back to the latter part of the nineteenth century, a certain intellectual interest in Arab and Muslim affairs and civilization was stimulated and it acquired the label of *africanismo español*. It was further promoted by various Spanish governments regardless of their ideological orientation on other issues. Thus in 1932, the Spanish Republic established The School of Arab Studies *(La Escuela de Estudios Árabes)* in Madrid and Granada.

General Franco took this policy a step further in 1938 by establishing two schools in Tetuan, the Muley el Mehdi and one named after himself, followed by *El Instituto de Estudios Africanos* in June 1947. Nevertheless, in the late 1940s and early 1950s the Muslim presence in Spain was limited to foreign diplomats and a handful of Civil War veterans and their families as well as Franco's "personal guard".

It may seem strange that a Muslim presence on Spanish territory was promoted during the rule of General Franco. This is all the more remarkable when the rights and privileges of the Catholic Church had been fully restored and there existed no framework whatsoever for public worship of any other religion in the country (not even Protestant). This was undoubtedly due to the personal gratitude felt by Franco to his loyal Muslim troops of the Army of Africa, who played such an important part in his victory over the Republic in the Civil War. He set aside a special area in the cemetery of San Fernando in Sevilla for fallen Muslim soldiers.

The Franco regime maintained a policy of friendship towards the Arab states as part of his desire to find allies for Spain and escape the diplomatic isolation imposed on the country by the victorious allies at the end of World War II. In the continued colonial administration of the

Spanish protectorate in Morocco, the authorities showed a positive attitude towards all expression of Muslim religious identity and facilitated the *hajj* (pilgrimage) to Mecca.

It must also be said that a favourable attitude was manifested at the same time towards the Spanish speaking Moroccan Jews as well. Their *Sepharadi* heritage was also acknowledged as a valuable part of Spanish tradition. In the 1950s, Spain expanded its contacts with the Middle East and increased its Arab orientation by refusing to recognize the State of Israel. Various intercultural programmes were established and visits made by prominent Spanish and Arab intellectuals.

A considerable amount of educational literature was produced dealing with the heritage of *Al-Andalus* (Medieval Muslim civilization in Andalucía) and distributed in the Arab world. In 1954, the *Instituto Hispano-Árabe de Cultura* was established with the support of the Spanish Ministry of Foreign Affairs, underlining the intense interest in promoting Arab-Spanish contacts, associations and close relations.

From 1967 to 1975

The first law of religious liberty was promulgated in July 1967, opening the way for the organization and free exercise of other religious communities in Spain. This measure was due in part to the increasing anachronistic position of the Catholic Church in the country, following the liberal tendencies of the Vatican II Council as well as an increasing desire of the Spanish government to be regarded more positively in Europe with an eye to eventually joining both the European Union and NATO.

Between 1968 and 1971, the first official Muslim communities/congregations were created in the Spanish overseas enclave territories *(plazas)* of Ceuta and Melilla, hardly surprising since the cities are surrounded by Moroccan territory and Muslims constitute significant minorities in both.

A national Muslim Association *(La Asociación Musulmana de España)* was formed in 1971 with its headquarters in Madrid. The Abu Bakr mosque, the first in the country in almost 500 years, was completed in 1971 with considerable Saudi aid. It was designed by a Syrian, Riay Tatary Bakry, who had become a nationalised Spanish citizen and led the new association.

From 1975 to 1989

It was not long, however, before the first tensions arose between the new religious community and the host society. The *Comunidad*

Musulmana de España, created in 1979 by a Spanish convert, opposed an earlier organization claiming to represent Spanish Muslims. Following the introduction of a new law on religious freedom in Spain in 1980, several new associations of a mixed national religious and political character appeared in Granada, Córdoba and Sevilla, and made their debut in the first democratic regional and local elections. Due to the prolonged period of Muslim rule in Andalucía, the new Muslim associations attempted to portray Islam as an integral part of the regional identity of Andalucía, in spite of the absence of any organized Muslim community there for centuries.

A movement began of conversions of disaffected Spanish Catholics to Islam, a trend that provided a ready-made community able to welcome any defections from the majority culture. More than a few Spaniards with previous grievances against the Catholic Church in such personal matters as marriage, divorce, and close ties with the Franco regime identified with Islam.

It did not take long, however, for the first "incident" to arise involving a challenge by Muslim society to the Spanish authorities. This occurred when members of the new Muslim association in Córdoba attempted to enter a building jointly used as a church (the Cathedral) and a mosque to pray, without asking the permission of the local municipal authorities. Eventually a compromise was worked out.

In 1981, a new mosque was constructed in Marbella, with the help of Saudi capital. The growing amount of immigration and flow of cheap labour from Morocco prompted the need to have workers' interests represented in the form of a special Moroccan community (1986), the *Comunidad Musulmana Marroquí de Madrid Al-Umma*, in close contact with Moroccan, Saudi and Kuwaiti diplomats.

From 1989 to 1992

In 1989, the Muslim presence in Spain was recognized with the creation of a national body, the *Federación Española de Entidades Religiosas Islámicas (FEERI)*, with 15 branches, followed by another rival "union" in 1990, the *Unión de Comunidades Islámicas de España (UCIDE)*. By 1992 the two rival associations had agreed to cooperate, but not merge. They presented a united front in dealing with the Spanish state in matters of common concern such as religious schools, licensing of ritually approved butcher shops, etc.

The cornerstone to the largest mosque and Muslim centre in Europe was laid in the presence of their majesties, King Juan Carlos and

Queen Sofía and Prince Salmán of Saudi Arabia on September 21, 1992. This mosque is often referred to as the "M-30" after the highway leading into Madrid, where it is located, and cost approximately 2,000 million pesetas (12 million euros in today's currency) and was also funded with Saudi money.

The second largest religious community and its divisions

Islam has approximately 500,000 adherents in Spain, making it the second largest religious community in the country. It is, however, in serious conflict with the host society. Converts are largely attracted by what they perceive to be the moderate face of Islam and find themselves largely unable to challenge the more radical fundamentalist elements represented by the immigrant community and the support of outside sources of finance. This conflict is clearly seen in the divergence of opinion regarding the status of women.

The more moderate *FEERI*, with most of the converts to Islam, was originally the larger group. The *UCIDE* is more in tune with strict orthodoxy. In addition there are other groups such as the Muslim Brothers *(Hermanos Musulmanes)*, who maintain a separate community. The state signed an agreement in 1992, according to which Muslim schools would be financed, but this has only been possible in the overseas *plazas* of Ceuta and Melilla, where the local Muslim population is not composed of immigrants and has long demonstrated its loyalty to the Spanish state.

The Albayzín of Granada, the centre of Islamic Spain today

The acknowledged centre of the Muslim community in Spain today is, of course, Granada. This last stronghold of Islamic Medieval Spain has been revived by immigration, conversion and the presence of the Great Mosque, the most important monumental remnant of Islam in the former "capital" of Muslim Andalucía.

The very heart of Spanish Islam today is in the midst of the narrow streets of the Albayzín quarter (The Falconer's Quarter) on the steep slope opposite the Alhambra. Before the fall of the city to the Catholic monarchs in 1492, the Albayzín quarter had at least two dozen mosques and hundreds of baths and teahouses, along with its own local judges, courts and administration. It was the centre of many tradesmen and included Christians and Jews. The houses of the quarter are still recognizable as "Moorish" with their typical white-washed walls and blue *azulejo* tiles and red roofs.

A considerable number of the inhabitants are converts from Christianity, many of whom had been searching for a new lifestyle with the advent of democracy and their rejection of the repressive Catholic-Francoist Spain that had dominated their childhood. Their biographies are often symptomatic of the trials, tribulations and searches of the younger generation of the 1960s in Spain and their experiences with counter-culture, drugs, sexual experimentation and Left-wing politics and ending in conversion to Islam.

Very few of these converts experienced their religious transformation as a "blinding flash of revelation". This movement appeared in Granada, Sevilla and Córdoba but quite quickly it was Granada, due to its historical associations and most specifically the Albayzín, that attracted the like-minded. It became a magnet for Muslim immigrants from North Africa as well as those who regarded the presence of these converts as a form of legitimisation for their own activities in the city.

Wife beating

The most serious aspect at odds with most of Spanish society today is the attitude of Spanish Muslims towards women. The notorious case of a book recommending physical punishment to be administered by Muslim husbands to their wives called attention to the existence in Spain of a community at odds with the host culture. It was nevertheless defended by the author, Kamal Mostafa, a Saudi-born imam.

Around 80 women's organizations, including several Muslim women's groups, brought a lawsuit against the author, accusing him of encouraging Muslim men to beat their wives. On 14 January 2004, Mostafa was sentenced by a Barcelona court to a 15-month suspended sentence and fined 2160 euros for publishing his book *The Woman in Islam*. It states that Shar'ia law confirms:

> Beating must never be in exaggerated, blind anger, in order to avoid serious harm [to the woman)... It is forbidden to beat her on the sensitive parts of her body. Instead, she should be beaten on the arms and legs," using a "rod that must not be stiff, but slim and lightweight so that no wounds, scars, or bruises are caused." Similarly, the blows "must not be hard... A wife must be reprimanded, then removed from the conjugal bed. Only if these two methods fail should the husband turn to beating.

The Spanish judge said that Mustafa's book contained incitement to violence against women, constituting a violation of the penal code. In defence, Sheikh Mustafa's attorney argued that his client was not expressing his personal opinion, but only reiterating the writings of Islam from the thirteenth to the nineteenth centuries. The book sold around 3,000 copies in Islamic cultural centres across Spain before being removed from the shelves.

In Andalucía, moderate Muslims largely identify with the Spanish Socialist Party *(PSOE)* and are critical of continued reliance on the influence of Saudi subsidies to mosques under their influence. Problems continue to grow due to the increase in illegal immigration and the presence of extremists, including agents of terror groups. Most come across the Strait of Gibraltar. Practically every night, the Spanish Coast Guard is on watch searching for illegal immigrants attempting to land on Spanish soil.

The prelude to the Madrid Massacre of 11 March 2004

For years, Spanish intelligence believed that the country was being used by Islamic militants as a logistical base or staging area, and several arrests had been made of suspects implicated in some way to the September 11 attacks in New York and Washington. The March 11 bomb attack on several trains in Madrid that cost the lives of almost 200 people was actually able to influence election results in a democratic state and led to a change of governments. The timing of the explosions during the rush hour, and coming only three days before the national elections, was designed to cause maximum mayhem and influence the outcome.

It was the work of Islamic fundamentalist extremists linked to or part of al Qaeda, and surprised the government. Spanish intelligence had not been able to uncover much evidence indicating that there were foreign agents among the Spanish Muslim community ready, able and willing to lend a hand in committing such a crime on Spanish soil. At first, the authorities were convinced it had been the work of ETA, in spite of the fact that more than a year earlier a bomb attack was carried out by Muslim extremists in Casablanca in Morocco directed towards Spaniards and Moroccan Jews and the *Casa de España*, resulting in 30 deaths.

The Spanish government had taken a risk by supporting American policy in Afghanistan and Iraq. On the other hand, it had been unable to divorce itself from considerable dependence on Arab economic investment (primarily Saudi) in downtown Madrid and many coastal resort towns. The Spanish people were not called upon to mobilize against a terrorist threat from this direction.

Fearful of a reaction among the half-million-strong Muslim

community under the influence of the strict Saudi *Wahabbi* sect, and the almost unanimous criticism of the pro-American government by a press in which many journalists have traditionally been hostile to the United States since the Spanish-American War (1898), the electorate reacted by swinging to the Socialist Party.

The Socialists charged that the government had lied and enough Spaniards were convinced at the last moment to switch their votes to elect them by a slim margin. The facts since then, however, indicate beyond any doubt that those arrested and their ringleader had planned the bombings well before the war in Iraq and Spanish participation in the "coalition" forces.

Renewed theological debate and its political consequences

In Medieval Spain, numerous theological debates were held to discuss the relative merits and claims of the three monotheistic religions. Even though many centuries have passed, there is still a fundamental division among them. Jews who first discovered a path towards salvation believed they were setting an example by serving God as a nation, demonstrating their way of life to other nations. This continued to be possible even after the destruction of the Temple and loss of Jewish independence in 70 AD. Christians, on the other hand, believed that this was possible on a purely individual level and could be achieved by anyone no matter what his or her nationality, race or sex.

For Islam, the world is divided between two hostile camps, and it is incumbent upon Muslims to subject the other camp to its will. The struggle intimately involves territory and ideology. The other camp is labelled the "Camp of War" *(Dar-il-Harb)*. Islam is the Camp of Submission to Allah's will. In this regard, territories such as Israel, Spain *(Al-Andalus)*, Chechnya, Kosovo or Albania, that were once submitted to Allah, cannot be allowed to return to the Camp of War.

"Moderate" Muslims may want to live in harmony with their neighbours, but this theological sword and the pressure it exerts suggest that the more militant strain will gain the upper hand. Now that *Al-Qaeda* has forced a change in Spain's foreign policy with a bombing, it is questionable whether European domestic policies will be able to remain free from the aims and goals of Islamic radicals. ●

The migrant impact in Spain

Spain has undergone an amazing transformation during the last thirty years since the death of its aged dictator General Francisco Franco and the end of his authoritarian regime. Older tourists who visited the country before 1975 remember it as a stagnant society with high unemployment, lagging behind the rest of Western Europe by more than two generations.

Since then, the country has emerged as a prosperous and flourishing nation, one that has gone from exporting people in search of work and a better life to one attracting tens of thousands of retirees and even younger people from Northern Europe, who have made a conscious decision to come to Spain, not just for the weather but for a better life in almost every respect compared to their homelands.

Their attraction to the coastal resort areas has provided massive investment and sources of employment that have lifted the entire Spanish economy to a new crest. The country has also become a "testing ground" for the vision of a "united Europe" which many advocates believe will eliminate the national jealousies, rivalries and tensions of the past.

Less optimistic observers see the presence of so many Northern

Europeans in Spain as a separate group, of whom the great majority are ignorant and oblivious to Spanish culture, language and traditions. Many foreigners live in gated communities forming a string of "golden ghettoes" growing as foreign bodies within the Spanish organism. They even go further and believe that the reality of the "ex-pat" communities of Brits, Germans, and Scandinavians is proof positive that the European Union will never be able to become the "United States of Europe" but will ever founder on the hard rocks of language, culture and tradition.

More than 2.5 million Spaniards continue living outside Spain. They are the migrants and children and now grandchildren of the migrants who left Spain during the economically stagnant Franco years. In contrast, about 1.3 million foreigners live for most or part of the year in Spain and are legally registered as residents with full social rights and medical insurance. However, a much larger number are resident in the country for at least part of the year and "commute" back and forth between Spain and their original homeland. This "foreign population" is still quite a small percentage of the total, but one that is particularly noticeable in several distinct areas of the country.

The trend is obvious. More and more Spaniards will return to their homeland and, as far as the eye can see, the number of migrants seeking work from both Morocco and overseas from Latin America, as well as retirees from the wealthy countries of the European Community, will continue to increase.

Among the first group of poor migrant workers, half of these (about 250,000) are Moroccans, Peruvians, Ecuadorians and Dominicans, most of whom speak Spanish but are at the very bottom of the economic totem pole and live in squalid conditions. They have created resentment for very different reasons than the other "foreigners" from Northern Europe. Although unemployment has dropped markedly during the past eight years from above 20 percent to about half of that today, there is much illegal employment and a reluctance or outright refusal on the part of many young Spaniards to take employment in competition with this cheap labour. The gap filled by this pool of cheap immigrant labour shows no sign of disappearing.

The reasons are due to the very low Spanish birth rate, at the moment only 1.07 children per fertile woman, among the lowest in the world! Since so many migrants among the wealthy North Europeans are retired, they are not providing any future reserve pool of labour (unless all their children come to settle in Spain while still of working age), so the need is all the greater.

The economic burden of the poorer migrants who are legal residents on the State is enormous. The law demands that they be provided with all the benefits of Spain's generous health, education (for their children) and welfare benefits, whereas the wealthy retirees draw upon their accumulated savings and the social security benefits provided by their countries of origin.

This latter group forms about one-half of the foreign population today and in selected resort areas along the southern and eastern coasts of Spain have established numerous communities where Castilian Spanish is rarely heard or encountered in shops, restaurants, cafes and in the street.

The "discovery"

Why have so many North Europeans "discovered" Spain? It was due at first to Spain being a much cheaper tourist attraction than rivals Italy and France. The country's image as a backward, under-developed economy with a rigid puritanical society dominated by the Catholic Church, and ruled by an ultra-authoritarian "leftover" from the Fascist regimes of the 1930s, was crumbling in Franco's latter years and collapsed entirely within a few years of his passing from the scene.

According to *Instituto Nacional de Estadistica*, the following numbers of North Europeans were registered in 2002 as residents and listed on the voting register of their local municipalities: Brits 90,000; Germans 66,000; French 45,000; Scandinavians 22,000; Dutch 19,000; Belgians 15,000; Swiss 8,000; Irish 4,000; There are also 45,000 Italians and 10,000 Russians resident in Spain but many of these are workers in construction rather than retirees.

These figures, however, are a gross underestimate and must be taken with a large grain of salt. An equal or greater number of foreigners from these countries have bought property in Spain but reside there for only a few weeks a year and maintain their own home in their countries of origin where they still prefer to draw upon social benefits such as medical insurance. Thus, the real impact of the Northern Europeans in the Spanish economy is much greater than the official statistics of "legal residents" would suggest.

Ask almost any Brit, German, Swede or Norwegian why they came to Spain and the answers (almost entirely enthusiastic) are amazingly similar: a desire to enjoy the sun and sea in a much more congenial climate; the chance to live at an affluent or at least significantly higher standard of living due to the rate of exchange; the much lower Spanish prices for property, food, liquor and tobacco; a realization of the extremely high level of Spanish health care, a much lower rate of violent crime, and a much more "easy-going" lifestyle all around.

Even though the property boom has witnessed an explosion in Spanish house prices, they still lag far behind the cost of housing in Northern Europe. The same applies to many food staples, not to mention alcohol and tobacco. Retirees, many of whom have taken up golf, would be unable to practise this expensive sport in their countries of origin, where joining a club is necessary or socially the "thing to do".

The boom

A fantastic economic boom has changed the country almost from head to toe. Spain is the unrivalled number one tourist destination in the world. In 2003, an astonishing 52.5 million tourists entered a country with some ten million fewer inhabitants. A growing migration of retirees from the wealthy North European nations has sought out Spain's nature, hospitality and booming market to settle permanently in the country. Others are happy to buy a second holiday home, perhaps for investment or to rent out and then retire a few years later.

Spain has become a magnet for investment as well as vacations. Its prosperity, excellent health services, new roads and spotless beaches (due to generous grants from the European Union's Structural Fund) have outdistanced its traditional rivals, the still more expensive resort sites of France and Italy. Of the 640,500 housing starts for 2003, about 100,000 were for foreigners.

Las urbanizaciones

The prevalence of ethnically homogeneous housing estates is due in large part to the popularity of living in planned communities that provide shared facilities such as swimming pools, on-site parking, maintenance, electronic entry and exit gates, cable television and year-round landscaping. Such communities, mostly of apartments, offer the newcomer from Northern Europe a much easier life style than buying and maintaining a private house and garden.

Builders and estate agencies project their advertising to partners and affiliates abroad to attract buyers, many of whom prefer these advantages, plus the additional factor of being able to communicate easily with others of a similar background and shared language. These urbanizations also exist for Spaniards, and there is a clear preference for each national group to congregate. Many of these estates are virtually deserted for parts of the year, when those residents who still maintain a home in their countries of origin return to spend holidays with family and friends.

The challenge to new settlers

Among the retired North European migrants to Spain, there is, however, a major division into two groups. There is a large majority who is content with living in "little England" or "Norway" or "Germany" among neighbours and friends they can speak to and continue to enjoy the same food, habits and forms of relaxation they were accustomed to before their move. Then there is a minority of those who are beginning to feel uncomfortable in their "golden ghetto".

Look at the comments below. I have heard them in more or less the same words dozens of times. Among a minority of North Europeans you will find many who agree wholeheartedly and a majority who will argue that there is no need to feel embarrassed by them:

This place is over-run with immigrants. Sometimes you have to remind yourself what country you are in. If you close your eyes and listen to the voices on the street, it can seem like Spanish is fighting a losing battle. Everywhere you go, there are road signs written in English, shops, mini-markets, pubs and Irish bars with foreign sounding names over the door and foreign products in the window. I confess I'm not particularly comfortable with it. When I came to Spain for a holiday, I wanted to hear the Spanish language, eat Spanish food, drink in Spanish bars and get a flavour of Iberian culture.

Where I live, close to the shores of the Mar Menor in the Costa Cálida region, I have taken my own survey of the North European impact. From reliable information gathered from Spanish neighbours and friends in the area, I learned that 12 years ago there was not a single Chinese restaurant within an hour's drive. There are well over 50 today! Chinese food is particularly popular with North Europeans but has yet to win over many Spaniards, at least in my area. On any given meal out at a Chinese restaurant, you would be lucky to find one table occupied by Spaniards.

Why learn the language ?

A common trap many ex-pats fall into is avoiding to learn the language – a chore especially for Brits who were never accustomed to dealing with anyone at home in any other language but the native and official language of the country. It comes as a particular shock to many English speakers that so few Spaniards (except in the major tourist areas of the Costa del Sol and Costa Blanca) are fluent or even able to use English at a minimal level.

For the first time they encounter television in a foreign language without subtitles. All films in Spanish cinemas and on television are dubbed in Spanish. Today, Spanish has approximately the same number of native speakers as English worldwide and there are something like 25 independent nations whose official language is Spanish.

This means that most elderly Spaniards (like most Americans and Brits) have had little or no incentive to learn a foreign language because in their opinion everyone speaks Spanish. For the first time, Brits have to deal with another people who have the same arrogant attitude as themselves – why learn a foreign language?

Who did the building work?

Many new residents therefore make the mistake of taking on an English speaking builder, carpenter, electrician or plumber through a casual encounter simply because they don't want the hassle of trying to communicate with someone in their broken or non-existent Spanish. It often turns out that many of these "handymen" are cowboys who realize they have an easy market in Spain among the ex-pats. The result is often months of shoddy and expensive work.

The advantage of dealing with local and competitive workmen becomes obvious after an initial disaster. The remarks below are also those I have heard many times. They are the majority view of those ex-pats who have stayed for at least five years:

> I have no desire at all to return to the UK. I love it here. It is so beautiful with the nearby sea and the mountains. Even with a limited income, living here has given me the opportunity to do all sorts of things and to lead a very pleasant and comfortable life. Everyone, both the foreigners and the Spanish, welcome you and are friendly. They seem much better tempered than they are in England. The open-air life makes it easy to meet people.

The final verdict

There is a major disagreement when it comes to views on a "social life". For those ex-pats who lack Spanish, their lives are limited to their nearest friends and neighbours from their country of origin. This makes them miss much of what Spanish society and culture has to offer. It also means that unless one has also prepared interests to pursue, life in Spain can be lonely and confining. For those who are willing to meet the Spaniards halfway, there are many more opportunities for new experiences.

Racism and resentment

There is, of course, another side to the coin – the Spanish reaction. Clearly, tourism and migration have been important ingredients that contributed to the economic boom and rising prosperity, most apparent in those areas of Spain along the coasts and on the Balearic islands that have always been the major tourist sites.

Naturally, this generates a certain amount of envy and/or resentment, particularly when most people working in the service industries who come into close contact with North European residents have a story to tell about the reluctance of these foreigners to learn Spanish or familiarize themselves with the Spanish way of life. In the Balearic Islands, notably on Ibiza and Mallorca, there is growing resentment against the German population which has bought up a significant amount of the land available for building. This has even taken the form of petitions and political activity designed to limit land ownership by foreigners.

There is also a widespread suspicion that much of the theft and numerous break-ins that plague large parts of Spain are due to the immigrants from Morocco and a growing number of East Europeans. The crime rate involving property is much higher in the resort areas and where foreigners have settled, posing an issue that Spaniards living in these areas must also face.

The issue here is not envy but contempt and, occasionally, racism. This is most obvious when the foreigners involved are non-Spanish speaking and Muslims, most often Moroccans involved in agricultural labour, and in the country without wives or other family ties. The same problems are familiar in many parts of the world.

Another issue increasing tension is the apparent reluctance of some *ayuntamientos* (townhalls), especially those with a socialist administration, to properly enforce rules and ordinances dealing with sanitary measures in slaughter-houses, butcher shops and rules of employment in small open-air markets in which many Moroccan immigrants are employed. Critics maintain that the socialist administrations want to avoid antagonizing Muslim immigrants.

The special problems of the Moroccans

The link between delinquency and immigration is no myth, although it is frequently presented with euphemisms designed to be "politically correct". More than a half million Moroccan citizens live in Spain (either permanently, or during particularly labour-intensive seasons) and an additional 100,000 are from Algeria and Tunisia. Among the Moroccans, more than 40 percent (about 225,000) are in the country illegally and are undocumented. Their presence is often quite visible due to language, religion, residential concentration and dress.

Various polls carried out by the Centre of Sociological Investigations in Spain report that more than half the population considers immigration, particularly from North Africa, to be linked with the increase in crime, especially theft, smuggling and illegal drug use. This is borne out by the Ministry of the Interior. Well known "downtown" areas such as Lavapiés and Tetuán in Madrid, Raval in Barcelona and the centre of Palma de Mallorca are recognized as "Moroccan ghettoes" and the main sites for the sale of drugs, especially *cannibis* and *hachís*.

The problems of assimilation and religious extremism

Unlike earlier immigrants, the growth of religious extremism and coercion against older more moderate immigrants has been noted in the Moroccan community. Ten years ago, Arab dress was much less notable among both men and women. Older Moroccans have complained to the police of coercion to appear more fundamentalist and readopt Arab dress, a process referred to by the new Spanish verb as *reislamizar*.

Its appearance has been linked to pressure exerted by hard-line tendencies as a result of the growth of Saudi influenced *Wahabbi*-sect teaching. The 19 Moroccans detained in the Madrid bombing atrocity of 11 March 2004, were all long-time legal residents of Spain, with contacts to extremist religious organizations in Morocco (see vignette number 6).

Ethnic violence

The most serious incident of rioting and vigilante activity of Spaniards against foreign workers occurred in the town of El Ejido, situated between the Sierra de Gádor and the Mediterranean, the focal point for a large agricultural area specializing in the cultivation of hot house winter grown agricultural produce.

The region has often been referred to as "a sea of plastic" to denote the protection covering greenhouses and in the fields. In early February

2000, El Ejido was the site of a series of attacks by the local population against immigrant farm workers in the locality.

The town has grown enormously from 4,300 inhabitants in 1975 to 55,000 today! This growth is a product of the enormous demand for agricultural produce and has led to the immigration of many thousands of agricultural workers, many of them from Morocco and the other North African countries. Estimates place the number of illegal migrants at one-quarter of the local work force. Many earn low wages and work long hours six days a week. Most live in temporary camps or the hot houses next to the fields.

Among the most veteran North African population, there are individuals who have established shops in town. The cause of local anger against the foreign workers was the killing of a 26-year-old Spanish woman by a mentally disturbed young boy. This was the third case of murder of a Spanish national by a migrant farm worker within a period of only 15 days.

Mobs attacked workers and burned down bars and other establishments frequented by the foreign worker population, some of whom were forced to seek shelter and protection in the local police station. A facility that provided showers and a laundry for the migrants was also destroyed and some employers immediately dismissed their illegal workers. Fortunately, no one was killed. Out of fear, many workers did not show up at their places of employment for several days.

The incident received widespread coverage in the Spanish media. The embarrassing events led to a much closer inspection of employers hiring illegal migrants and the establishment of better living conditions and facilities and compensation for whoever had suffered property damage. The incident shed light on the less attractive side of Spain's appeal for migrants.

Many Spaniards are still grappling with how to better integrate the two diverse groups of migrants into Spanish society. The solution will have to depend on both sides making an effort, starting with better communication through a common language. ●

The pilgrimage to Santiago de Compostela

For 800 years, a small town in the peripheral province of Galicia has drawn millions of pilgrims. The pilgrimage has rivalled those to Rome and Jerusalem and it is likely that, due to its greater proximity for most Europeans and less dangerous surroundings, was an experience shared by more ordinary people in Europe than at the other two more traditional holy sites.

It is unquestionably true that it continues to far surpass its rivals in terms of the number of pilgrims who actually walk great distances and who consider the journey itself as a spiritual experience. Nothing better represents the different rhythm and link with the medieval past that makes Spain a country that has not yet jettisoned its past.

Today, as for centuries long ago, "All roads lead to Santiago de Compostela". Santiago de Compostela was proclaimed the first European Cultural itinerary by the Council of Europe in 1987. This route from the French-Spanish border passes by some 1,800 notable buildings along the way, both religious and secular and of great historic interest. The pilgrim route played a major role in encouraging cultural exchanges between the Iberian Peninsula and the rest of Europe during the Middle Ages. It is the most visible artefact of the power of the Christian faith among diverse people of all European nations and social classes.

Understanding the nature of this experience and its attraction – not only for observant Catholics but for the many thousands of pilgrims, travellers and tourists who seek to walk in the footsteps of their ancestors – reveals in part some of the mystery our modern world has lost. "Santiago" is a corruption of the Latin Sant Iago (Saint James) and Compostela (a corruption of the Latin *Campous Stellae* – Field of Stars).

The particular James in question was not the brother of Jesus but of John (the Evangelist). The Gospels (Matthew 4, 21-22; Mark 1, 19-20; Luke 5, 10-11) tell us that James and John were fishermen, the sons of Zebedee, and sailed with Simon called Peter and his brother Andrew. All four were called by Jesus from mending their nets beside the sea of Galilee at the beginning of his ministry. James and John were present at various miraculous events and spoke with Jesus on the Mount of Olives (Mark 13, 3). They themselves, asked Jesus to accord them places on his right and his left when he came into his kingdom, and declared themselves ready to drink from the same cup as Jesus – i.e. to accept martyrdom.

Finally, they are mentioned as present at one of the post-resurrection appearances (John 21, 2), on the lakeshore of Tiberius. He is thought to have been the first bishop of Jerusalem (Galatians 1, 19 and 2, 9). The martyrdom of James (Acts 12, 1-2) at the hands of Herod Agrippa I (about 41-44 AD) is also mentioned. So how did he come to be buried in Galicia in the northwest of Spain?

Legend has it that when the Apostles divided the known world into missionary zones, the Iberian Peninsula fell to James. Seventh and eighth century documents refer to the belief that he spent a number of years preaching in Spain before returning to Jerusalem, and martyrdom. His followers are supposed to have carried his body down to the coast and put it into a stone boat, which was carried by angels and the wind back across the Mediterranean to land near Finisterre, on the Atlantic coast of northern Spain. The local Queen, Lupa, brought the body to the site of the marble tomb a little way inland, where he was believed to have been buried with two of his own disciples, but the site of his tomb was forgotten for some 800 years.

Origins of the legend

Early in the ninth century a hermit, Pelayo, was led by a vision of falling stars *(Campus Stellae)* to the spot. The tomb was rediscovered, and the relics authenticated as those of St James by the local bishop. Galicia and the mountains of Asturias and Cantabria and the Basque country at the foot of the Pyrenees were the only areas of the Iberian Peninsula that had not been conquered by the Muslims. At this time, Spain was very much in need of a new champion to inspire Christian hopes against the invading Moors. The "rediscovery" came therefore at a very fortunate moment to rally religious fervour.

Even before this "rediscovery" of the remains of the Apostle Saint James, many people as far back as pre-Roman times had gone on a pilgrimage along the route that goes to the *Finis Terr* (the End of the Earth) on the extreme north-western corner of the *Peninsula*. There, they believed that they saw the sun being extinguished in the waters of the ocean. Perhaps this was part of a ritual in an ancient pagan religion.

The legend's connection with the Re-conquest – and St. James *Matamoros* (The Moor-Slayer)

The importance of the tomb site took on a new significance with the rallying of Christian forces determined to win back territory lost to the Muslims as part of the idea of The Re-conquest as a religious crusade. In the early ninth century when the tomb was discovered, Christian Spain had been reduced to the far North of the Peninsula and was fragmented into small kingdoms. The long-standing antagonism and rivalry between old Roman-Iberian Catholics and Arian Christianity among the Visigoths persisted.

It was not long afterwards that Ramiro I of Galicia saw a vision of St. James and led his forces under the banner and war-cry of "Santiago!" before which the Moors fled in 834. This victory suddenly propelled the image of Santiago – *Matamoros* – to the forefront of the battle to evict the Muslims entirely from Spain and unify the country under a common Catholic faith and the eventual ascendancy of the Kingdom of Castilla-Leon, which had assumed the protection of the site.

Although pilgrimages to Compostela had begun, a Muslim army under Muhammad ibn-abi-Amir, Arab advisor to the Caliph Hisham II, was not deterred and re-took the town, destroying the shrine in 997. Aware of its significance, the basilica's doors and bells were carried off to Córdoba to embellish the great mosque there. This setback did not result in Christian despair but only encouraged renewed devotion to Santiago and the determination to persist in the Re-conquest. This second Christian victory cemented the image of the town, its tomb and Cathedral as the pre-eminent pilgrimage site for believers motivated as much by hatred of the Muslim enemy as by Christian religious devotion.

This vision was enhanced by a monk and later saint, Francis of Assisi (1213), and monarchs such as Jaime I, "The Conqueror", who made the pilgrimage to Santiago de Compostela to give thanks following his victory in taking control of the Balearic islands, and by the monarchs Ferdinand and Isabella in 1488 and 1496 to pray for the conquest of Granada and to give thanks for the discovery of America.

By now, the participation of masses of common people from all over Spain and much of Western Europe had made the pilgrimage an act of devotion and penitence that acquired a growing following. Numerous "miracles" and "cures" were reported by pilgrims, while the Church and monarchs of a unified Spain fostered participation by the improvement of roads, the building of bridges and the installation of hostels and other facilities to aid travellers.

The Road

One of the two most traditional routes of the pilgrimage begins in Saint Jean Pied de Port on the French side of the Pyrenees and stretches 772 kilometres to Santiago. The somewhat longer second route from the Somport starts at the French border, beginning in what was the Kingdom of Aragón in north-eastern Spain and covers a distance of 846 kilometres. Both routes lead through the towns of Logroño, Burgos and León.

Pilgrims walking to Santiago de Compostela from the French border cover between 20 and 25 kilometres a day and take about 30 days to reach their destination in good summer weather. The great majority of pilgrims undertake the journey in the months of July and August (more than 50 percent), whereas a scant three percent set out in the coldest months between December and March.

Who are they?

There are more than two dozen associations to aid pilgrims and provide overnight accommodations in hostels, although many come equipped with their own tents. According to official statistics maintained by the associations and the Church, about 75,000 pilgrims undertook the journey, using one of the two major routes, in 2003. Men outnumber women about 2:1 and Spaniards account for about 60 percent of the traffic, followed by French, German, Italian, Ibero-American and North American pilgrims. In 2003, about 60,000 made the entire journey by foot, almost 14,000 by bicycle, three in wheelchairs and 266 on horseback. A majority were students and teachers, followed by workers, the retired, priests and housewives. About 70 percent of the pilgrims reported that their prime motivation was religious, whereas the remainder cited cultural and social reasons.

Even in medieval times, not all participants in the event were devout Catholics. They donned the traditional outfit of a cape, curling felt hat adorned with scallop shells, the symbol of the saint, and carried a long staff and gourd for water. The commercial opportunities presented by such a mass of itinerant wayfarers quickly became apparent. At first, before their total conversion to Catholicism, some Basques preyed upon the traffic, offering "protection" (i.e. blackmail). Jewish merchants provided needed goods, farmers and shepherds sold their products, gypsies from as far away as India turned up, as well as beggars, many prostitutes, thieves and what might just be called riff-raff.

The pilgrimage clearly did not enjoy universal respect and a number of clerics, including such famous personalities known throughout Europe as Erasmus and Bertoldo of Ratisbona, spoke out against the abuses and immoral acts frequently committed by the unscrupulous. Famous Spanish writers including Cervantes and Quevedo even poked fun at the pilgrims in some of their novels and stories satirizing the great diversity of human types. Among today's famous celebrities, Hollywood actress Shirley MacLaine has taken part (on the advice of her psychiatrist!).

The Santiago years

Ranking as the most favoured times for the pilgrimage are the "Santiago Years" when the Saint's Feast Day (July 25) falls on a Sunday. This occurs at intervals of 6, 5, another 6 and then 11 years. The last such events were in 1993 and 1999 and the next ones will be 2005, 2010 and 2021. Since next year (2005) almost corresponds to the one thousand and two-hundredth anniversary of the tomb's discovery (dating back to 813), a great many festivities and memorial events are planned, and 2010 will be even more eventful.

The geography

Certainly, the striking landscape of the two most famous routes are among the most appealing aspects of the journey for everyone, no matter what their degree or absence of religious motivation. It is often said that for the true pilgrim, it is the journey along the road rather than the destination that provides the greatest satisfaction. The tranquil landscapes of striking mountains, swift-flowing rivers, vineyards, forests and fields of verdant northern Spain provide ample rest for the soul on both the religious and existential levels.

It offers one a chance to get to know oneself without constant reference to the clock, the noise of the workaday world or material things, and to share in the joy of nature and communion with others and with God. This is the *Senda Jacobea* (or *Xacobea* in the Galician language), the route or "Path of James" that is the experience of the pilgrimage.

Santiago de Compostela – the destination

Looming above the town and seen by the pilgrims from a distance are the twin towers of the Cathedral dating from the eleventh century. The buildings facing the Cathedral on the elegant Plaza de Quintana share the same granite colour, and together give a harmonious unity to the several different architectural styles. The Cathedral houses the tomb of St. James lying in a crypt under the altar in the original ninth century foundation.

Visitors who set out on the pilgrimage with the cooperation of one of the many associations, and had their overnight stays validated at the various hostels, are awarded documentary proof in the form of a "passport" that they have made the journey by foot, bicycle or horseback. The entrance to the Cathedral is formed by the *Pórtico de Gloria* with magnificent twelfth century statues of the apostles and prophets.

For most modern visitors, including those tourists who have driven all the way to simply get there, the most impressive aspect of the town lies less in its stone than in the human spectacle of pilgrims from all over the world, many of them bearing their walking sticks, backpacks and displaying a scallop shell, symbol of the pilgrimage. Their diversity in appearance and language, visible exhaustion and, most of all, the look of contentment on their faces at having reached their destination and shared in this experience, is heart-warming even for the cynical. ●

HISTORY AND
FOREIGN RELATIONS

The Gibraltar dispute

ew, if any, other places in the world of such small size (5.8 square kilometres in area or just 4.5 kilometres long and 1.2 kilometres wide) have been the subject of international controversy for so long as Gibraltar. Centuries of history have turned "The Rock" into a symbol of British naval power and a synonym for security, so much so that it was adopted by the Prudential Life Insurance Company as its trademark.

Although driven from the headlines by Spain's three-decade-long confrontation with the Basque separatist-terrorist organization ETA and the recent discovery of extremist Islamist groups allied to *Al-Qaeda* who were responsible for the Madrid Massacre on 11 March 2004, the "recovery" of Gibraltar remains the longest standing and highest profile goal of Spanish diplomacy. This is all the more poignant in that it is the sole fly in the ointment which disturbs the otherwise excellent relations between Britain and Spain.

In spite of all the changes in technology and transportation in the past century, the strategic importance of Gibraltar continues to be paramount. The Rock provides a first-rate natural harbour, and is more easily defended than Spanish Tarifa at the most southerly point of the coast facing Africa. The strait separating Spain from Africa is only 8.6 miles wide at Gibraltar. The port is not of great economic importance but the naval base has safeguarded the link between the Atlantic, Mediterranean and Suez Canal, and acts as a guardian for international shipping (especially oil tankers) supplying Western Europe and Britain with oil from the Persian Gulf.

It is no exaggeration to describe Gibraltar as "the link between two continents, two civilizations, two great religions, two ways of life, physical environments and two great seas". The Spanish claim to Gibraltar was perhaps the sole issue on which the government of General Franco fully agreed with the losing Republican side, which maintained a government-in-exile in Mexico.

Gibraltar's population

Gibraltar's population of 28,000 firmly supports the current status of the territory as a British possession and has twice given overwhelming support to the continuation of the present arrangement in referenda. In both votes, a majority of 99 percent rejected proposals to full or shared Spanish control. This "rejection", unprecedented for the size of its majority in a true democratic vote, has wounded Spanish pride.

The *Gibraltereños* are quite a mixed bunch. They are decidedly not "English roses" in their physical appearance, origins and heritage, although all speak fluent English. They included the Sepharadi-Jews, Cypriots, Maltese, Italians (primarily from Genoa), Portuguese, Indians, Pakistanis, Moroccans and finally English. All these people came to work and eventually settled in the city, due to its lively commerce and need for their entrepreneurial, work and handicraft skills.

The growth of a Gibraltarian consciousness was stimulated during and just after World War II. The civilian population was forcibly evacuated and many deeply resented being sent into a temporary exile for the duration of the war in Northern Ireland, Madeira, and Jamaica. The exile made the Gibraltarians miss their homes and all the more determined to return and take a more active part in governing themselves.

To this was added the fact that Spain's leader for more than a generation (from 1939 to 1975) was General Francisco Franco. The Spanish leader was actively aided by Hitler and Mussolini in the Spanish Civil War. Franco was sympathetic to the Axis powers for the first few years of the war, even allowing Spanish volunteers to fight with the Germans against the Soviet Union. These wartime experiences strengthened the feelings of many Gibraltarians that they are a distinct people with their own right to self-government and their independence from any Spanish interference.

Among part of the population there is a profound respect for Spanish culture. Ironically, this is most true for the Sepharadi-Jews who retained the language of their oppressors of five hundred years ago. Sir Joshua Hassan, a Jewish governor of the territory for 42 years, was a correspondent reporting on bullfighting for the Spanish daily *La Republica*! Nevertheless, in the two referendum campaigns, the most popular slogan used by the winning side was "British we are, British we stay".

The Gibraltarians' desire to remain a British colony but still exercise more independence does not sit comfortably with the British government. In 2002, a referendum organized by the Gibraltarians themselves without the approval of either the British or the Spanish governments voted by an overwhelming majority of 17,900 to 187 against the idea of "shared" British-Spanish sovereignty.

The proposal would have given the territory greater autonomy within the European Union as well as the retention of the British naval base and intelligence facilities under the NATO banner. In spite of these "sweeteners", it was a stinging rejection of Spain's long-standing demand to reacquire the territory. The 2002 vote result saw a small advance on the numbers who voted for a deal with Spain the last time round in 1967.

Ironically, this arch-British patriotism is an embarrassment for Great Britain, which would like to resolve the issue with Spain. It formally endorsed the "shared sovereignty" formula in the last plebiscite. UK Foreign Minister Jack Straw has repeatedly told the House of Commons that both Spain and the British government agree that "shared sovereignty" is the best way forward.

Things were different when Spain was isolated internationally, outside the European Union and run by General Franco as a dictatorship. Technically, as the colonial power, Britain has the right to impose new arrangements, although it has repeatedly said that no change in sovereignty would be implemented without the approval of the people of Gibraltar. The stark reality of the Gibraltar problem at the moment is either a continuation of the status quo or fruitless attempts at serving up the same idea of a future referendum which will only lead to a rousing endorsement of the status quo.

A lot of history

The Moors first drove out the Visigoths in the eighth century, and held The Rock (*El Peñon* in Spanish) of Gibraltar until just prior to the Spanish conquest of Granada. The Spanish crown took possession of the peninsula following victories over the Moors and held it for 242 years until 1704, when it was seized by a joint Anglo-Dutch military force under Admiral Sir George Rooke during the War of Spanish Succession. The peace treaty that settled that war was signed in Utrecht in 1713 and ceded Gibraltar to the United Kingdom "in perpetuity". The territory has remained under uninterrupted British control ever since. In terms of length of ownership, it has been British for longer than it was Spanish!

Spain has eyed the recovery of Gibraltar with immense envy ever since its loss. The year 2004 is the 300th anniversary of its seizure and the inability to restore it to Spanish sovereignty is a bitter pill for Spain to swallow. The 1713 treaty confirmed British naval power as the dominant force in the Mediterranean, a fact resented by both France and Spain and eventually Italy when it became a united country.

The treaty forbids the introduction of any smuggled goods from Gibraltar into Spain and, in deference to Spain's eighteenth century "judeophobia", prohibits the settlement of Jews or Muslims on The Rock! This anachronistic clause has had no practical significance for more than 200 years and there is a thriving Sepharadi-Jewish (the descendents of those expelled in 1492) community in the city that has supplied the territory with several of its governors.

Valiant but vain Spanish attempts to recover The Rock

Spain has made several valiant but vain attempts to recover The Rock. Several times, the British made proposals to return Gibraltar in return for strategic advantages in the Mediterranean – yet each time the Spaniards had other more important concerns. This occurred in 1718 when Britain proposed returning Gibraltar if the Spaniards agreed to lift their siege of Sicily. The Spanish crown had other priorities and valued its dynastic ties in Sicily or its hold on the Dominican Republic in the Caribbean and rejected a British proposal to trade it for Gibraltar.

In 1728, the Spaniards made a major assault accompanied by a mammoth bombardment of The Rock, but failed to take it. Between 1779 and 1783, while the British were occupied with the American Revolution, another Spanish siege and artillery bombardment failed for a second time to recover Gibraltar by force.

Franco refuses Hitler's offer

With the fall of France in June 1940 and the entry of Italy on the side of Nazi Germany, Franco was confronted with a dilemma. It seemed a golden opportunity to recover Gibraltar, but the British fleet was still powerful and Spain was exhausted from a long civil war, and suffering from both hunger and poverty on an unprecedented scale.

Much of the rich farming land had been on the Republican side and their retreating forces had destroyed considerable amounts of modern farming and irrigation equipment. The country's gold had been sent to the Soviet Union to buy arms and for safe storage. Spain's only major economic resource was the important metal tungsten, a vital element in hardening steel for artillery shells. In return for tungsten, Spain was able to receive much needed food supplies, but it had to maintain neutrality and trade with both sides.

Although sorely tempted, Franco had to refuse Hitler's attempts to force Spain to become an Axis ally. He was in no doubt that Winston Churchill meant what he said at the close of 1939 that, if Spain sided with Germany, Britain would apply a massive blockade and that "No ship would be able to leave or enter Spanish waters".

Franco and Salazar, Portugal's ruler, proclaimed their neutrality upon the outbreak of the war, but Franco made it known to Germany that he would "tilt" whenever he could. German submarines were allowed to provision secretly in Spanish ports, notably Vigo, Cartagena and Las Palmas in the Canary Islands. The British ambassador to Spain was greeted by jeering crowds shouting *"Gibraltar para España"* whenever he was recognized in public.

Franco gave permission for a German military team to visit Spain. It was led by Admiral Wilhelm Canaris and, in July 1940, plans were made for a joint German – Spanish assault on Gibraltar. German reconnaissance teams observed Gibraltar's preparations, the 1,400-foot-high limestone mountain bristling with gun emplacements, guarded by 12,500 soldiers and laced with intricate supply tunnels. Hitler agreed to Canaris' plan in August and a special training camp for the assault was set up in occupied France.

Franco answered Hitler's plea for entry into the war with a long list of essential goods that Spain lacked. He demanded that Spain be adequately provided with food supplies and assured possession of Gibraltar, most of Morocco and parts of French North Africa and French Equatorial Africa. Franco continued to play both sides for all he could and sent letters to London and Washington promising to stay out of the war.

Hitler made a pilgrimage to personally convince Franco of an alliance. He travelled to Spain and met with the Spanish dictator at Hendaye on the French-Spanish border on 23 October 1940. The meeting was set for 3pm, but Franco arrived an hour late, putting the Führer under psychological pressure. The two dictators argued for nine hours and Franco was able once again to promise to enter the war only when "convenient" for Spain. Finally, after being kept waiting for another hour while Franco took an after-dinner siesta, Hitler had to leave with a worthless piece of paper, stating that Spain would decide the time of her entry into the war.

"Operation Felix" to conquer Gibraltar never got beyond the planning stage and was scrapped after Mussolini visited Franco, attempting to prod him into joining the Axis in 1941. The Spanish dictator soothed his conscience after the German invasion of the Soviet Union in July 1941 by allowing Spanish Volunteers (47,000 men of the Blue Division) to fight alongside the Germans against communism.

In November 1942, Franco met with the American ambassador who assured him that Allied landings in French North Africa had no intention to intrude upon Spanish territory. Franco then gave orders not to allow any German troops to move across Spain to reinforce their troops in North Africa. Franco had ended his romance with the Axis and his dreams of recovering Gibraltar.

The dispute remains

In its attempt to work our a deal, the British government has only succeeded in arousing the ire of many Spaniards who cannot accept a referendum leading to a lopsided outcome. Many observers feel that the end result would be the worst of all worlds, the dashing of raised expectations in Spain and a complete loss of trust in the British government by the people of Gibraltar, who regularly criticize the Foreign Office. They never grow tired of reminding the British government that any proposal on joint sovereignty must be approved by Parliament as well as in a popular referendum. Gustavo de Aristegez, a Spanish spokesman on foreign affairs in the previous government, has said any referendum is "not legally binding".

British-Spanish relations reach a low ebb

Both before and after Franco, the border between Gibraltar and Spain was closed by the Spanish, imposing considerable economic hardship on the territory. The low point was reached in 1954 when Queen Elizabeth II and the Duke of Edinburgh visited Gibraltar on their royal yacht as part of the Coronation Tour. This was waving a red cape in front of the Spanish bull and Franco took it as a personal insult. Mobs chanted and waved Spanish flags, screaming insults and cries that "Gibraltar is Spanish" and "Down with Churchill". Even the British embassy in Madrid was practically besieged. For 13 years, telephone communications between Gibraltar and Spain were blocked.

The maximum point of tension occurred in 1969 when Spain cancelled the work permits of almost 5,000 Spanish workers, who were unable to continue working in Gibraltar. Franco even ordered a boycott of ships that had used the port of Gibraltar and prohibited their entry into Spanish territorial waters. Further pressure limited incoming and outgoing flights through Spanish airspace. These measures greatly increased the dangers to international flights.

To demonstrate that the "return" of Gibraltar remains an essential Spanish goal, the new King Juan Carlos in his first address to the Spanish Cortes (Parliament) in 1975 declared that "It would not be faithful to the tradition of my blood if I did not recall that during generations we Spaniards have fought to restore the integrity of our homeland."

Following Spanish entry into the European Union and NATO, tensions have subsided and no further attempts at massive disruption have been made. Spain and the UK signed an agreement known as "The Brussels Accord" in Belgium in 1984, eliminating the various restrictions and sanctions that had been used to blackmail Gibraltar. The border was reopened in 1985, after having been closed for the preceding 15 years.

Negotiations with the Pope, and U.N. meddling

The issue remains an open wound, the only border dispute between two members of the European Union. When Harold Wilson was Prime Minister, he made approaches to the Vatican to mediate the dispute. Spain's campaign to "decolonise" Gibraltar was submitted in a U.N. resolution in December 1967. The entire Arab bloc voted in favour.

This was bad enough, but the Israeli delegate had the "bad taste" to explain his opposition by recalling that Franco had allowed Spanish volunteers (The Blue Division) to fight on Hitler's side, while Gibraltar held out as a British bastion of freedom. These remarks were ill received in Spain and revived many of the old biases against the UK and Israel as well as the United States.

The press played on Spanish sentiment against what they perceived as an "unholy alliance" between the Anglo-American Protestant powers and the Jewish state. The Blue Division was a particularly sore point since the soldiers had volunteered only out of anti-communist zeal and had no impact or influence on German policies. Moreover, they had been kept in Soviet prisons long after all other Axis prisoners of war had been released.

Renewed U.N. language over Gibraltar

Spanish representatives have re-stated their position on Gibraltar many times and have invited the current Chief Minister of Gibraltar, Peter Caruana, to participate in the negotiations. Spain has made it clear that it intends to continue conversations with the UK to reach an agreement that satisfies all the interested parties. But all members of the Caruana government have replied that various Spanish-UK negotiations are not genuine because they do not give Gibraltar an equal say, leaving it open for both the UK and Spain to reach agreements over their heads. The people of Gibraltar will continue to fight to uphold their rights as had been the case in the past throughout their 300-year-old tie with the UK.

British representatives at the United Nations have come under continued criticism with regard to both the Falkland Islands and Gibraltar, and face a hostile alliance of Spain, the Latin American nations and the Arab world. Nevertheless, the UK representatives make a clear distinction between the two. No reference is made by the U.N. to the "right of self determination" with regards to Gibraltar, in contrast to the line taken over the Falklands.

The UN Committee on Decolonisation is to consider whether a reference to Gibraltar in the conclusions to their annual regional seminar should be amended to the effect that the wishes of the people of Gibraltar need to be taken into account in resolving the dispute. Previous draft references to Gibraltar make no mention of Gibraltarian wishes and are strongly pushed at every opportunity by the Cubans, who wish to embarrass Great Britain and the United States.

While the idea of an independent Gibraltar may seem absurd (compare with Andorra's population of 65,000, Liechtenstein's 32,000 and San Marino's 26,000), there are those in Spain who look forward to some sort of arrangement that would make Gibraltar an equal autonomous region, on a par with the other 17 autonomous regions, but with even more rights.

Another alternative is the one known as the "Andorra solution". It means independent status under some sort of joint patronage. That could be the British Queen and the King of Spain, or the Prince of Wales and the Principe de Asturias, perhaps. Although this smacks of something out of the Middle Ages, it could prove to be the least provocative solution.

Gibraltar is clearly unique, but Britain cannot expect any support in a confrontation, due to the composition of the United Nations with a potentially large majority of Latin-American, Arab-Muslim and African states hostile to what they see as colonialism. The return of Hong-Kong has only whet the appetite of such states who won't accept that Gibraltar is different. After all, many people in Hong-Kong opposed the move but it was enshrined in a treaty, so even the "holy" issue of "self-determination" could not be raised. ●

The Basque conundrum

The dictionary defines a conundrum as a problem admitting of no solution or a riddle in which a fascinating question is answered by a pun. Both seem to fit the problem of *El País Vasco* – one of the 17 autonomous communities in Spain and part of the ancient homeland of the Basque people.

It is not only a Spanish problem. Part of the Basque country extends into south-western France (the departments of Labourd, Basse Navarra and Soule), and the Basque campaign to achieve independence has been categorized by growing and ever more extremist violence beginning in the last days of the Franco regime.

Political unrest

More than 800 Spaniards have been killed in acts of violence perpetrated by the separatist organization ETA. *(Euskadi Ta Askatasuna* – The Basque Country and Liberty) since its founding in 1959. Prior to that, the problem had largely been suppressed following the end of the Spanish Civil War.

The Basque provinces had traditionally been integrated within feudal, medieval and contemporary Spanish society for almost ten centuries. They were often involved in dynastic and political struggles almost always on the side of the most reactionary elements on behalf of a traditional monarchy, feudal privileges and the Catholic Church. Yet remarkably, ETA and most Basque separatists who envision either an "associated status" or independence as a just claim of the Basque cause, drape themselves in the vocabulary of Marxist, left-wing and "revolutionary" jargon.

ETA has increasingly followed a campaign of violence, intimidation, and subscribed in the past to the racist doctrine of Sabino Arana, the modern founder of Basque nationalism. Even more absurd in the light of their past devotion and loyalty to the Catholic Church are recent alliances with forces of radical Arab nationalism and Islamic extremism.

The Basques are perhaps the best case of what has been termed "The Fourth World" – consisting of ancient peoples who have been denied political independence but maintained their own distinctive languages and a sense of solidarity. The Basque people have never formed a politically independent state as is true of the Kurds and was, until the collapse of the Soviet Union, true of the Armenians as well.

The political party enjoying the largest amount of popular support, but far short of a majority in the Basque country, is the *PNV* – the *Partido Nacionalista Vasco* (Basque Nationalist Party) – whose current leadership has argued for increased autonomy or self-rule with the future goal of either independence or as a condominium alongside Spain. They claim to respect due process of law, democracy and reject ETA's violent approach, but many observers are suspicious of their true policies, motives and goals.

Antiquity of the Basques

The Basque case is particularly fascinating because of the involvement of anthropological, racial and linguistic claims regarding the antiquity and long residence of the Basque people extending back to the Stone Age, depending on various claims, theories and arguments. Extreme claims by Basque nationalists assert that the language was even spoken throughout the entire Iberian Peninsula before the arrival of the Iberians, Phoenicians or Romans. All these assertions are likely never to be proven since they go far back to the remote past, predating written languages by thousands of years.

What is incontrovertible are the following four facts about the language and political struggle.

1. The extremely archaic character and apparent lack of any close linguistic affinity with other languages in Europe (see vignette 22 on Spain's Languages). A few linguists have argued for a remote similarity with the languages of the Caucasus mountains and Berber dialects in North Africa, which may seem to indicate a remote origin and original migratory path by which the Basques entered their homeland. This territory in the western Pyrenees and adjacent shoreline of the Bay of Biscay includes steep sided hills and valleys in what are today the provinces of Alava, Biscay (Vizcaya), Guipuzcoa and Navarra.

2. The extraordinarily high percentage of type B blood and RH negative factor (to which some observers would add unusually large ears!) indicating a long period of settlement in their homeland and isolation, during which there was little mixture with other peoples.

3. Whatever the merits or demerits of the claims regarding antiquity, blood type and language, the Basque country has been an integral part of the Kingdoms of Navarre and Castile, and later of a united Spain, for close to a thousand years. During that time, especially with the development of modern industry, the area has attracted migrants from other parts of the country. They and their descendents are at least 40 percent of the population of the four Basque provinces (Navarra, however, is not a part of the autonomous community of *El País Vasco* but has its own autonomous charter), and whether or not they speak the Basque language (known as Euskera), they are Spanish citizens. They are thus entitled by the constitution to the same rights as other citizens and have thoroughly justified suspicions and concerns regarding their status in any future political arrangement.

4. There is much evidence to support the concerns of those who oppose any future arrangement that would countenance further "autonomy". This view is shared by Spaniards of Basque origin as well as others, including some who heroically fought in the Civil War against Franco and, as a result, spent years in prison for their activities. Charges have been made by prominent Basque personalities that famous institutions such as the renowned Guggenheim museum in Bilbao, as well as businesses of all types and sizes, are subject to a campaign of blackmail and intimidation, leading to the payment of protection money to ETA – "or else".

Early history

The Romans by and large avoided Basque settled areas that were entirely rural. Roads were built through the area and the Romans established some settlements of their own. Whatever order, discipline or administration the Romans managed to impose disappeared with their retreat. The Basques had not accepted Roman rule or the Latin language.

They likewise resisted the Germanic tribes of the Franks and the Visigoths who took control of what are today France and Spain. They resisted Christianity as well and, in 788, ambushed a Frankish army returning from an unsuccessful campaign against the Moslems in Spain. The Franks were wiped out and their defeat was immortalized in one of the most famous medieval ballads, the *Chanson de Roland*.

Those who wrote the ballad turned the ambushing force into Muslims, apparently to spur on religious conviction. Another motive may have been to avoid the embarrassment that a humble illiterate and non-Christian pagan tribe of Basques had defeated one of the most powerful peoples in Western Europe.

Rival kingdoms – Castilla-León, Asturias and Navarra – contended for control of the Basque country. Some Basques undoubtedly were already part of the Kingdom of Navarra and did not hesitate to try and absorb their kinsmen into a state in which they felt there was common cause and mutual interests.

As late as the twelfth century, there are accounts of Basque pagans harassing pilgrims on their pilgrimage to Santiago de Compostela. The wildest country of "uncivilized Basques" lay in the coastal and mountainous regions, whereas those in Navarra had already accepted Christianity.

The form of political organization in much of the Basque country consisted of tribal elders – in Biscay and Guipuzcoa and an elected council of nobles in Álava. In comparison with the rest of feudal Spain and Europe, the common people were not serfs. They enjoyed such liberties and rights as bearing arms, freedom to hunt and fish and make use of common woodlands and pastures.

Eventually all three regions fell under the rule of Navarra and then Castilla. Their association was voluntary, however, and the kings accepted the Basque claims to traditional rights and privileges they had previously enjoyed.

The *fueros*

These rights, known as *fueros* became the cornerstone of the Basque sense of political identity as freemen in a wider kingdom. The abstract idea of "nationalism" based on language and/or territory did not enter into the equation. From the twelfth to the fourteenth centuries, the Basque councils voted voluntarily to offer the "over-lordship" of their regions to the crown of Castilla.

Navarra remained an independent kingdom until 1512, when it refused the passage of the King Ferdinand of Aragón's troops. It is an irony that Navarra, which is the "least Basque" in terms of the ethnic-linguistic origins of its inhabitants, was the only one to be forcibly absorbed by Castilla into what later became part of a unified Spain.

A great deal of self-rule continued to be permitted, especially in Guipuzcoa where a local assembly could refuse a royal order from the King of Spain simply by rejecting it with the words "We obey but do not comply". Navarra had its own "Viceroy", the only such title to be granted within continental Spain, and retained its own legislature and judiciary.

Basques played a major role in the development of a united Spanish state and army under the domination of Castilla. They provided many administrators, explorers, conquerors of the Americas and religious figures such as St. Francis Xavier and St. Ignacio de Loyola.

They became expert whalers and dominated this profession, often going abroad to serve in this capacity under contract. They also played an important economic and police role in the Spanish economy and enjoyed a special status with their own customs control on the French border.

Basque traditions and life style

Some sociologists, who have studied the Basques, maintain that they have always had a higher status and respect for women (see vignette 23 on *La Dama de Elche*). Women traditionally did the farm work (while the men were at sea or off to war) and inherited property. The Basque countryside was also quite different. Farms were widely dispersed instead of concentrated in villages.

Even in cuisine and drinking habits, the Basques could not be considered as typical Spaniards. Their original preferences were for beer and cider, relied on whale blubber and dried cod for much of their sustenance, and they had a different tradition of sports and games (see vignette 3 on *pelota*), poetry and music.

The Basques even bequeathed to the world their typical headgear, known as the *boina* (or beret in French). A large red *boina* became the uniform of the Basques supporting the Carlist cause and is worn today by the local Basque police force. Ironically, because of their status as "underdogs", the beret became the symbol of the political Left in much of Latin America – a la Castro and Ché Guevara – in spite of its origin as a symbol for the most reactionary Right in Spanish politics during the nineteenth century.

Quite a few unique traditions, home crafts, musical instruments and dance, games, sports, customs and folklore survive in the rural heartland of the Basque country, and it is easy to understand why there is a legitimate concern that a way of life – not just a language – is in danger of withering away under the impact of modern economic development, increased migration and further urbanization.

Some of the sports and competitions are reminiscent of those practiced in Scotland, Wales and Ireland and on the American frontier in the nineteenth century, such as wood chopping, log-throwing, cutting corn with a scythe, pulling carts, and straw bale hoisting. Others such as catching a greased pig were a favourite of rural humour for generations but now seem quite old-fashioned.

The impact of the Inquisition

Eventually, the Basques embraced Catholicism and became devoutly religious. Nevertheless, the traditional fondness for fortune telling and the survival of pagan superstitions made Basque women susceptible to charges of witchcraft. In the last major *auto-de-fé* (public ceremonial execution of death by being burned alive at the stake), in 1610 in the town of Logroño, more Basques were sentenced for witchcraft and heresy than those condemned for practicing Judaism, Islam or Lutheranism.

In spite of their Catholic faith, the Basques should have been aware that they would become an easy scapegoat. In fourteenth century Huelva, a town to the east of Navarra, a law was passed that forbade the speaking of Basque and Hebrew (languages of the Devil).

The impact of industry and nationalism

With the advent of modern times and the new idea of nationalism, the Basques showed their antipathy to everything new and modern. They rejected the idea of a centralized state that might threaten their traditional *fueros*. They rejected abstract liberties such as freedom of religion which seemed to contradict the teachings of the church. In various conflicts and civil wars, the Basques showed their determination to support the reactionary Carlist cause in the nineteenth century.

However, they could not ignore modern industry. The ample resources of iron, timber and water power attracted capital and a new workforce drawn from migrants who entered the region from every part of Spain The newcomers were immediately regarded with suspicion and looked down upon and given the derisive name of *maketos* or *belarri motx* – those with stumpy ears.

It is from this period that modern Basque nationalism can be dated. Before, there was no doubt regarding the loyalty of the Basques to the monarch as the legitimate ruler of Spain, and this included *El País Vasco*. It subsequently changed from being an abstract term to one of Basque uniqueness in the face of a "foreign" invasion that threatened their way of life. Ironically, though, many of the capitalists and artisans who benefited from the new economy were Basques.

Sabino Arana and the Nationalist Cause

The instigator of modern Basque nationalism, looked upon by ETA as their founding father, was Sabino Arana, the son of a Carlist exile in France. Born in 1865, like many other nationalists, his first interest and obsession was to "purify" the Basque language from an accumulation of Hispanicisms. He went on to provide the language with what had been its major shortcoming and inability to handle the modern industrial society that was then developing – the almost total lack of words for abstractions.

Abstractions were not needed for a stone-age language but Arana grasped how to utilize the innate properties of the language to create a whole new vocabulary. In spite of this, he was entirely reactionary and envisioned a Basque homeland that would return to its pre-industrial, devoutly religious rural and pastoral past. On the most gut-level, his doctrine preached hatred of everything "Spanish" – from the bullfight to *flamenco* music – and "foreign" (i.e. the immigrants from other parts of Spain and the outside world).

He helped establish the PNV in 1894 and subsequently spent several months in prison. The authorities found him guilty of sedition for his congratulatory telegram to President Theodore Roosevelt in May 1902, thanking the American leader for "having liberated the Cubans from Spanish slavery" as a consequence of the American victory in the 1898 war. He then changed tack and proclaimed his ambition was "autonomy" rather than secession and the authorities realized he would become a martyr if sent to prison for a long time.

The Spanish Civil War (see vignettes 17-19) provided a unique opportunity for the Basques to realize most of their ambitions within a democratic framework. Although conservative, the Basque leadership chose to support the Republican cause and fight against General Franco. Their hatred of the Franco regime and international Fascism was cemented by the German Luftwaffe attack on the historic centre of Basque nationalism, *Guernica*, immortalized by Picasso's most famous painting (see vignette 18). The *Juntas Generales* (General Assembly) of the Basque country met in Guernica under an oak tree to legislate and administer the *fueros*.

After the Civil War

With the Franco victory in 1939, severe measures were taken against the Basque country. All the traditional *fueros*, use of the Basque language and even other cultural organizations and activities that smacked of any indication of Basque separateness were forbidden. These punitive measures were less harsh in Navarra, due to its mixed population.

A Basque government in exile was established in New York City (the remainder of the Republican government in exile met at Mexico City). During World War II, many Basque and Spanish volunteers in exile served the Allied cause in the hope that they would be recognized as combatants for a Republican Spain to be re-established with the overthrow of the Franco regime.

Anti-Franco Basques had aided downed allied pilots and refugee Jews escaping from Vichy France into Spain. The Basque government in exile in New York, led by Jose Maria Aguirre, tried to make the case that they were an integral part of the Allied cause and should be helped in the common struggle against Fascism and Franco, a view that evaporated with the final Allied victory in Europe in May 1945.

The Cold War helped rescue Francoist Spain from its isolation and pariah status and, in so doing, doomed the Republican and Basque causes. A Spanish-American defence pact was signed in 1953, American airbases were established and Spain was admitted to the U.N. two years later.

According to material published by Basque nationalists with the endorsement of the PNV, more than 25,000 Basque prisoners were executed following the Civil War in revenge for their support of the Republic. An ineffectual underground resistance was abandoned after a few premature unsuccessful operations in 1946-57, and the Basque nationalist cause languished until the establishment of ETA in 1959. The organization was originally led by intellectuals and did not subscribe to Arana's racial doctrine or his automatic loyalty to the Catholic Church. It even believed that it might be possible to absorb the "foreigners" in the Basque country who had learned the language.

Strange bedfellows

Politics makes strange bedfellows. Originally, the Basques greatly admired Israel for the successful anti-colonial struggle that drove the British from Palestine and for their defeat of the invading Arab armies, as well as the immediately obvious achievement of great interest to the Basques – the successful revival of the Hebrew language. Several Basque intellectuals had read *The Revolt*, the biography of Israeli leader Menahem Begin, and strove to have ETA imitate the *Irgun*, the right-wing Jewish underground in British-mandated Palestine.

Many Basques and Republican sympathizers remembered the heroic contributions of thousands of Jewish volunteers who flocked to the International Brigades during the Civil War. Basque sea captains piloted some of the immigrant ships that successfully ran the British blockade attempting to strangle the newborn state of Israel by preventing the arrival of immigrants and supplies.

They remembered, too, the lively Basque woman communist delegate to the *Cortes* (Spanish Parliament) during the Republic, Dolores Ibarruri, who had gone into exile in the Soviet Union and from there issued a proclamation saluting the new State of Israel and comparing the invading Arab armies to the Fascist uprising that had destroyed the Republic.

This pro-Israel orientation was also fuelled by the open pro-Arab orientation of the Franco regime, but things began to change in the 1970s when ETA stepped up its violence and blackmail and abandoned its policy of taking care to prevent injuries to innocent bystanders. They gradually became more and more anti-American and, with it, anti-Israel. Their admiration changed to the PLO and other Arab terrorist groups who attracted world attention to what had been considered a lost cause.

Eventually, extremist and mercurial Arab leaders, such as Libya's Muammar Ghaddafi, became open supporters of ETA, supplying it with explosives and funds. It is no wonder that the government was not sure at first whether it was Islamist terrorists or ETA (or both) who were behind the March 11 atrocity against the train passengers in Madrid's Atocha Station. There is an active *Al Qaeda* cell in Spain and a number of arrests have been made in such locations as Alicante, Marbella and Madrid.

Al-Qaeda is not the only radical Islamic group operating in Spain. Others include the armed Islamic Salafist Group for Call and Combat (responsible for tens of thousands of deaths in Algeria), and members of the Syrian branch of the Muslim Brotherhood. These groups have cooperated with ETA in the past and with *Al-Qaeda*, too, and the fact that so many of the suspects arrested thus far are from Spain's near neighbour, Morocco, looks suspicious.

Many of ETA's leaders felt that the movement should openly proclaim its belief in Marxism and identification with the "oppressed". This was in spite of the fact that many Basques, even those favourable to greater autonomy, tend to be devout Catholics. This has caused some *PNV* spokesmen to occasionally denounce ETA as a communist organization.

The present impasse

The 1978 Spanish constitution, adopted three years after Franco's death, speaks of the Basques and the Catalans as a "nationality" but only Spain as a "nation". The constitution failed to achieve a majority only in the Basque country, where 40 percent of eligible voters abstained. This is the sticking point. The Basques today have all the same (or more) rights and freedoms they had under the Republic.

ETA's political wing *Batasuna*, now banned as a political party, is able to operate "on the street" and "behind the scenes" to exert blackmail against many ordinary citizens in the Basque country, where supporters of the status quo (even those who spent years in Franco's prisons) are liable to be targeted and denounced as *Españolistas* ("Spanish lovers"). The conundrum continues. ●

The African *plazas*

B
eyond the Spanish mainland (The Peninsula) lie three overseas island chains. Many tourists are familiar with two major ones – the Baleares in the Mediterranean and the Canary Islands off the coast of Northwest Africa, opposite Morocco and Mauritania. The remaining "overseas" territory along the Moroccan coast, however, has traditionally been a forgotten curiosity until suddenly projected into the headlines by the recent Moroccan attempt to seize control of uninhabited Perejil (Parsely) island.

This rock, however, is not the real issue of contention. It has become a "test balloon" for a much greater dispute – the issue of Spain's sovereignty over its overseas African *plazas*. One needs to find a very large-scale map to locate these small territories. Much Spanish blood has been shed in the past to keep them, but their importance to Spain is more than just emotional.

What is at stake is nothing less than Spanish sovereign territory in the form of two major cities and their hinterlands (Ceuta and Melilla) surrounded by Moroccan territory – and several small but strategic islands, the Chafarinas and the *plazas* of Velez de la Gomera and Alhucemas, located a few kilometres from the Moroccan coast.

The last three island groups are important for the maintenance of Spanish fishing rights, navigation and supervision of illegal migration and smuggling. Spain has carried on an aggressive campaign for more than two centuries to recover Gibraltar and would not countenance the loss of its overseas territories in the same region. All the areas involved have traditionally been considered important for Spain's control of the Mediterranean's entrance and exit.

Potential for future conflict

The potential for conflict is both very imminent and far-reaching. No one on the Spanish political landscape, except the extreme far Left, contemplates surrender or withdrawal from these areas that Spain considers an integral part of its territory.

Both Ceuta and Melilla are autonomous *comunidades* and their status as such is part of the Spanish Constitution. The Organization of African Unity has gone on record proclaiming support of what they term Morocco's "current fight for the liberation of its territories occupied by the Spanish". Spain is the only European Community and NATO nation that shares a common boundary with an Arab state.

What makes this situation so fascinating and potentially explosive is that the question of the *plazas* has in the past involved other issues, such as the struggle to achieve independence for the Western Sahara claimed by Morocco, the UK's interest in reaching an accord with Spain over Gibraltar, and Spain's relations with Israel and the Arab world. Spain has had to walk a tightrope in trying to maintain the status quo in the face of periodic bouts of Arab nationalism and growing Islamic extremism.

Ceuta and Melilla are valuable economic resources, important fishing and free ports, although small in size (19 and 12 square kilometres respectively) and population (75,000 and 60,000 respectively). The majority of the population in both areas are native-born Christian Spaniards, and both cities have age-old Jewish communities, synagogues and schools. Moslems constitute about one-third of the population and there are many Moroccan workers who cross the frontier daily to work in the two cities.

How did Spain acquire these possessions? Ceuta was originally conquered by the Portuguese in 1514, as part of the *Reconquista*, which drove the Moors from the Iberian Peninsula. When Portugal was absorbed by Spain (1580), it passed under Spanish control and Spain simply refused to return it to Portugal when that country regained its independence in 1640.

It later was used as a Spanish penal colony and military base that withstood repeated Muslim sieges. Melilla was conquered by Spain in 1497. Like the Portuguese seizure of Ceuta, it was good strategy to acquire a major naval base on the North African coast to prevent any further attempts by the Arabs to re-enter and try again to conquer the Iberian Peninsula.

Spain further insists that these territories were thus legitimately acquired to ward off further aggression and have been Spanish for 500 years. They are much closer to the mainland of Spain than the Canaries or the Baleares and the UN has never regarded them as colonial territories. A list of such territories drawn up in 1947 by the UN does not mention them and a statement by the UN proclaiming the "territorial integrity" principle in 1960 is regarded by Spanish authorities as proof that legal grounds outweigh any "geographic argument" put forward by Morocco.

Peñón de Vélez de Gomera is a minor plaza, a conical island, barely more than a barren rock of 15 acres, which serves as a relay station halfway between Ceuta and Melilla. During low tide, the island becomes a *tómbola* – a 100-metre-long narrow sand spit attached to the mainland. It was awarded to Spain in its dispute with Portugal by the Treaty of Cintra (1509), and has been used as a prison.

Peñón de Alhucemas, located to the west of Melilla, is four kilometres from the coast. It consists of three small islands and was occupied in 1673 as part of the Spanish naval strategy to prevent Turkish domination of the Mediterranean. The village of Alhucemas is within sight of the Moroccan mainland.

The Chafarinas islands occupied in 1848 are located almost midway between Melilla and the Algerian-Moroccan border. They are used as a fishing base. There is an important natural anchorage for all types of ships.

Spain's involvement in Morocco, the Western Sahara and the Gibraltar question

Spain's attempts in the nineteenth century to become an imperial power, after the loss of its South American and Caribbean colonies, focused on expansion of influence in Morocco and West Africa. The *plazas* were important staging grounds for penetration into Morocco, the Spanish Sahara and Equatorial Guinea.

Eventually, Spain gained control of its own Protectorate in Morocco. From the Moroccan point of view, its demands to acquire the *plazas* are part of its own struggle for liberation against colonialism. They don't accept the Spanish arguments about the fine historical distinctions.

Spain's campaign to "decolonise" Gibraltar was submitted in a UN resolution in December 1967. Israel abstained and, of course, the entire Arab world voted in favour. In spite of these policies, Spain received a rude awakening when, at an OAU conference, Libya's Colonel Ghadaffi included the Canary Islands, Spanish territory for centuries, as part of "un-liberated Africa". At the same time Morocco insisted on annexing the entire territory of what had been the colony of Spanish Sahara.

Spain's first reaction was to win the support of President Nasser of Egypt although, for the first time, some voices were raised that perhaps Spain should seek some sort of approach to Israel as a counterbalance. Arab opinion backed Morocco fully. How could Spain legitimately request Great Britain to return Gibraltar to Spanish control and yet adamantly refuse to return the *plazas* to Morocco?

Egypt's response was to reward Spain for refusing to recognize Israel. The Egyptian leader defended the "Spanish character" of the Canary islands but, along with Libya and Algeria, pressured Spain into accepting the principle that the people of the Saharan territory should have the right of "self-determination." Spain was, of course, anxious to have the "entire Arab world" on its side in any vote on the issue of Gibraltar and was willing to pay a high political price for it.

Renewed crisis in Africa and support of the Arab world

Spain needed the support of the Arab world to soothe its dispute with Morocco and to peacefully resolve its withdrawal from the West Sahara territory. After all of Spain's efforts, the Arab countries most assured of Spain's friendship – Egypt, Saudi Arabia, Syria, Iraq, Tunisia and Kuwait – all supported the Moroccan King's open defiance of Spain in organizing the "Green March" in 1975 to win control of the territory. This dealt a blow to Spain's prestige.

Arab demands

Following the Yom Kippur War (1973), The Organization of African Unity revived the issue of independence for the Canary Islands, and the Algerian and Libyan governments decided to give political asylum to members of the two most active Spanish terrorist groups – ETA and the revolutionary communist GRAPO – as well as stepping up its Spanish language broadcasts in favour of independence for the Canary Islands.

Following heated debate, Spanish diplomats came to the conclusion that it was better to pacify the Arabs and continue non-recognition of

Israel as the best way for Spain to deflect the issues of the Canaries and the *plazas* (Ceuta and Melilla) from reaching the U.N. for resolution.

In a meeting between Franco and King Hassan II, there was a reported agreement that Spain might cede the minor *plazas* (the three island groups of the Peñones and the Chafarinas) and retain Ceuta and Melilla, but Franco's successors did not have the authority to carry out the agreement.

Suspicion of Moroccan expansionism

Spain views the predictable renewed Moroccan demands to "regain" the plazas with great apprehension. This issue has re-emerged with the impending final status agreement affecting Gibraltar. Spain's insistence that the "principle of territorial integrity" justifies its claim to regain Gibraltar is a double-edged sword. Morocco claims the same right over the *plazas*.

The muted and divided reaction of the European Community, which first backed Spain's actions to reoccupy Perejil island and then backed off from any future pledge of support, does not bode well for Spain, especially with the new volatile Moroccan king Mohammed VI on the throne. Perhaps strong Spanish support for American actions against Iraq expressed by Prime Minister Jose Maria Aznar was in part an attempt to ensure that Spain is not without friends in any future confrontation over the *plazas*.

The reader interested in additional information regarding the *plazas* and the boundary dispute should consult *Ceuta and The Spanish Sovereign territories; Spanish and Moroccan Claims* by Gerry O'Reilly. Boundary and Territory Briefing, vol.1, No. 2. 1994. ISBN 1-897643-06-3. International Boundaries Research Unit, department of Geography, University of Durham, South Road, Durham, UK. ●

The long thaw in Spanish-Israeli relations

A curious tale of diplomatic intrigue lies behind the 38-year wait for Spain and Israel to establish diplomatic relations. In so doing, Spain became the last country in Europe to recognize Israel. The move was a symbol of new Spanish confidence and prestige into facing up to what had been a long policy of tagging along after the Arab World to gain diplomatic leverage elsewhere. It also destroyed one of the last illusions of the power of the Arab League to threaten blackmail or retaliation of some kind in a relationship with Spain which had become much too one-sided.

The Sepharadim – "Spaniards without a country"

The expulsion of the Jews by Spain in 1492, and the sad memory of the Inquisition has haunted Jews through five long centuries of exile. Even so, their descendents known as Sepharadim retained their loyalty to the Spanish language and many customs and traditions.

Spain remained a country without Jews until about the time of the French Revolution and the liberal Constitution of 1868. Following the corrupt rule of Queen Isabel II, Spain implicitly recognized the right of Jews to live in the country, although it did not officially rescind the edict of expulsion.

Several noted Spanish historians had also begun to publicly question the policy Spain had followed, and speculated on how much Spain had injured its own interests through the loss of a highly skilled, literate and commercially astute population. Many of them and their descendents had made enormous contributions to the economic life of Great Britain, the Netherlands, Italy, Germany, Greece, Turkey, Bulgaria, the United States and many of the Caribbean islands.

The most notable of these historians was Angel Pulido, who devoted much of his life to working on behalf of improving Spanish-Sepharadi relations. He visited the leading Sepharadi centres of the Ottoman Empire, wrote dozens of articles in the Spanish press, a book on the use of Castilian Spanish by the Sepharadi Jews and two influential books whose titles clearly indicate his sympathies. These were *Españoles sin patria y la raza sefardi* (Madrid, 1905) and *Reconciliación hispanohebrea* (Madrid, 1920).

He met with the Ottoman Chief Rabbi and spoke before the Spanish Senate. He also met King Alfonso XII, who was so impressed with Pulido that he declared that it was his dream, too, to renew a "Greater Spain" in which the Sepharadim would play a major role.

Spain even voted on behalf of the British Mandate for Palestine in 1920 under the League of Nations to help create a Jewish homeland there, and Republican leaders welcomed Chaim Weizmann, later to become Israel's first president, on a visit to Spain in 1932, thereby indicating support for the Zionist programme in spite of opposition and disquiet within the Catholic Church.

The shadow of the Spanish Civil War

The Spanish Civil War cast a long shadow over Spanish-Jewish relations for more than a generation. It is estimated that close to 20 percent of all the volunteers in the International Brigades who volunteered for the Republic to fight against Franco and Fascism were Jews (see *No Pasarán: The Jews Who Fought in Spain* by Colin Shindler in The Jewish Quarterly, Vol. 33, No.3, 1986, pp. 34-41).

Their heroism and experiences have been vividly recorded and gave proof that Jews would not wait passively for others to solve the problems of anti-Semitism and International Fascism. It also shaped a simplistic Jewish view of Franco as an ally of Hitler and Mussolini.

This was intensified by the short sighted decision of Franco to allow Spanish troops (The Blue Division) to volunteer in a unit of their own as allies of Nazi Germany in the campaign on the Eastern Front against the Soviet Union. Franco was an opportunist and a fervent anti-Communist and represented arch conservative Spanish traditions and aspirations, such as the recovery of Gibraltar, but he was not a Nazi or an anti-Semite.

Franco did not whip up anti-Semitism, nor did he employ anti-Semitic rhetoric in his campaigns, although several extreme-right parties had labelled some of the prominent Republican personalities as "secret Jews". There were even persistent rumours that Franco himself was of "New Christian" origin from his native Galicia in north-western Spain. The names Franco (and Castro) are among the most common Sepharadi names!

What is undeniable are the deeds of Spanish authorities, acting with Franco's knowledge and consent, to rescue Jews during the Holocaust. Few Jews were aware that Spain was responsible for accepting and saving more than 30,000 Jewish refugees and others of Sepharadi background who claimed a connection with Spain and who were provided with Spanish visas to escape from the occupied Balkan countries.

Israel's War of Independence and Franco's search for respectability to end Spain's diplomatic isolation (1948-49)

Concern in Spain, especially among high-ranking clergy in the Catholic Church, at the prospect of a Jewish state alarmed public opinion, and Spain viewed with dismay that its position as one of the traditional Catholic Powers in the Holy Land might be compromised.

An additional factor was that the Franco regime had been isolated by the United States and its West European allies as a result of Franco's early pro-Axis stance during World War II, and had therefore sought to build up a relationship with the newly independent Arab Middle Eastern and North African states. Large numbers of Moslems had served in the Spanish Army of Africa and had been with Franco's invading forces since the beginning of the Civil War.

Ironically, in spite of all of Franco's lip service to the cause of Catholic values and Western civilization and the propaganda line that the Nationalists had rescued Spain from atheistic communism, his triumph would not have been possible without the massive participation of Muslim troops from Morocco who had been feared and hated by most Spaniards, especially in those areas where these troops had participated in the fighting and subsequent occupation.

In spite of the Jewish underground's resistance against Great Britain, most Spanish public opinion courted by the Church viewed the Jews in Palestine both as Russian influenced communists and tools of Anglo-American "Protestant" influence. Years later, the Spanish Communist Party echoed the Moscow party line and preferred to completely forget Soviet and Czech aid to Israel in 1948.

Israel says NO to Franco

Franco, being a political realist and anxious to break out of the imposed diplomatic isolation he found himself in, decided that establishing relations with the newly independent Jewish state would be a clever strategic move and ingratiate himself with the United States.

In his view, there was little chance of Israel becoming a Russian ally and he was hesitant about the long-term reliability of the Arab World with which Spanish diplomacy had built up relations. Israel soon found itself in the enviable position of being courted by Spain. As a member of the United Nations and influential with Republican Spanish leaders, Israel also enjoyed good relations with many Latin American states.

On the first major UN vote involving a Brazilian motion to lift the diplomatic boycott against Spain, Israel naturally looked askance at Franco's previous friendship with the Axis powers and wanted to cultivate good relations with noted Spanish intellectuals and artists such as Picasso, who still resisted the Franco regime from their exile abroad.

Thus, in spite of the initiative put forward by Spanish diplomats to recognize the new Jewish state, Israel under the leadership of David Ben-Gurion and his socialist government voted a resounding "no" in 1949 to abolishing the diplomatic boycott of Spain. This was a slap in the face that Franco never forgot.

Ben-Gurion was in a coalition government at the time with more Leftist socialist parties and was reluctant to give them an emotional issue they could use against him. Nevertheless, the move was definitely short sighted. Many Sepharadi leaders, not only in Spain but also in Latin America, Greece, Turkey and North Africa, urged the Israeli government to reconsider.

Spain could have used its influence with the Vatican to modify its stance of non-recognition and the internationalisation of Jerusalem, two positions that Israel would ardently have liked to convince the Pope to change. The Israeli vote also offended some Sepharadim who became convinced that an Israeli government dominated by Jews from the "Ashkenazi tradition " (Central and Eastern Europe) had no sympathy for them.

Missed opportunities

Spain began more and more to cultivate Arab opinion and as a result refused subsequent Israeli overtures to begin normal relations. It turned down an Israeli request for a commercial consulate and even barred Israel from participating in various athletic competitions in Spain.

Many Arab kings and leaders were luxuriously entertained in Madrid and in return they lavished praise on Spain (and Portugal, also under its own dictator Salazar) for their principled stand. In December 1955, Israel made an about-face and voted for the admission of Spain to the United Nations, but it was too late.

The 1956 Suez campaign

Franco was not simply a "Fascist Dictator" in a one-party monolithic state. The Falange was the most important, radical and populist of several right-wing groups that had formed a coalition during the Civil War. Two other movements were monarchist, more conservative and ultra-Catholic.

All shared in the construction of The National Movement headed by Franco, who received the title *Caudillo* (The Leader), and who continued with his military rank of *Generalísimo* (Commander-in-Chief). Nevertheless, these groups maintained their own existence and party political newspapers.

The Falangist press was the most traditionally anti-British, due to the age-old conflict over Gibraltar, and therefore anxious to show its pro-Egyptian stance during the Suez Crisis in 1956. The party newspaper *Arriba* praised Nasser and labelled Anthony Eden, Guy Mollet and David Ben-Gurion as "war criminals".

This view was not endorsed among most of Spain's military elite, who were unsympathetic to Soviet designs to stir up trouble in the Middle East, and even expressed secret admiration for the tough and gallant Israeli army.

Franco was still anxious to win American support and eventually join NATO. He was therefore not pleased by the Falangist press and worried, too, about continued Moroccan agitation against the Spanish *plazas* (enclaves) on the Moroccan coast. Within a few days the word "from on high" came down to *Arriba* to change the editorial line.

Spain's aid to the Sepharadim in Morocco

Through secret contacts and with the approval of General Franco, several thousand Moroccan Jews were secretly smuggled out of Morocco through the Spanish *plazas* of Ceuta and Melilla in 1956 and allowed to move by ferry to Spanish ports and Gibraltar. Israel then belatedly called upon them and traditional Sepharadi leaders in Spain itself to begin steps towards normalization.

The Spanish government agreed to a purely cultural event suggested by the World Sepharadi Federation to jointly sponsor an exhibition of books on the Sepharadi experience. This very successful exhibition involved the presence of a Spanish minister, evoking protests from Arab governments who were politely reminded that "relations with the Sepharadi communities are based on a mutual recognition of very ancient ties and acknowledgment of their attachment to Spanish cultural values".

In 1960, Franco received a distinguished Sepharadi delegation that included the Chief Sepharadi Rabbi of Great Britain, and the following year Spain established The Institute of Sepharadi Studies.

The Six Day War and more missed opportunities

In the 1967 war, the Spanish government, and the far-left illegal communist opposition in the country, were united in defending the Arab position, but a number of Spanish journalists raised the issue of whether it was wise or self-defeating for Spain to uncritically endorse every Arab position in the wake of Israel's lightening victory against overwhelming forces, supported to the hilt by the accumulated might of the Soviet Union and its block of satellite states.

This was all the more poignant in the light of what was clearly a favourable public reaction that expressed satisfaction at the Israeli victory. This change in public opinion lasted only a few months before it was offset by a misguided Israeli UN vote regarding the Gibraltar dispute.

Spain's campaign to "de-colonise" Gibraltar was submitted in a UN resolution in December 1967. Israel abstained and, of course, the entire Arab world voted in favour. This was bad enough but Israeli UN envoy Arie Eilan, in explaining Israel's vote, repeated the old charges that Franco had allowed Spanish volunteers (The Blue Division) to fight on Hitler's side while Gibraltar held out as a British bastion of Freedom.

These gratuitous remarks were badly received in Spain and revived many of the old biases. The Blue Division was a particularly sore point since they had volunteered only out of anti-communist zeal and had no impact or influence on German policies. Moreover, they had been kept in Soviet prisons long after all other Axis prisoners of war had been released (see vignette 9 on Gibraltar).

In spite of Spanish-Arab cooperation and friendship, there were several disturbing elements threatening to rupture the relationship, notably over Spain's relations with Morocco and the disposition of the last outposts of its African possessions. This conflict was subject to the mercurial mischief of Libya's unstable ruler, Muammar Ghaddafi.

At a conference of the Organization of African Unity (OAU), Ghaddafi included the Canary Islands, a Spanish possession since before Columbus, as part of what he termed "unliberated Africa". Morocco also made demands on the "return" of the Spanish Sahara without any attempt to offer the inhabitants a choice. In 1970, there were secret meetings with Israel made with a maximum of discretion and care through the guise of international meetings, at which the Spanish and Israeli foreign ministers participated.

Yom Kippur War, Franco's Death, and restoration of the monarchy

As a result of American pressure, Spain made available its airbases for American supply of Israel during the Yom Kippur war, although this was officially denied. General Franco's death raised new hopes of a continued and accelerated rapprochement.

His successor was the eccentric Admiral Luis Carrero Blanco, a strange reactionary and throwback to Medieval Spain who believed that the country's "real enemies" were the Communists, Jews and Freemasons. He was assassinated in December 1973, probably by the Basque terrorists of ETA. In any case, Israelis sighed in relief.

Meanwhile Spain and the PLO reached a mutual understanding that Spain would maintain its pro-Arab stand and that Palestinian guerrillas would avoid any operations on Spanish territory. Although this appeared satisfactory at the time, many Spaniards were dismayed when, despite Spain's efforts to placate the Arab world, Egypt, Saudi Arabia, Algeria, Syria, Iraq, Tunisia, Kuwait and Libya all supported the Moroccan king's open defiance of Spain over the Sahara and "recovery" of the Spanish *plazas* of Ceuta and Melilla.

This was all the more hypocritical because several Arab states such as Algeria opposed Morocco's take-over and actually were scheming to support rebels in the territory and gain influence or even seize part of its territory.

This was followed by a turnabout in Spain's UN votes. At the famous meeting in which the General Assembly blindly approved an Arab resolution condemning Zionism as a "form of racism", Spanish delegates were absent from the hall.

The new King Juan Carlos I also awakened Israeli hopes. On several occasions, he had expressed the opinion that the establishment of normal diplomatic relations would be beneficial and aid in improving Spain's still poor image in American public opinion.

It would end the anomalous situation of Spain being a lone voice in Europe, especially after Portugal had recognized Israel in 1981. However, Spain remained very vulnerable to threats of an Arab economic boycott involving oil, all the more so following the fall of the Iranian Shah.

Post-Franco Spain

A new prime minister, Adolfo Suárez, chose a careful path. In 1976, he re-established relations with Mexico and even the Soviet Union, two states that had remained part of a boycott against Francoist Spain, but he insisted on various Israeli gestures such as complete withdrawal from all territories the Arabs considered "occupied".

Moreover, on a visit to the United States, Suárez became involved in a dispute with the Jewish American former U.S. ambassador, Arthur Goldberg, who had accused Spain of pandering to the Arabs. The election of Israeli Prime Minister Menachem Begin halted any plans to recognize Israel. The proposal was put "on ice" even though, a short time later, Egyptian Prime Minister Anwar Sadat visited Jerusalem and Egypt established formal diplomatic relations with Israel.

In 1979, Spain became the first European state to officially receive PLO chairman Yasser Arafat as though he were a head of a state. This move was met with much criticism in the United States.

Spain joins NATO and gets a new government

By the end of 1981, the future outlook for Israel changed dramatically with the end of the Suarez government and Spain's adherence to NATO. A new government sought the appropriate moment to begin a new policy. They were upset, however, by Israel's Peace in Galilee Operation and the subsequent events at the two refugee camps in Lebanon, in which Palestinian civilians were massacred by Maronite-Christian Lebanese gunmen.

Pro-Israel circles were dismayed by the callous and hypocritical nature of the Spanish press that held Israel responsible and found no space to criticize the Lebanese Christians for taking revenge against Palestinians for a previous appalling massacre carried out by the PLO in the village of Damour in South Lebanon.

Instead, attention was focused only on "The Jews", reinforcing the worst and oldest prejudices. However, the approach of the 500th anniversary of the expulsion edict of 1492 made many Spaniards reflect that the image of the country would be blackened irrevocably if nothing were done by then.

New elections in both Spain and Israel brought about a convergence. The young dynamic leader and head of the Spanish Socialist Party (PSOE), Felipe Gonzalez, had criticized previous governments for their failure to establish relations with Israel. The PSOE, however, was divided.

The old timers who had fought Franco and spent years in his prisons remembered the Jewish effort on behalf of the Republic, the thousands of Jewish volunteers of the International Brigades, the achievements of the Kibbutz movement, and the affection of so many Jewish people for great Spanish intellectuals and artists who had fled from Franco's Spain or been its victims and critics, such as Garcia Lorca, Unamuno, Picasso, Casals, Miró, León Felipe, Antonio Machado and Américo Castro.

The younger generation in Spain, however, was brought up on legends of Fidel Castro and Che Guevara. For them, the kibbutz was not the socialism they dreamed of. Israel was regarded as a "Yankee Satellite". González used his sophisticated charm and received the unanimous support of the world's Sepharadi communities and congregations. By this time, many Spaniards had reached the conclusion that there would be no end to Arab blackmail.

Another main factor in the new equation was the "Hispanic Caucus" in the United States Congress – the representatives and senators of Hispanic extraction who were proud of being American and of Spanish origin. Many were active in the Democratic Party and friendly towards Israel.

On 22 June 1984, at a secret meeting in the Waldorf-Astoria Hotel in New York City, Prime Minister González assured Edgar Bronfman, head of the World Jewish Congress, that Jewish-Spanish reconciliation and recognition of Israel were "historic questions" and not just tactical matters.

Spain's admission into the European Community would also be hard to engineer if its foreign policy on the question of recognition of Israel was so out of line with the other member states. A series of small steps began, starting with direct flights between Madrid and Tel Aviv, followed by cultural events and mutual visits of Spanish and Israeli dignitaries and personalities from every walk of life. The ground was being prepared.

Last ditch Arab efforts

A last ditch effort was made to convince Spain to stop the proposed recognition. Wild talk by Ghaddafi was discounted, but even González was surprised to learn that the Libyan leader had written a check for $900,000 to the Basque terrorist movement ETA.

Even more shocking was the first terrorist action on Spanish soil by an Arab organization. On 12 April 1985, the *PFLP* (Popular Front for the Liberation of Palestine) carried out an attack on a Madrid restaurant at random, murdering 18 Spaniards and wounding 82. Even such blind terrorism would, however, no longer deter Spain.

The welcome

On Friday, 17 January 1986, Felipe González announced to the Spanish cabinet that the establishment of diplomatic relations would take place at The Hague on that day. The Spanish ambassador to Israel, Pedro López Agirrebengoa, presented his credential to President Herzog on 14 April 1986, and was greeted with the words "welcome after 500 years!" – while King Juan Carlos declared in a welcome to the diplomatic corps on the occasion that "Spain had overcome a situation that did not correspond with our own history nor with the present course of our country."

The Great Iberian Rivalry (Spain vs. Portugal)

In the European Community envisioned by politicians three decades ago, it was felt that old antagonisms would vanish. No one expected them to re-emerge as the result of a dramatic football match. Indeed, this has not happened in matches between Germany and France or England and Germany. Although these nations have been at odds for centuries, their rivalry does not extend back into the Middle Ages as is the case between much older rivals – such as Spain and Portugal, England and Scotland, Sweden and Denmark – where peoples speaking the same or very similar languages have an intertwined history and were united for long periods within one nation.

Football matches between these older rivals tend to excite the most heightened passions among spectators, although these countries have been formally at peace with each other for many centuries. Spanish and Portuguese, while mutually intelligible in their written form by educated people, are still far enough apart in their spoken forms to mask irony and sarcasm. Spanish and Portuguese folk music, church architecture, dance, food, humour and national character are quite distinct and may even have been cultivated to exaggerate a sense of being different

Psychiatrists use the term "sibling rivalry" to express the jealous and sometimes resentful feelings between brothers and sisters in the same household, and apparently this applies to nations as well as individuals.

Newcomers from abroad living in Spain are often surprised at the latent jealousy and even hostility between neighbouring Spain and Portugal.

To this day, the Portuguese and Brazilians are much bemused or sometimes angered when mistakenly addressed by foreigners in Spanish. The popular Portuguese press continues to delight in teasing and taunting the Spanish "Big Brother complex", much like the Scots' attitude towards the English, the Slovaks towards the Czechs or the Danes towards the Swedes.

What makes the Portuguese different

Why did Portugal become an independent nation, whereas other parts of modern-day Spain (Galicia, Cataluña, Aragón, Asturias, Navarra, Valencia and Andalucía), with original vernaculars as distinct from Castilian as Portuguese is – and all with their own sense of identity eventually – became absorbed into a united Spain?

One factor is probably the very rugged mountainous terrain and low population density that characterise the Spanish-Portuguese border region along the course of swift flowing rivers. However, several renowned Portuguese historians and geographers have highlighted human and historical-dynastic factors rather than language or physical-geographic barriers as the reason for Portuguese independence.

They point out that the Portuguese national character is more sentimental, ironic, mild, more mindful of women and children, and even more melancholic than the ardent and often arrogant and aggressive characteristics of the typical Castilian-Spanish temperament.

Two scholars, who have dealt with this question at length, find both cultural and geographic factors at work. Pierre Birot put it this way (*Le Portugal: Étude de Géographie Regionale* 1950):

Thus, the typical characteristics, that so gracefully distinguish the Portuguese soul from its peninsular neighbours, were able to ripen in the shelter of frontiers which are the oldest in Europe. On one side, a proud and exalted people (the Spaniards), ready for all kinds of sacrifice and for all the violent acts that inspire them to be concerned with their dignity; on the other hand a more melancholy and indecisive people (the Portuguese), more sensitive to the charm of women and children, possessing a real humanity in which one can recognize one of the most precious treasures of the patrimony of our old Europe.

Oliveira Martins, the dean of Portuguese historians had this to say:

There is in the Portuguese genius something of the vague and fugitive that contrasts with the Castilian categorical affirmative; there is in the

Lusitanian heroism, a nobility that differs from the fury of our neighbours; there is in our writing and our thought a profound or sentimental ironic or meek note... Always tragic and ardent, Spanish history differs from the Portuguese which is more authentically epic and the differences of history are translated into differences in character." (Historia da Civilizaçao Ibérica, 1897).

Portugal as the "Little Brother"

There is, of course, a shared common heritage embracing all the peoples of the Iberian Peninsula, but it was the Portuguese who first achieved independence and national unity and then established a far-flung colonial empire, only to lose out later in large part to Spain. The result was a prolonged feeling towards its neighbour as an upstart and arrogant "Big Brother". As late as the sixteenth century, Portugal's greatest national poet, Camõens, could describe the Portuguese in his epic *Lusiadas* as *"Uma gente fortissima de Espanha"* (Canto 1. verse 31). He used Espanha in much the same sense as the term Iberia is used today for the entire peninsula.

It was the great successes of Portugal's explorers, seamen and mapmakers that made such heroic achievements in the Age of Discovery and cemented the essential feelings of national character that made separation from Spain a matter of national pride rather than regional distinctiveness.

The Portuguese love to reassert their great imperial past, which outlasted Spain's, even though the final remnants eventually disappeared after World War II (Mozambique, Angola and the Cape Verde islands in Africa, Goa in India, Macao in China, and East Timor in the Pacific). Quite a few Portuguese, while bemoaning the loss of empire, at least have the satisfaction of knowing that there are almost as many speakers of Portuguese as Spanish.

Some were therefore recently dismayed to learn that Brazil, the largest Portuguese speaking nation, has adopted a new educational curriculum making Castilian Spanish a required subject (as the obligatory first foreign language studied) in schools, and resent their great partner in the Portuguese language in taking what appears to be an overly conciliatory step.

The dispute over who discovered America

Any visitor to Lisbon will have seen the great monuments to the early Portuguese explorers, seamen and cartographers, but may not have read the monument on the Avenida da Liberdade stating that João Vaz Corte is the real "Discoverer of America". Portuguese resentment of Spanish claims to Columbus' greatness has even encouraged considerable speculation by serious Portuguese scholars that Columbus was a Portuguese spy (see *The Portuguese Columbus; Secret Agent of King John II* by Mascarenhas Barreto; translated by Reginald A. Brown. Macmillan Press Ltd. 1992.)

They claim he purposely misled the Spanish throne in advance of his journey, well aware that the route westward would not lead to a short-cut to the Indies but drain Spanish resources, whereas Portugal had already established itself as the sole European commercial maritime power in the Orient and wanted to maintain its superiority. None of Columbus's written work and notes are in Italian (strange if he were born in Genoa) and his Castilian Spanish is full of the type of mistakes a Portuguese speaker would make; also his wife was a Portuguese noblewoman.

Whenever either side feels aggrieved, they both refer to the fifteenth century diplomatic manoeuvres that allowed the Portuguese to alter the original line of division of Spanish and Portuguese territories in the New World (Treaty of Tordesillas negotiated with the Pope, the corrupt and Spanish-born Alexander VI).

The treaty put the line at 100 Leagues West of the Cape Verde Islands in 1493 but was changed to 270 leagues in 1494, thereby enabling the Portuguese to take control of Brazil, while ceding the Canary Islands to Spain. Spain maintains this was deception, while Portugal claims it was its more advanced cartographic skills. This famous division of "undiscovered lands" beyond Christian Europe between the two Iberian nations gave them an unprecedented status and contributed to the sense of rivalry between them.

Spanish role as "big brother" resented

Intense Spanish pressure forced the Portuguese to follow the Spanish example of expelling the Jews in 1497, a step which deprived Portugal of some of its best merchants, diplomats, mathematicians and mapmakers. Feelings of resentment were aggravated by Spanish attempts to absorb Portugal, which temporarily succeeded between 1580-1640, a period known as "The Spanish Captivity".

It was a political mistake that only encouraged a strong and proud reaction that cemented the identity of an independent Portuguese nation, a separate state and culture. Imagine what problems Spain would have today if, on top of contentious separatist sentiment in the Basque country and Cataluña, Portugal were added to the list!

There is great resentment, too, that Portugal was drained of resources and forced to provide a substantial number of the ships in the "Invincible Armada", its nautical expertise and thousands of trained seamen. Many of the ships and men ended up at the bottom of the sea as a result of the vain and foolhardy attempt to invade England in 1588 and restore it to Catholicism.

The Portuguese often reflect sadly that their loss of empire was the result of attempts to seize control of much of Morocco and North Africa from its base in Ceuta. There, they faced a numerically superior enemy armed with equivalent weaponry, while the Spanish obtained their great empire in Mexico, Peru and the rest of South and Central America by fighting people who possessed a stone-age technology.

Why is Galicia Spanish and not Portuguese?

In today's Spain, the Constitution grants the three autonomous regions of Cataluña, Galicia and the Basque country control over their cultural identity and education. The result is that education in those parts of Spain is today bilingual and the minority languages are recognized by the local administration and courts as absolutely equal to Castilian.

Galicia in the north-western corner of the Iberian Peninsular has been closely associated with Castilla, the heartland of Spain, for more than 600 years, although its climate, landscape, vegetation, indented Atlantic coast and language all resemble Portugal more than the rest of Spain.

At one time in the Middle Ages, Galician and Portuguese were identical and have only diverged slightly after many centuries. How and why Galicia came to be part of Spain rather than Portugal proves that the long cherished ideal of so many poets, patriots and philosophers that "language is the heart and soul of the nation" is not necessarily so. If it were, then Galicia would have been part of Portugal, not Spain.

Galicia was liberated from Moorish rule before the independence of Portugal with the help of nearby Asturias-León (later to merge with Castilla). The early development of the great pilgrimage centre in Santiago de Compostela tied Galicia to other parts of Spain, even though the original language was basically Portuguese. A great lyrical, poetic tradition developed in Galicia and spread to other parts of Spain including Castilla, where Galician became the accepted vehicle for court poetry.

By the fifteenth century, Galician had declined as a result of dynastic wars in which most of the local nobility supported the losing side in the struggle for the throne of Castilla. From the sixteenth to the eighteenth centuries, Galicia became firmly integrated into the centralized Spanish state and Castilian Spanish became the only language of government, literature, the church and administration. Very little literature was then written in Galician until a revival in the nineteenth century, following the French invasion under Napoleon that stimulated local patriotism.

In the middle of the nineteenth century a renaissance of Galician took place and competitions were held for poetry and serious literary works, modelled after the movement to revive and promote Catalan. During the last decades of the nineteenth century, a great deal of work was done to devise modern grammars and dictionaries to standardize the language. Galicia remained a poor region and suffered considerable emigration abroad, provoking a further effort to preserve the language lest it die out.

Galicia is the least problematic of the autonomous regions. Most *Gallegos* have a relaxed attitude towards the language question and are satisfied with the current status of the language There are some activists who constantly berate the local administration for lagging behind in efforts and subsidies to make Gallego more popular and widely used (see vignette 22 on Spain's Language and Regional Diversity"). A small but vocal group regards Galicia as originally having been severed from its shared homeland with Portugal and agitates for independence.

The two regimes in the Iberian Peninsula

Relations between the two countries have been marked by mutual suspicion, fear and scheming. The successful Portuguese revolution in October 1910, deposed the corrupt monarchy and established a republic, setting an example that remained a nightmare for the Spanish monarchy. Overnight, the Portuguese broke with the past by introducing a new flag, national anthem, separated church and state and adopted a new constitution as well as ending the monarchy – all anathema to the ruling circles in Spain.

These fears made Spanish King Alfonso XIII play with the idea of Spanish aid to the Allies in World War I and eventual entry into the war in return for British recognition of a Spanish "re-integration" (conquest) of Portugal. This scheme encouraged Portugal to outbid Spain.

Spain remained neutral and devoted itself to serving as a meeting ground for peace advocates. Alfonso XIII even succeeded in using his personal prestige to back several humanitarian projects, such as putting pressure on Germany to persuade its ally Turkey to rescind the expulsion order against the Jews of Jaffa in Palestine. These measures only increased Portuguese suspicions that Spain was capitalizing on its neutrality to gain increased recognition and prestige on the international stage

Fear of losing their independence and their African colonies in the event of a German victory drove the Portuguese to enter the war on the Allied side in 1916. The British had no problem in promising the Portuguese they could keep what they already had of their colonial empire, whereas they were hardly ready to bargain away their important naval base in Gibraltar in order to buy Spain's promise to join the Allied side.

The popular reaction to Portugal's disastrous losses in the trenches of France provoked a renewed debate over the country's individuality. For many, it was the outrageous and exaggerated sense of the "Spanish danger" that had impelled the leaders of the various factions which made up the Republican movement to actually force Britain to accept Portugal as an ally.

The Portuguese leaders were aware of schemes and secret treaties that had been made by Germany and Britain to eventually dispose of Portugal's great African empire in the event of serious disorders affecting mainland Portugal or its African colonies. (A British anti-slavery society was also extremely critical of Portuguese colonial policies).

They feared that the Spanish government, anxious to restore the Portuguese monarchy, had schemed with exiles and even aided insurrection and would always be waiting in the wings to march on Lisbon unless Portugal could prove its worth as an ally of Great Britain.

Ironically, it was the most conservative and pro-German of the Republican leaders, Sidonio País, who seized power in a three-day armed uprising in early December 1917, and promised to limit further Portuguese participation in the war and grant full democratic rights to the country's largely illiterate peasant population, who had been sent to the front as cannon fodder to rescue and save the Republic and the Empire. The more radical Republican leaders had denied them the right to vote and entered the war without any popular mandate.

Post World War I trauma in Portugal

Portugal's rewards were pitifully small – a disputed border town

(Quionga) in Mozambique that the Germans had seized in 1894 and the promise of reparations amounting to three-quarters of one-percent of Germany's obligations. País was assassinated on 14 December 1918, and the country was plunged into near anarchy and chaos.

This thoroughly justified the suspicions and fears of King Alfonso XIII and his ministers that Republican Portugal was a dire threat to the stability of Spain. The reaction of the Spanish popular press was that Spain would be justified in any form of intervention to prevent this chaos from spreading across the border.

The Olivença question

There has also been a lingering border dispute between Spain and Portugal that continues to be officially "unresolved". Spain seized the border town of Olivença from Portugal during the Napoleonic wars in 1801 and has subsequently refused to return it, in spite of several treaties promising to do so.

The town (population of less than 9,000) is located along the left bank of the Guadiana River, about 24 kilometress to the south of Badajoz. Together with seven small villages, the area of 750 square kilometres (about the size of Singapore) has a population of about 12,000 people. According to the Portuguese, the present population is descended from Spanish settlers who dispossessed the original Portuguese population in the mid-nineteenth century.

Although both governments ignore the problem and the local population today is thoroughly Spanish in outlook, an activist pressure group called *O Grupo dos Amigos de Olivença* keeps the issue alive through demonstrations and propaganda. It maintains that Portugal has right on its side through historic treaties agreed to by Spain, more than Spain has in its claim to regain Gibraltar from the British.

It is true that there is an official Portuguese position, reiterated many times during the long dictatorial rule of Prime Minister Salazar and over the last 25 years of democracy, as well as international forums for the settlement of boundary questions. The official position is that Olivença *de jure* belongs to Portugal and no Portuguese government official has ever refuted this.

It is an embarrassment, since so much legal evidence through treaties supports the Portuguese case – yet both governments have agreed to simply regard it as a dead issue. For the "Friends of Olivença" this is due to Portuguese subservience. The group maintains a website and continually researches the extent of Spanish involvement in the

Portuguese economy, pointing out that many firms employ cheaper Portuguese labour and market goods as "Made in Spain".

Portugal's lament at the Versailles Peace Conference

In World War I, some nationalists hoped to regain Olivença as a reward for participation, and prepared a legal case to present at the Versailles Peace Conference – a thoroughly utopian idea as the British had no interest whatsoever in offending Spain. In fact, Portugal had to face the ultimate humiliation that, despite its decision to actively participate in the war and the grievous casualties suffered on the Western Front, neutral Spain won a seat on the Council of the League of Nations at the suggestion of President Wilson and the approval of Great Britain.

The Spaniards had indeed played their cards well as a benevolent neutral and Alfonso XIII had become a respected figure on the world stage. The Portuguese on the other hand could only lodge an official protest that the "traditional, reactionary, Germanophile Spain" had usurped its rightful position at the League of Nations and that Portuguese blood had been shed in vain for the Allied cause.

As late as the Civil War (1936-39) and, in spite of Portugal's aid to Franco and the friendly alliance between the dictator and Portugal's authoritarian leader Antonio de Oliveira Salazar, part of the Portuguese high command under the leadership of Colonel Rodrigo Pereira Botelho plotted to seize Olivença and restore it to Portuguese sovereignty. However, the Fascist uprising quickly took control of the town and its leaders were careful to expel any local sympathizer who might have joined in a Portuguese attempt to assault the town.

The rivalry continues even under fascist dictatorships

Another important consideration of the different behaviour of the two countries in World War II was the strategic importance of Portugal's Atlantic island possessions in the Azores. These "stepping-stones" on the way to North America were seen by the German high command as critical for the threat to strike the United States. New York City lies only 2,500 miles from the Azores. German control of the islands would have aided their U-boats and posed a real threat to the U.S. East coast.

In 1940 (the three-hundredth anniversary of Portugal regaining its independence), a leading Spanish magazine wrote that "it was God's will that the two countries be reunited again." In April 1941, President Roosevelt declared that the Azores lay in the Western Hemisphere, implying that they came under the protection of the American Monroe Doctrine.

Their significance for the American and British navies to combat the German U-boat threat was paramount. Franco maintained a position of neutrality in the war and permitted thousands of Spanish volunteers to serve with the German Army in a special "Blue Division" (5,000 killed and missing in combat on the Eastern Front) to fight communist Russia.

The Portuguese knew where their most vital interests lay and, in June 1943, the British formally invoked their ancient alliance with Portugal, requesting the use of airfields on the islands. Portugal agreed. Following the war, Portugal was an honoured ally – a founding member of NATO in 1949. Spain under Franco remained a pariah state for another decade and was not even admitted to the United Nations until 1955.

The curious case of de Sousa Mendes – and how Salazar outfoxed Franco

It is unlikely that Portugal would have been so well regarded by the Allies had it not been for an amazing turn of events that worked to the advantage of Portuguese dictator Antonio Salazar. Along with the noble Swedish ambassador to Hungary, Raoul Wallenberg, another diplomat of much lesser rank, Aristides de Sousa Mendes, the Portuguese Consul in Bordeaux at the time of the German conquest of France in June 1940, deserves to be regarded as a truly "Righteous Gentile".

An austere career diplomat, he was struck by the awful human tragedy engulfing so many refugees, among whom were many Jews trapped in France. He took it wholly upon himself to use his office to help all of them in contradiction to strict orders. Mendes Sousa provided families with Portuguese documents to legally enter Portugal and transit Spain from France. He did this knowing that he would be severely punished – and was in doubt that his documents would be honoured by Spanish officials.

Salazar had signed the very demanding *Pacto Ibérico* – the Treaty of Friendship and non-Aggression with Spain's Generalissimo Franco in March 1939. The clever Portuguese dictator knew that he was most vulnerable to a German-supported Spanish attack if suspected of treachery or if Spain decided to realize its age-old ambition to annex Portugal. He therefore played for time and demonstrated pro-Axis sympathies by shipping supplies of much needed foodstuffs to Spain and expressly forbade his diplomats from granting transit visas to Jews.

He reinforced this with another directive on 17 May 1940 that "under NO circumstances" was any visa to be issued unless previously authorized from Lisbon on a case-by-case basis. De Sousa Mendes personally intervened at the border when Spanish guards questioned the authenticity of the visas at the border towns of Bayonne, Hendaye and Irun.

Approximately 30,000 refugees owed their lives to the Portuguese Consul who was recalled and declared insane, the official explanation later reported in the Spanish and Portuguese press. The Portuguese Ambassador to Spain, Pereira, had to intervene and relieve Sousa Mendes of his post.

Salazar demanded an enquiry and "appropriate punishment" but, before a decision could be taken, Life magazine featured a headline story on 29 July 1940, calling Salazar "the greatest Portuguese since Henry the Navigator." The naive Life reporters could not accept the story that a minor Portuguese consular official had acted according to his own conscience and were unaware of the press reports of insanity or the charges to be filed against him. They concluded that this magnificent act of humanity must have been the work of Portugal's leader, Salazar.

The simple reality of the situation demanded a cover-up from the Portuguese and Spanish officials who could not admit to such incompetence and risk losing the good will earned by Portugal. Sousa Mendes was removed from office and declared guilty of "professional incapacity" but the entire matter was handled with the utmost tact so as not to ruin the good press the country had received in the United States.

It was also a kind of insurance for Salazar that Spain could not threaten Portugal in the future using its "German card" since Portugal could then retaliate with both American and British support. So, although he never forgave Sousa Mendes, he did not close the Portuguese border for the remainder of the war and Lisbon became the chief embarkation point to the New World for refugees who managed to flee Nazi occupied Europe.

Franco responds in kind

Franco was an opportunist, a fervent anti-Communist who represented arch conservative Spanish traditions and aspirations, such as the recovery of Gibraltar, but he was not a Nazi or anti-Semite. He did not personally whip up anti-Semitism or employ anti-Semitic themes in his campaign to seize power and topple the Republic.

Embarrassed by the favourable American press received by Salazar in June 1940, Franco made it Spanish policy to accept all refugees who legally entered Spain and even gave special attention to Jews of Spanish-Portuguese descent (the *Sepharadim*). He, too, realized that it could conceivably be in Spain's interest to maintain a decent and humanitarian respect for the refugees, and he was determined not to play second fiddle to Salazar.

The fall of two authoritarian regimes and an empire

In 1968, after 36 years at the head of the government, Salazar suffered a stroke and was replaced, although this fact was kept from him until his death two years later. Finally, the Portuguese army had had enough and drew the conclusion that Portugal must finally bite the bullet and let go of its vast overseas territories.

On 25 April 1974, units of the army, fed up with trying to fight the long arduous guerrilla war in Africa and calling themselves the Armed Forces Movement (MFA), seized power and in a brief skirmish defeated government loyalist units. This brief uprising put an end to Portugal's old regime that had survived Salazar. The MFA had no political programme except to withdraw from Africa, and the country was plagued by unrest and coup attempts, strikes, and demonstrations.

Eventually, a democratic system became installed by July 1976, and many Spaniards pointed to their neighbour as the way to go, even if it meant temporary unrest. With the death of Spanish dictator Francisco Franco in November 1975, Spain began a successful transition to democracy under a restored monarchy.

Within a short space of time, Spain joined NATO (Portugal had been a founding member) and the European Economic Community and made substantial economic progress. The result has been a marked reduction of the old tensions. Both countries have widened their horizons and are no longer obsessed with the old rivalry.

There are a few remnants of envy and competition among die-hards, especially in Portugal. Celebrations of the restoration of Portugal's independence (1 December) are still occasionally marked by such anti-Spanish signs as "Better Poor than Spanish" and letters of protest continue to be featured in some Portuguese dailies expressing resentment at Portuguese national television for bringing Spanish language news reports from Spanish TV without subtitles in Portuguese.

To most observers, this only proves that some Portuguese still have an inferiority complex. There is popular opposition in Portugal to the far-reaching economic and planning proposals for a trans-national

Euro-region embracing the Portuguese province of Alentejo and Spanish Extremadura, but in all other areas the two regimes and peoples have never been closer or so harmonious.

The new harmony

The two countries have drawn closer than ever before, due to membership in NATO and the European Community. The war in Iraq was fully supported by both Prime Ministers Jose María Aznar and Durrão Barroso. Both leaders value their traditional economic ties with Great Britain and the United States.

Iberian cooperation is still a fragile flower but it has been carefully cultivated and is finally bearing fruit. However, more could be done to increase public awareness of events and issues in the two countries. In the Spanish press and media, for example, whilst there is extensive coverage of international events from all over the world, it is rare to make any mention of Portugal. Moreover, there is still no direct motorway link between the two EU capitals of Lisbon and Madrid. ●

Spain's Phoenician, Carthaginian, Greek, Roman and Visgothic past

Spain at the western end of the Mediterranean has had a long history of fertile contacts with the civilizations located at the eastern end. There is an historical Phoenician-Carthaginian connection to the Iberian Peninsular. The Bible tells of their settlements that were already established at the time of the alliance between the Phoenician King Hiram of Tyre and King Solomon (recalled in Kings 20-22). Cádiz (Gadir) was founded by the Phoenicians in the twelfth century BC.

From the Phoenician colony of Carthage in what is today Tunisia, migrants and merchants settled in and traded with much of the southern part of the Iberian Peninsula, beginning sometime in the sixth century BC. Archaeologists have identified the existence of similar settlements in Ibiza, Sardinia and Sicily.

The Phoenicians were originally attracted by the natural resources of the Peninsula, principally silver, bronze, tin, gold and amber. They later found themselves in competition with the Greeks and shortly afterwards with Rome. The meeting point for all three of these foreign influences with an advanced local Iberian culture lay in the southwest of the Peninsula near the mouth of the Guadalquivir River.

A region of advanced culture, stretching from the Algarve (in what is today southern Portugal) to Cartagena, included an indigenous civilization and its chief city, Tartessos (possibly recalled in the Bible by the name "Tarsis"). Remains of pottery found in this area reveal Phoenician and Greek borrowings.

The name "Iberian" refers to this early civilization that prevailed in much of southern Spain and extended along the Mediterranean coast as far north as southern France. The language spoken may have been Basque or a close relative that became extinct. Linguists have not been able to decipher inscriptions that have been found. Their religious life seems to have closely resembled contemporary worship practices of the pagan cults – dedicated to goddesses, rivers, trees and mountains – found elsewhere in Italy and Greece at that time.

The pre-Roman pagan population worshipped a variety of local gods, among which a female goddess of the moon was particularly prominent. Perhaps the remnants of such statues as *La Dama de Elche* (see vignette 23) are evidence of an early female-oriented pantheon of goddesses. Also prominent among the animals worshipped were the bull and horse.

The great rivalry between Carthage and Rome (see vignette 31) ended with a total Roman victory after a prolonged campaign, extending from the third century BC until the reign of Augustus (26 BC- 4 AD), to gain control of the entire Peninsula, now called Hispania. Roman power, the worship of various gods of the Greco-Roman pantheon and the use of the Latin language all expanded, moving from the earlier Romanized southeast (*Hispania Citerior*) towards the north and west (*Hispania Ulterior*).

Roman Hispania and early Jews and Christians

Spain is mentioned in the Apocrypha and the New Testament Book of Romans (XV, verses 24-28) and was the scene of early missionary work by St. Paul and others who came to seek converts among both Jews and gentiles. A Jewish community flourished as early as the second century BC. Its existence and way of life had clearly become a matter of concern to the Church authorities in the twilight of the Roman Empire before Spain was overrun by a series of barbarian invasions by Germanic tribes.

Evidence exists that some Jews held considerable political power under Roman rule. Mention is made of a Jew appointed as *Defensor Civitatis* and another Jew who became governor of a Roman province in Spain. With the conversion of the emperor Constantine (336 AD), legislation was introduced that gradually established Christianity as a favoured state religion and restricted Jewish rights. From about the fourth century AD, the Church sought to eliminate Judaism as a potential rival. It legislated limited social contact between Jews and Christians, with the explicit aim of restricting Jewish influence, power and attempts to gain converts.

Although the destruction of the Temple in Jerusalem in 70 AD and the suppression of a major revolt in Judea in 135 AD resulted in the expulsion of many thousands of Jews, who fled into exile, it is unlikely that they would have been welcomed to settle in Roman Hispania in very large numbers. What is certain is that a Jewish community of some size was already in existence and had begun to move inland from the Mediterranean coast to areas around Sevilla, Córdoba, Carmona in Andalucía, and further north in Zaragoza, Cuenca and Astorga before the earliest Christian missionaries arrived to seek proselytes. The new faith thus faced an established competitor.

The Elvira Council Edicts and what they suggest

An important church council at Elvira occurred sometime between the years 295 and 314 AD, when Christianity was well on the way to becoming the official majority religion of the Empire and not just another tolerated minority faith. Fragments of these edicts have survived in various written forms and are an early codification of laws that attempted to segregate and limit Jewish economic and social activity. All of the five Roman provinces of Hispania sent bishops and other clerical representatives to the Council.

Four of the Elvira edicts (numbers 16, 49, 50 and 78) relate to the Jews in Hispania. The first prohibits marriage between Jewish women and Christian men with a penalty applied against the parents of the Christian husband, and provide for excommunication from the church for five years.

Edict 49 is hard to interpret and prohibits Jews from blessing the harvest of land owned by Christians and implies that some Jews were wealthy landowners or had contracted Christian-owned land to work for their own benefit. It may have even signified that at the time there was some religious confusion and that many Spanish farmers were not entirely aware of the crucial differences between Christian and Jewish prayer.

Edict 50 prohibits Jews and Christians from eating meals together at the same table and provides excommunication as a penalty. This edict aimed at social segregation may also have been designed to prevent Christians from following Jewish dietary regulations as a first step in ensuring that closer social relations did not develop between the two communities.

The last edict (number 78) is also against intermarriage and prohibits adultery by a Christian man with a Jewish woman and provides a penalty of excommunication for five years. All four edicts are remarkably lenient in the light of later Church policies. It is indeed striking that the penalties are directed towards Christians who transgress the edicts and that the sole issue, apart from the threat of intermarriage and adultery, deals with Jewish-Christian cooperation in working the land.

They may be seen as an early attempt to severely limit what was already the fact of close social interaction between the two religious communities, and later rigid residential segregation in distinctive geographic areas that produced the segregated Jewish urban districts *(juderías)* may have been the outcome of the failure of these earlier edicts. In any case, we do not have any evidence from this early period of Christian rule in Spain that Spanish towns were divided into religious quarters.

Visigothic Spain and the Arian "Heresy"

As long as the Roman Empire endured, Jews did not suffer any more problems in Spain than elsewhere and indeed seem to have enjoyed a kind of formal equality before Roman law. The same thing cannot be said about the late Visigothic period, during which the Arian "heresy" held sway. This heresy was named after Arius of Alexandria, who taught (c.318) that God created, before all things, a Son who was the first creature, but who was neither equal to nor co-eternal with the Father. According to Arius, Jesus was a supernatural creature not quite human and not quite divine but with a nature that could not be co-equal with God the Father, thus denying the Trinity.

Jews were forbidden to own Christian slaves and Christians were encouraged to redeem a slave or bonded servant in Jewish service. Other measures were adopted to prevent pressure from being applied by Jews to prevent conversions to Christianity. These measures also seem to indicate that the Jews enjoyed a high social and economic status at the time. Although Jewish merchants were already present and active in the neighbouring Frankish kingdom to the North, Jews in Spain were not yet overly prominent in commerce.

The new society: Visigothic Spain

The decline and final collapse of the Roman Empire in the west was a consequence of the movement of the so-called Germanic "Barbarian" tribes, the Vandals, Suevians and others who crossed the Pyrenees in 409. At this time, the early Christian Church as endorsed by the Emperor Theodosius, himself a Roman of Spanish birth, had accepted the Nicean Trinitarian creed according to the orthodox doctrine of Atanasius as the official religion of the entire empire. Rome itself was sacked in 410 by the Visigoths (Western Goths), a group that had previously accepted Christianity in its divergent "heretical Arian" creed.

The period of Visigothic rule was chaotic and extremely violent. Most Visigothic kings died violent deaths. They were out of step with a majority of the population who adhered to the Catholic version of Christianity. Nevertheless, as a form of bribery and blackmail, the Visigoths were enlisted as "allies" by Rome and charged with taking power in Hispania and exercising control over the other Barbarian tribes that had begun to settle down.

In the religious sphere, pagan practices and customs were still prevalent but increasingly subject to the authority of the newly established Arian Church. The Jews were considered on the same level as the pagans and for a while not subjected to onerous restrictions. During the last decades of Visigothic rule, however, religious legislation proved more and more discriminatory and was designed to bring both the remaining pagans, other "heretical" Christians and the Jews into line.

After suffering a major defeat in a battle with the Franks, the Visigoth ruling class began to seek ways to integrate the Hispano-Roman and Catholic majority into the affairs of state. In 589, the Visigothic King Racaredo converted to Catholic doctrine with the aim of achieving both political and religious unity over the Peninsula. Until that time, the Visigothic rulers had supported Arianism and caused the Hispano-Roman majority to feel persecuted. Under several early Visigothic kings, intermarriage between Arian and Catholic Christians had been prohibited, thus predating the same ordinance against Jews and Christians!

For several generations in the seventh and eight centuries, Visigothic laws were aimed primarily at the Jews, subjecting them to all kinds of onerous taxation and humiliations. Pagan practices were also subject to growing restrictions, although some of them, such as trial by ordeal, were still widespread until the end of the Visigothic rule.

The new Visigothic rulers apparently tried to demonstrate their newly found Catholic orthodoxy to the majority Hispano-Roman population by their anti-Jewish laws. Later kings added a specific ordinance prohibiting Jews from managing Christian owned estates.

This testifies to the fact that Jews must still have exercised considerable economic and agro-technical skills.

The next to the last Visigothic king, Egica (ruled 687-702), believed in a Jewish conspiracy to aid an invasion launched from North Africa and messianic ideas about the end of the world. He sought to bring about a forced conversion to the newly established Catholic doctrine. This attempt predates the later successful unification of the country and the establishment of a single permitted religion by the Catholic monarchs Ferdinand and Isabella more than 700 years later.

Egica forbade the Jews to own lands and houses, to engage in trade with North Africa, and even to transact business with Christians. He claimed to find evidence of a Jewish-Arab plot to overthrow Visigothic rule, sentencing all Jews to slavery and ordering that Jewish children over the age of seven be given to Christians to be educated. The provisions were not fully carried out when the Moors invaded Spain in 711 and with Jewish help they defeated and killed the last Visigothic King Roderic. The Jews obtained their liberty and were enlisted to help the new Muslim rulers administer the country.

Las Tres Culturas: multi-cultural medieval Spain

Medieval Spain was the scene of a unique encounter among the three great civilisations of Roman Christianity, Arab-Berber Islam and *Sepharadi* Jewry. The multi-cultural synthesis that emerged following the Muslim conquest left behind a stunning legacy, but one that was uneven, sporadic and marred due to political fragmentation, intermittent warfare, religious intolerance and eventual excessive religious zeal that ended in the expulsion of the Jews and Muslims or their forced conversion as a step in the consolidation of political unity.

During the several centuries of sporadic coexistence under the rule of enlightened kings and caliphs, both Christian and Muslim Spain were the envy of the rest of Europe and regarded as the seats of great learning, science, medicine, mathematics, geography, cartography, navigation, astronomy, philosophy, law, and the most sophisticated achievements in literature, poetry, translation, architecture and the arts.

In these fields, Maimonides, Nahmanides, Yehuda HaLevi, Abraham Zarko, Hasday Crecas, Ibn Gabirol, Hasday ben Shaprut, Averröes,

135

al-Jwarizmi, al-Fazari, Ibn Hazm, Ibn Hayyan, Azarquiel, Al-Farabi, Ibn Sina, al-Ghazali, Ibn Said, and al-Muqradir, became known throughout much of Europe as well as Caliphate. Much of the great scientific and philosophical treatises of the ancient world in Latin and Greek were translated through Hebrew and Arabic into Latin, Castellano and other European languages.

Muslim rule in Spain was continuous for a long period of time only in Andalucía and most notably in Granada. Elsewhere, it was limited and short-lived. A good indicator of the Muslim presence is the large number of sites that bear Arabic place names (toponyms), starting with either the article *"Al"* (the) or the prefix *"Beni"* (sons of). These sites show a strong concentration in the south of Andalucía and along the Mediterranean coasts of what are today the provinces of Murcia and Alicante.

There is abundant evidence of social coexistence and considerable cultural interchange between members of all three religions in the early period of Muslim rule in the south, participation in holidays (even Christmas) and celebrations such as weddings and baptisms across religious lines. Noted Spanish historian Antonio Dominguez Ortiz, in his classic essay *Las Tres Culturas en la Historia de España,* put it this way:

> *Conversion to Islam had not eroded the taste of many for good wines, the woman's veil had not yet become a widespread custom (such a requirement does not appear in the Koran) and the happy sensual and cultivated environment that has always characterized the peoples of the South of Spain was not compatible with a rigid interpretation of the Koranic precepts.*

Centuries later, the dynamic Zionist leader and great poet, Ze'ev Jabotinsky, explained his support of the *Sepharadi* (Judeo-Spanish) pronunciation of Hebrew as due, in part, to appreciation of the gayer, more carefree, less inhibited nature of the *Sepharadim* and their Mediterranean traditions than the heritage of the more morose and sombre Ashkenazi (East European Jewish) past.

The Arab Conquest and the beginning of Muslim Spain (Al-Andalus)

Much of the Christian population had little stake in continued Visigothic rule and, even among the Visigoth ruling class, several clans found it expedient to cooperate with the Muslim rulers in order to preserve their property and privileges.

These Germanic rulers were still considered "foreigners" by many ordinary native Spaniards and their formal conversion to Catholicism had only been an initial step designed to integrate the different elements of the population into one society. The harsh anti-Jewish measures adopted by the last Visigothic king were made to appeal to Christians and unite the kingdom in the face of the Muslim invasion (711). Consequently, the Muslim invaders were welcomed by the Jews, who initially regarded them as liberators

For Muslims, both Christianity and Judaism were tolerated but decidedly "inferior" religions. Their adherents were not forced to convert as they were considered "protected peoples" *(dhimmis)*, who possessed a divinely inspired book of revelation (but an incomplete one). They had to pay a "head tax" from which Muslims were exempt.

The Jews, being more literate and whose Hebrew closely resembled Arabic, felt much more able to adapt to the new State at once and began to specialize in those activities and professions that Arabs regarded as "beneath them" (especially trade and tax collecting), administration, or onerous and "defiling" (working with leather). The term "Golden Age" most correctly applies to a period from the eighth to the eleventh century. The *Omayyid* Dynasty, owing loyalty initially to the Caliph in Damascus, practised a considerable degree of tolerance towards their "minority" Christian and Jewish subjects.

The Berber-Arab division

From the very beginning of the Muslim domination of Spain, a considerable antagonism existed between a minority of Arab overlords and their predominantly Berber followers who had joined the Muslim crusade after their conversion to Islam. The majority of these Berbers lived in Morocco and Mauretania and for this reason were referred to as *Moros* (Moors), a term that has continued in use today and is more prevalent than *musulmanes* (Muslims) or *árabes* (Arabs) in contemporary Spanish.

Many of the Berbers had remained pagan or converted to Byzantine Christianity before accepting Islam and had long been in contact with the south-eastern corner of Spain separated from the Moroccan coastline by the narrow strait of Gibraltar. They provided the majority of the manpower for the invasion as "shock troops" but were regarded with contempt by an Arab ruling class who felt a racial superiority and purity of faith connected with the Caliph in Damascus.

The Muslim conquest of Spain was greatly aided by internal divisions among the "Christians", especially the land-owning class of Visigoth nobles who were anxious to maintain possession of at least part of their holdings under Muslim rule. The Muslim Conquest of Spain was accomplished in the short space of five years (711-716) but society did not change abruptly. The newly won territory was given the name *Al-Andalus* and became a dependency of the *Omayyid* Caliphate of Damascus, and its capital was established in Córdoba. "Al-Andalus" was a corruption of the term meaning Land of the Vandals.

The Muslim Arab Elite – a small minority

In Al-Andalus, the Muslims did not constitute a majority until more than three hundred years after the initial conquests of 711-716. At the time of their arrival in the Peninsula, the original Hispano-Roman-Gothic Christian population and "Sefardies" (Jews) together numbered approximately seven million. By the beginning of the tenth century, it has been estimated that the Muslim population of Arabs, Berbers and *Muladies* (Christians who converted to Islam) was approximately 2.8 million. By the beginning of the eleventh century, this number of Muslims had doubled (see *Judíos, Moros y Cristianos; Tres Pueblos, ritos y cos-tumbres* by Pastora Barahona, Libsa. Madrid, Spain. 2004).

Within the Muslim community of believers referred to as the *umma*, the Arab ruling elite was a small minority. In spite of Muslim religious theory that all believers must be regarded as equal, there was a jealously guarded ethnic and hereditary factor of Arab descent among the elite who looked down upon the Berbers as ignorant and crude.

A number of revolts by Berber troops against their Arab masters enabled Christian princes in the north to withstand further advances by the Muslim armies. These factors also explain why the Caliphate established at Córdoba rapidly disintegrated after the subsequent Berber incursions of the Almohades and Almoravids.

The new intolerant dynasties: Almoravids and Almohades

New Berber incursions of tribesmen from North Africa further fragmented the Muslim-occupied areas of the country. The Almoravids who arrived in 1086 were military commanders and also administrators. Their authority was fragile and soon deposed by rivals, the *Almohades*, in 1147. Even before the arrival from North Africa of the *Almoravids*, Jewish-Muslim relations had begun to suffer a serious reversal that makes much talk of Jewish-Arab coexistence in a so-called "Golden Age" a pure myth.

In December 1066, a serious anti-Jewish disturbance occurred in Granada. It was part of an uprising against the ruling caliph. Twenty years later in 1086, the exodus from the Muslim south to the Christian north became a mass movement as Jews abandoned their ancestral lands in the face of muslim intolerance. In the following period (twelfth to fifteenth centuries), a steady stream of Christian and Jewish migrants fled to the Christian north as the *Omayyid* Muslim Caliphate of *Al-Andalus*, with its capital in Córdoba, fragmented into rival and intolerant feuding mini-states known as taifas .

The new Berber Moslem rulers from North Africa practiced the fundamentalist dogma of *din-Allah bi-sayf* ("The Judgement of Allah is by the sword"). In a few cases, however, their lust for booty and plunder made them relent and several Jewish communities were spared in return for a blackmail payment.

Their theological foundation was one of simple rules. They became the ruling social class and were immediately recognizable by the face scarf they wore. The Jews had barely managed to reach a modus vivendi with the *Almoravids* when the more extreme *Almohades* arrived. However, coexistence with the new rulers was much more difficult and consequently most Jews fled to the Christian part of Spain and sought refuge and a new life there.

Muladies and Mozarabes

In the early centuries of Muslim rule, a small ruling minority dominated the original Hispano-Gothic Christian population who were still subject to special taxes, discriminatory treatment and a prohibition against mixed marriages. The threat of severe penalties, including death, for apostasy hung over the Christians who accepted Islam and were still suspect. The growing movement to re-conquer the Peninsula and win it back from the Muslims, thereby restoring "Roman-Christian Hispania", intensified Christian-Muslim tensions and suspicions.

As always, the Jews without a state of their own were inevitably caught between major opposing forces. The see-saw balance of power and shifting majority-minority rule in various parts of the peninsula resulted in great instability and mutual suspicions.

The existence of the many terms (coincidentally all beginning with the letter M) is therefore a consequence of the complex and shifting nature of Spanish society, in which the border between Muslim and Christian dominated territories shifted continually, and religious conversions were often a matter of expediency rather than ideology.

The *Muladies* were initial converts to Islam. The *Mozárabes* were those Christians who maintained their Christian faith but adopted many aspects of Arab culture and were mostly bilingual. We also speak of Mozárabe as an artistic "mixed style" in jewellery, wood, silver and stone. It was developed and diffused by Christians who eventually left Muslim controlled *Al-Andalus* and brought with them the skills which had been learned from Muslin craftsmen. Its principal manifestation was in church architecture and wonderfully embellished manuscripts.

Mudejars and *Moriscos*

As the Christians regrouped and counter-attacked, pushing back the frontier with Muslim *Al-Andalus*, a Muslim population of either Berber and Arab invaders, or the original inhabitants who had converted to Islam and their descendants, were left behind. A tolerant tradition survived for periods of time in several of the Christian kingdoms of the north, although in these regions local Muslims were often under severe pressure to convert.

These former Muslims who became "new Christians" were called *Mudejars* (those left behind) and remained Arabic speakers or were thoroughly bilingual. They inherited the traditions of the early emirate of Córdoba and made important contributions to Medieval Spanish art and architecture.

Generations later in a united and Christian Spain, they were still recognized as being the descendents of converts and became known as *Moriscos*. Just as with the *Mozárabes*, a tradition developed and defined a mixed artistic style of two civilizations. The *Mudejars* and later the *Moriscos* used Arab geometric designs or copies of fruit, nuts and vegetables for their designs on ceramic tile and pottery with a striking use of colour.

The *Maragatos*

A fascinating remnant group that preserved its social and perhaps ethnic identity from the Middle Ages are the *Maragatos*. They still reside in and around the town of Astorga in León. For generations they have specialized as trustworthy carters and muleteers. Their distinctive dress, folklore, dialect and certain customs have interested sociologists and historians.

It may well be that they were originally Berbers with possible Jewish antecedents who accepted Christianity and were first subdued by the Visigoths with whom they intermarried and then converted to Islam, only to return to Christianity later. If so, they encapsulate the entire history of Spain! They also verify the considerable ethnic and religious "mix" that resulted from the invasions, cultural influences and great religious civilizations that have shaped the history of the country and the Spanish people.

Sepharadim and *Marranos*

The history of the Jews in Spain suggests several surprising conclusions and hypotheses that dispute many previously accepted views regarding the more than 1500-year/old Jewish presence in Spain before modern times. These are:

Many, perhaps most, of the Spanish Jews were quite likely descendents of converts to Judaism. They held high social and economic positions in the Roman-occupied province of Hispania, under the first Visigoth kings, and later between the eleventh to mid-thirteenth centuries were considered as vital assets of the Kingdoms of Castilla-León and Aragón-Cataluña, in spite of prevailing hostile attitudes of the Church. They called Spain by its Hebrew name *(Sepharad)* and referred to themselves as *Sepharadim* (*Sefardíes* in Spanish). Only later, after centuries of persecution and violent attacks resulting in forced conversions and exile, was the term *marranos* (pigs) used by anti-Semitic Spaniards to denounce the *Sepharadim* who ostensibly converted to Christianity but did so insincerely and maintained their Jewish traditions, faith and identity in secret.

The evidence for the origin of the *Sepharadim* is indirect. It is the hypothesis that offers the best explanation for the numerical strength of the Jewish communities in Iberia, even before the appearance of the first Christian converts, the wide geographic dispersion of the Iberian Jews, their prevalence in the rural economy and involvement with agriculture including land ownership, their high social status, and the edicts of the Christian Church to limit Jewish influence among Christians who had been pagans and became proselytes after their conversion by missionaries. There is also no evidence of the arrival of Jews migrating from abroad during the Middle Ages. In addition, some of the *juderías* (Jewish quarters), notably in Valencia, had been granted as a special award of royal favour.

Early Christian Church Council edicts, rather than Jewish Orthodox-Rabbinic law, promulgated much of the physical-social separation into distinctive residential quarters and separated and limited social contact between Jews and Christians.

Most Jews found Christian Spain much more tolerant and attractive after the twelfth century, when the fundamentalist Islamic *Almoravids* and *Almohades* arrived from North Africa.

Many Spaniards converted back and forth from Arian to Catholic Christianity, between Islam and Christianity, between Judaism and Christianity, and from Judaism to Islam!

The Jews were not the only group to be segregated into distinctive residential quarters. The same applied to other minorities such as Christians in Moslem dominated southern Spain (Andalucía) and Moslems in Christian dominated northern Spain (Castilla-León and Aragón).

Under enlightened rulers of both the Christian north and early *Omayyid* period in the Muslim south, all three religions were much more tolerant, materialistic and even hedonistic than anywhere else in Medieval Europe. This phase of Medieval Spanish civilization deserves the title *Las Tres Culturas.*

The final decline and expulsion of the Jews resulted in part from dynastic rivalries and the growing intervention of the Church to lessen the power of both the nobility and the monarchy by appealing to the "masses". In this scenario, the Jews were used as scapegoats, casting them as responsible for spreading poisons in wells that caused the Black Death and as having supported evil dynastic rivals claiming the throne.

Although modern Spain has followed a pro-Arab and anti-Israel foreign policy for much of the last 45 years (see vignette no. 12), the *Sepharadim* are still regarded as an authentic part of the "Great Hispanic Family" whose homeland is Spain.

The *Sepharadim* – a barometer of tolerance

A vital part of the "Golden Age" of Medieval Spain was the coexistence of *Las Tres Culturas* under enlightened Muslim and Christian rulers. The status of the Jews as minorities under both serve as a barometer of tolerance. Whereas in early *Omayyid* Muslim Spain, Jews reached a high degree of comfort and culture, there were only a few scattered Jewish communities in the small Christian kingdoms of the north. The main one was situated in Barcelona outside Cataluña, while most of them were located in the commercial centres of the pilgrims' way to Santiago de Compostela, the most important of them being the one in León.

In these Christian kingdoms, Jews had a special legal status from the very beginning. They were considered as "belonging" to the royal treasury, a personal property of the monarch, which left them halfway between free men and servants. But this situation also had several advantages. Monarchs were interested in protecting them for their own purposes and the status of the Jews as belonging to the royal treasury made it possible for them to have direct access to the monarchs.

By the end of the eleventh century and the early years of the twelfth century, the Christian re-conquest had made considerable advances. Alfonso VI conquered Toledo, Aragón and Cataluña and included the Ebro River valley. Thus, numerous Jewish communities became subject to the Christian kings.

As Christian Spain extended its dominion over areas previously under Moslem control, the internal structure of urban residential areas underwent a reversal of the majority-minority order. Jews remained as a minority almost entirely limited to the *juderias*. The distinct neighbourhoods of the minority, Arabized but now Christian Mudejars, became the dominant social group, and the Muslims were converted en masse and mostly remained where they were as a new minority (*Moriscos*) feigning Christianity.

Another way for Jews to get to the court was through their knowledge of medicine and the Arabic language. Some of them made fortunes and became the real financiers in the kingdom. Several served as Ministers of Finance to the monarchs of Castilla and Aragón. Restrictions against Jews in such high posts were put in place in Aragón in 1283-84, but not in Castilla until much later. It is perhaps for this reason that even long after the expulsion, Jews whose families traced their ancestry back to Castilla maintained a sense of superiority among all *Sepharadim*.

The intolerance of the *Almohades* led to the abandonment of many *juderías* in the south and a major exodus of Jews and *mudejars* to the Kingdoms of Aragón and Castilla-León, where they were welcomed and soon achieved considerable prosperity and prestige. By the mid-thirteenth century, the whole of the Peninsula, except for the kingdom of Granada, was already Christian. These were the best times for Jews in Castilla and Aragón. Toledo was at that time a most important centre of Jewish life. The city produced great rabbis, writers, financiers and statesmen in Castilla and similarly in Barcelona and Saragosa, for the Crown of Aragón.

The *Fueros de Castojeriz* of Castilla (974) and those of León (1017 and 1020) established a juridical basis that provided Jews and Christians with official equality before the law. Nevertheless, social interaction was limited by a Royal Council (*Concilio de Coyanza* in 1050) that followed Church practice in ordering the social separation of Jews and Christians, so that they could not intermarry, dwell in the same house or even eat together.

It is particularly noteworthy that, as in a much earlier period, this degree of social separation did not apparently result primarily from orthodox Jewish religious ordinances but were instituted as legal social measures in which the Church and Kingdom acted jointly. This further supports the assumption that many Spanish Jews were converts and not migrants who brought with them the rigorous orthodox rituals and social codes distinguishing Jews and gentiles.

Alfonso VI, "The Brave" (1072-1090), appointed a Jewish minister and treasurer. The "philosopher-king" Alfonso X (1252-1284) collaborated on many of his projects with Jewish scholars and translators and proclaimed them as valued citizens, specifically forbidding the use of force to bring about conversions to Christianity. Jaime I, the conqueror of Valencia, was an equally enlightened king who promoted his Jewish subjects to positions of prestige and influence. As a sign of special favour, he offered a distinct part of the town for Jewish residence in 1239 at their request.

Although decimated by pogroms in a large part of Christian Spain in 1391, resulting in many conversions to Christianity out of fear, *juderías* persisted throughout much of Spain. At the time of the expulsion in 1492, there were still well over 200 Spanish and Portuguese towns with distinct *juderías*. The most notable were in the largest towns and most of them still have some recognizable features such as an entrance gate, a *mikve* (ritual bath), decorations, Hebrew inscriptions, and a *mezuza* (a small box containing a portion of the *Shema* prayer attached to the doorpost of a house).

There exists a website "*Red de Juderías*" providing additional information and guided tours for interested tourists. The dimensions of the *Juderías* have been recorded and remnants are apparent in several of the largest ones, especially in Toledo, Córdoba and Sevilla that have, not surprisingly, devoted a considerable part of their souvenir trade to attracting Jewish tourism. Readers interested in examining the *juderías* are advised to consult *Guía de la España Judía – Itinerarios de Sefarad* by Jose Luis Lacave (Ediciones Almendro, Córdoba, 2000).

Self-rule in the *Aljamas* (*juderías*)

The Jewish Community was a legal entity known as an *aljama*, but its actual physical space referred to as the *judería* was reserved for the residence of Jews only. The community was regulated by an Old Men's Council, a sort of governing body, composed of venerable middle-aged or older men who counted as the richest and most powerful and determined the actual running of the community. Normally the senate consisted of seven men. In Barcelona, it was widened to include 30 individuals and in other communities, too, the governing council was expanded in times of crisis.

Below them were the judges *(dayanim)*, who met in a *bet-din* in groups of three to rule in lawsuits among Jews according to rabbinic laws. There were also tax assessors who fixed the amount of tax to be paid by each family according to their wealth, officials responsible for charities, and an official notary in charge of keeping documents. In many *aljamas*, the old men of the governing council also filled these posts.

In the fifteenth century, a national federation of all *aljamas* in the kingdom started to function in Castilla. In 1432, a set of by-laws were written in Valladolid, using Hebraic letters and in the *Judeo-Español* or mixed Hebrew and Spanish language. A *rab de la Corte*, appointed by the king maintained liaison with the court, commanding the *aljamas* in the kingdom. Besides serving as a court of appeal for all Jews, it supervised Jewish life. This system was even more strictly regulated in Portugal where there was an officially recognized Chief Rabbi.

Specific rules forbidding Jews to live wherever they wanted within the city were enacted sporadically on both national and local levels but the natural tendency was that they gathered in their own section of town, the Jewish Quarter, which varied in its features and size depending on the particular city. The one in Toledo was the largest, while the one in Barcelona, *the Call*, situated in the very centre of the city between the cathedral and the castle, was much too small to encompass natural population growth.

In the twelfth century, there were a few cities such as Tudela where Jews lived in the castle. Normally, however, the Jewish quarter consisted of narrow twisting lanes and cul-de-sacs, all of them with a miserable appearance. The same was true of the *Morerías* (Muslim residential quarters within Christian dominated Spain). *Morería* is still the name of one of the oldest residential quarters in Lisbon. There was usually a main street, the *Calle Mayor de la Judería*, and a *Plaza de la Judería* or *Plaza de la sinagoga*, which also contained a *Talmud Torah* (academy), *mikveh* (ritual bath), *beit-din* (Rabbinic court), and butcher. The cemetery was always outside the walls of the city, usually on a little hill nearby.

The rationale of the *judería* was to maintain the social segregation that allowed the Jews to have a measure of autonomous government. Self-rule meant that the Jewish institutions of self-government would administer the community independently of the civil authorities of the municipality and collect taxes. The same system of self-government characterized the *morarías*, and in both cases the degree of self-government facilitated the efficient collection of taxes known as the *capitación*.

The tolerant Spain of *Las Tres Culturas* contracted and was eventually extinguished as the struggle for the Re-conquest took on the dimensions of a religious crusade in which there could be only one winner. The gains of territory achieved by the Re-conquest under Christian domination brought about several serious problems of national unity. It was necessary to re-populate the conquered territories, to organize the administration and defence of the great cities conquered, as well as the ruling of states that were now larger and more populated. Kings had to use all the resources they could, and Jews were one of them.

Many of these Jews, and those coming from Muslim Spain above all, were experts in administrative tasks, and managed to become civil servants to the king, especially as tax collectors. The services of these Jews were originally indispensable, as witnessed by the tolerant attitudes towards them by the rulers of Castilla, Valencia and in the Balearic islands in areas won from the Muslims. After the passage of a century, Christian rulers no longer needed these services and were able to cast the Jews as the unpopular tax collectors (whom the king and court had appointed) or unbelievers, in league with the devil.

The three sources of Hispanic civilization

At first glance, it may appear that Muslim Spain, at the height of its cultural achievements during the *Omayyid* dynasty's rule in Córdoba (population of well over 100,000 in the mid-tenth century), dwarfed those of the petty Christian kingdoms in the north (the largest city, León, had a population of about 7,000 at the same time), but it would be a mistake to conclude that the differences were between two opposing civilizations.

The small minority of Arab-Berber conquerors of Spain had first conquered much of the Near East and North Africa with its Byzantine and Roman-Christian cosmopolitan cities, the technical skills of Roman engineering and Greek science along with their artistic heritage in mosaic work and architecture. They absorbed and integrated these skills and techniques along with the original Christian and Jewish artisans, merchants and administrators who served them. The "Golden

Age" of Al-Andalus should not be solely identified with Islam but with the common heritage of the Three Cultures.

English readers interested in Medieval Spain, and *Las Tres Culturas*, are referred to *Convivencia; Jews, Muslims and Christians in Medieval Spain* by Vivian B. Mann. George Braziller (1992) and *Moorish Spain* by Richard Fletcher, University of California Press (1993). ●

The Re-conquest and the expulsion of the Jews and the Moors

The Re-conquest of Spain *(La Reconquista)*, as so many other great historical events and conflicts like the Spanish Civil War, is often simplified and presented as a black and white struggle. Certainly the end result was the unification of Spain under the Catholic Monarchs and the expulsion of the Jews and Muslims, thus creating a homogeneous state, at least with regard to religion.

As subsequent events so clearly demonstrated by four civil wars in the nineteenth and twentieth centuries, this homogeneity did not prevent a fratricidal conflict based on political ideology, language and ethnic identity. Even the unification of the country in 1492 did not create a unitary state. Castilla, Aragón, Cataluña and Navarra remained independent kingdoms, even if ruled by the same monarchs. Not until 1711 was a unitary state created, but this was largely an illusion that would be shattered within another hundred years.

Far from being a simple conflict between Christians and Muslims (with Jews caught in the middle), the Re-conquest was a shifting see-saw, a back and forth flow of hostile encounters between Muslims and Muslims, Christians and Christians and only ultimately between Muslims and Christians. Within each warring camp there were opportunists, mercenaries and contending royal houses ready, willing and able to make a deal by temporarily enlisting the support of allies from among the "infidels" to aid in defeating opponents of the same religion, who nevertheless were perceived as "the enemy".

The legend of *El Cid*

Charlton Heston played a magnificent, gallant and heroic Christian hero in the person of *El Cid Campeador* (Rodrigo Díaz de Vivar), but the 1961 Hollywood film, winner of three Academy Awards in which he co-starred with Sophia Loren, omits or obscures his readiness to serve several Muslim rulers in alliances with King Sancho II of Castilla. His very title *Cid* (*said* or *sidi* is Arabic for gentleman, lord or chief) was given to him in recognition of his service to the Moors. To put it in the least emotional and most objective terms, *El Cid* sold his services to the highest bidder.

He was, in fact, an unprincipled adventurer and by no means alone in this capacity. He battled with equal heroism and fervour against Christians and Muslims to further his own ends. He was no more averse to destroying a church as a mosque and plunder was an expected reward. His name and heroism are nonetheless preserved in Spanish legendary history as the model of ideal husband and father, gentle courageous soldier, a generous noble conqueror, unswervingly loyal to his country and his king.

Ferdinand I of Castilla died in 1065 and divided his kingdom between three sons Sancho, Alfonso, and Garcia, and his two daughters, Elvira and Urraca, but the eldest son Sancho naturally objected to weakening his dominion over the most powerful Christian kingdom. He therefore enlisted the services of Rodrigo Diaz de Vivar, who had commanded his father's troops. Rodrigo helped the king to first eliminate the rival kingdom of Aragón and then dispossess the king's brothers and sisters. He furthered Sancho's ambitions by defeating and annexing the Christian kingdoms of León and Galicia, which had been promised to Sancho's brothers.

Sancho was treacherously killed in a plot organized by one of his sisters and was succeeded by his brother, who became King Alfonso VI. The new king bore a natural animosity towards *El Cid*, who would only swear allegiance to Alfonso if the new king took a holy oath that he had had no part in his brother's death. The new king was suspicious that Rodrigo would prove to be disloyal and so engineered to accuse him falsely of having kept part of the plunder obtained from a victorious battle against the Christian King of Sevilla, a vassal of Alfonso.

In 1076, the king banished Rodrigo, who began his soldier of fortune career, warring against both Christians and Moors. Had the Christians truly been motivated by religious fervour and patriotism, it is quite likely that they would have been able to conquer the last Moorish stronghold of Granada centuries earlier than 1492.

His victory over the Moors, and recapture of the major city of Valencia shortly before his death in 1094, was the result of his quest for power. A monumental epic poem by an anonymous author, *The Song of the Cid (Poema del Cid* or *Cantar del Mio Cid)*, made him into a Christian hero.

Both the Christian and Muslim sides were fractured by rivalries, sporadic conflict, antagonisms between contending dynasties, and animosities, just as the Germanic Visigoths had been. The fanatical Islamic sects of the *Almohades* and *Almoravids* had driven out many of the most creative scholars, merchants and artisans, who then went on to enrich the Christian kingdoms of the north.

The Re-conquest was a long drawn-out tedious affair but it eventually became a crusade to expel the unbelievers. Only following the marriage of Ferdinand and Isabella was there a concerted drive to grasp control of the entire peninsula. A patriotic motivation was thus joined with a religious crusade and fused with the personal ambitions of a powerful expansive monarchy.

The Christian-Muslim frontier

The invading Muslim forces were stopped at the Battle of Covadonga, their first major setback in 718, north of the Asturias mountains that formed the initial line of defence against the Moors reaching the north coast of Spain. To this day, the heir apparent to the Spanish throne is given the title of Prince of Asturias in recognition of this valiant and crucial role to save the last vestiges of Spanish independence in the Middle Ages.

A new Muslim attempt to reach further north by crossing the Pyrenees and skirting the last few Christian princes of Spain resulted in a major defeat at the Battle of Poitiers. After this battle, the Caliphs in Córdoba were content to hold most of the Peninsula along a line extending from just south of Oporto on what is today Portugal's Atlantic coast, and continuing north of León, south of Pamplona, and ending at the Mediterranean east coast just South of Barcelona.

By the year 800, a Christian counter-attack based in Asturias and León pushed the Muslims back to south of Segovia and Salamanca. By the year 1095, additional Christian victories had won back Coimbra, Salamanca, Toledo, Tortosa and even Valencia with an army led by *El Cid*. By this time, the main centre of Christian efforts to retake the Muslim south had become centred on the Kingdom of Castilla. At the dawn of the twelfth century, the Peninsula was roughly divided equally between Christian and Muslim rule.

This should have been a clear warning to the many small and fractured Muslim *taifas*, that their days were numbered. The expanding Christian kingdoms had momentum on their side, further stimulated by the powerful attraction of the pilgrimage site at Santiago de Compostela, a symbol for all of Christendom of Spain's attempts to carry on a religious crusade, one that would prove ultimately more satisfying to the Spanish Church and even Rome than the loss of the Holy Land after four failed crusades. On the Christian side, the Re-conquest also had the effect of increasing the power of the king at the expense of many noble families.

By 1240, only Andalucía and a part of Valencia, that had been retaken, remained of *Al-Andalus*. By 1250, Sevilla had fallen to the ever-more powerful Kingdom of Castilla, which had absorbed a large part of Andalucía, including the strategic and historic towns of Córdoba, Cádiz, Sevilla, Valencia, Jaén and Murcia. All that remained of *Al-Andalus* was the Kingdom of Granada that managed to hold out for almost another two hundred and fifty years.

The rationale for the expulsions

The background to the expulsion and the end of the distinct Jewish quarters was a social and political consequence of the determined policy and drive towards Spanish unification, dynastic rivalries and the perceived threat of an established, wealthy and competitive Jewish middle class as an obstacle to the power of the throne.

The absolutist plans of the new monarchy in a unified Spain linking Castilla, Aragón and Navarra craved power to create a new hierarchy dependent on the patronage of the Court and Church. The assets seized as a result of the expulsion, including homes, lands, goods and money, placed a major new instrument in the hands of the State, allowing it to carry out its policies.

The monarchs had previously been restrained by a powerful noble class that enjoyed traditional rights and privileges. Often, the Jews had been useful pawns serving either the monarch or the nobility in administration, tax collection, commerce, translations, medical treatment and other services. Their removal and the use of the Church as an ally of the throne to weed out heretics and Judaizers tipped the balance to the side of the monarchy. The nobility dared not oppose the expulsion for fear of being labelled as allies of the Jews.

Several prominent Spanish historians (Eslava Galán, José Amador de los Ríos and Américo Castro) have concluded that in the long run the expulsion had disastrous consequences. Had the Jewish financiers, merchants, artisans and bureaucrats remained in Spain during the following centuries, the gold and silver arriving from America would probably have been wisely invested for the creation of new wealth and directed towards industry.

Instead, it was disastrously wasted on extravagance and on attempts to maintain Spain as the ruling power in the Holy Roman Empire, to dominate the Netherlands and parts of Italy as well as launch the "Invincible Armada" in a vain attempt to invade and regain England for the Catholic Church.

During the fifteenth century the so-called "Jewish problem" became the "Convert problem." At first, these converts easily integrated into the Christian community and many of them obtained public jobs and even high positions in the clergy. But around the middle of the century it was discovered that many of these converts and their descendants still practised Judaism in secret. They were the *Judaizantes* or *Crypto-Jews*.

When the Catholic Monarchs, Isabel and Fernando, began their reign, "open" Jews had a relatively quiet life, whereas converted Jews represented one of the kingdom's most serious problems. With priority given to state unity, those *Judaizantes* were an obstacle to be overcome. The division of society between old Christians and the "New Christians" (Jews who had converted to Christianity) had already been divisive. The Spanish Inquisition was created in a large part to solve this problem. Its mission was to prosecute, judge and condemn, even to burn at the stake, all those converts suspected of continuing to practise the Jewish religion, and other "heretics".

The eve of expulsion

The Jewish presence in the Iberian Peninsula was the largest in Europe. About one-third of the entire European Jewish population of the late fifteenth century lived in Spain and Portugal. Estimates in 1492 place the Jewish population in Castilla at 160,000, in Aragón at 75,000 and in Navarra at 15,00 – i.e., close to a quarter of a million in the lands ruled by Ferdinand and Isabella.

Another 80,000 lived in Portugal. Spanish municipal documents show Jews living in 216 settlements of diverse size, and estimate the number of households at 15,000. More than 100,000 Jews chose exile in 1492 and fled to the Ottoman Empire, Portugal, North Africa, France and Italy.

Many subsequently continued on to the Netherlands, England, the city state of Hamburg and Denmark as well as the Caribbean islands. (Readers interested in pursuing the subject of the *Sepharadim* after the expulsion are referred to *The Jewish Nation of the Caribbean; The Spanish-Portuguese Jewish Settlements in the Caribbean and the Guianas* by Mordechai Arbell, Gefen Publishing House. Jerusalem. 2002.)

It is quite likely that in addition to the number of Jews who left in 1492, there were others who had officially converted to Christianity earlier but seized the opportunity to escape from the threat of the Inquisition. The very large Jewish population in the Peninsula would have been much greater still had it not been for the violent anti-Jewish disturbances and mass conversions of 1391. This further supports the thesis that many Spanish Jews were the descendents of converts to Judaism rather than the result of a mass migration from Judea or other areas of the Diaspora.

Both the Inquisition and the monarchs reached the conclusion that it was not possible to make good Christians out of converted Jews if they continued living in a society where "open Jews" were publicly allowed to live. Consequently, the Catholic Monarchs decreed the expulsion from all their territories of all Jews (in 1492). In a short period of time, all those who were not baptized would be obliged to leave the country.

An itinerant Spain

These banished people's descendants are the *Sepharadim*. Over the centuries, they maintained their unity thanks partly to their Hispanic language, in which they produced an important literature between the eighteenth and twentieth centuries. It is no accident that in the ceremony bestowing the most prestigious Spanish cultural award (Prince of Asturias Prize) on the *Sepharadi* communities throughout the world, in 1991, King Juan Carlos I proclaimed that the *Sepharadim* "...are a much beloved part of the Great Hispanic family who have created an itinerant Spain all over the world and after five centuries of estrangement are assembled for an encounter with their origins and for whom their ancient homeland has opened its doors wide."

In recent years there has been a small movement of native-born Spaniards aware of their Jewish roots seeking to identify in some formal way with Judaism and the Jewish community in Spain or worldwide. They and their ancestors never left the country but maintained an awareness of their heritage for five centuries.

Some of them began to seek an alternative sense of distinctiveness by first identifying with the Masonic movement in Republican Spain (1931-1939) and have become more daring since the death of Franco. Several formal conversions to Judaism have taken place and such small groups have been elated and growing in confidence with the recent discovery of the remains of a synagogue in Lorca, in Murcia province, the only case of a synagogue that had not subsequently been altered and redesigned as a church.

By the end of the fifteenth century, a large degree of intermixture had taken place that had largely erased the social distinctions of such diverse peoples as the Iberians, Celts, Romans, Goths and, to a lesser degree, even among those Arabs and Berbers who had accepted Christianity *(Moriscos)*. Yet, suspicions remained that many Jews who had converted *(conversos* and sometimes contemptuously referred to as *Marranos)* had been insincere.

This feature of Spanish society would eventually be viewed as detrimental and convince the victorious Catholic monarchs Isabella of Castilla and Fernando of Aragón to ensure the integration of diverse regions, peoples and religions by a monolithic policy of centralizing political power and expelling the minorities.

The last of the *Moriscos*

With the final victory over the last Muslim stronghold of Granada in 1492, the peace terms offered included an option for those Muslims wishing to remain to be resettled. They were even allowed to keep their arms in the spirit of medieval chivalry. They could continue living under the supervision of their own magistrates. Most of those who remained, however, were of the poorer social classes. The wealthy followed their leader, the emir Boabdil, into exile in North Africa. Most of the *Moriscos* were resettled in the Alpujarra mountains around Granada.

However, no matter how generous in theory the terms were, they were often not honoured in practice. Muslims resident in other parts of Spain had already been forbidden to bear arms and buy land. The monarchs and the Church both agreed that ultimately the best solution would be to follow the example of the expulsion of the Jews and insist on exile or conversion to Christianity.

It did not take long before insurrection broke out in the Albaycín, the Muslim quarter of Granada, whose population had refused to be removed to the rural areas in the countryside. Their example was followed in 1500 by the *Morisco* population in the nearby mountains. In 1502, only a decade after the expulsion of the Jews, an edict required the forcible conversion of the *Mudejar* population, which had lived for several generations as a tolerated Muslim population in the Christian realm of Andalucía, and forced them into exile or into accepting Christianity.

An estimated 300,000 accepted Christianity overnight and a scant few hundred chose exile in Morocco. The remaining converted population of *Moriscos* in Spain were, like the *Marranos*, outwardly Christian – but a majority feigned their acceptance of the new faith and retained old customs, traditions and beliefs.

Firstly, Arab and Berber dress was prohibited and then the public use of Arabic and Arab names. No *Moriscas* were allowed to act as midwives and circumcision was strictly prohibited – a sure sign of loyalty to Islam or Judaism. The "godparents" of a newborn child had to be "old Christians". Even taking baths was considered a sign of secret Jewish or Muslim loyalties. Charges were made against some local priests for extorting money from the *Moriscos* as a payment for protection so as not to be denounced.

Marauding Berbers (later to be called the Barbary Coast pirates) began to raid the south-eastern Spanish coast for booty and their incursions became the source of intense suspicions that they were being aided by local *Moriscos*. King Carlos I (1516-1556), the grandson of the Catholic Monarchs, visited Granada in 1526 with the object of finding out to what degree the *Moriscos* had been successfully assimilated. The investigation found a systematic persecution and humiliation of the *Moriscos* by their old Christian neighbours. Nevertheless, a new inquisition was established in 1528-29 in both Valencia and Granada to punish recalcitrant Muslims.

The Visigoths had preserved their identity as a ruling elite long after they had assimilated into Spanish society by giving up their Germanic language and adopting the Romance Hispanic language that evolved into Spanish. Similarly, the Arabs had maintained their higher social status as a class within the Caliphate where the Berbers remained the majority of soldiers and the lower class of labourers; the "Old Christians" in the newly united Spain were determined to prevent the intrusion of the *Marranos* and the *Moriscos*.

In Spain's conflicts with the Protestant powers and its fear of confrontation with Ottoman Turkey as well as marauding Berbers, the Inquisition was used as a weapon not just to enforce religious conformity but to ensure that Spain would not be subject to a fifth column of *Moriscos* and *Marranos*. To prevent the possibility of any Morisco insurgency in future conflicts, the Inquisition imposed harsher taxes and expropriated *Morisco*-owned lands.

Even harsher measures were imposed in 1566, designed to force further assimilation and root out any lingering Muslim customs and traditions, although most *Moriscos* had been nominal Christians for more than a generation. Protests and petitions to the King were of no avail and even warnings by various nobles pointing out the disastrous effects upon Spanish agriculture, irrigation works, production of silk, rice and sugar, transport (largely by mule caravans), leather and ironwork that would result from a *Morisco* uprising and the loss of their labour, both the Church and Court failed to alleviate the situation.

The inevitable rebellion broke out in the Alpujarra region in December 1568, causing alarm that Granada might be subject to a Turkish invasion. It took two years to suppress, after which a forced round-up of all *Moriscos* was instituted, including those affirming they were Christians, and among those who had not joined the uprising. They were housed in detention centres and about 80,000 were escorted by armed guards to be dispersed throughout the country or shipped abroad to North Africa.

In 1571 the Spanish fleet in alliance with Venice and the Papal States defeated the Ottoman fleet in the famous battle of Lepanto (in which Cervantes was wounded), putting an end to the nightmare of a Muslim naval threat in the western Mediterranean. In 1609, the remaining *Moriscos*, estimated at between 275,000 and 300,000, mostly in the areas of Cataluña, Aragón, Valencia, Andalucía and Castilla, were expelled to North Africa after only three days notice.

Unlike the Jews more than a century earlier, there was no other choice such as the New World to flee to. The result was a considerable reduction in agricultural productivity and the problems of under-populated areas with insufficient manpower to undertake economic recovery. A remnant few who had been permitted to remain were expelled a few years later in 1611. *The España de las Tres Culturas*, that included fifteen centuries of Jewish existence in Spain and 900 years of a Muslim presence had come to an end. The long lasting effects proved devastating for Spain's economic development, deprived of valuable human resources in many productive fields of commerce, agriculture and industry.

Spain's self-inflicted wounds were apparent to many foreign observers and even a number of Spanish contemporaries, most of whom were cautious enough to keep their eye-witness accounts and expressions of sympathy in their private correspondence.

Three centuries later in 1910, the highly respected Spanish writer and philosopher José Ortega y Gasset, in commenting on the expulsions and the resulting racial obsession of Spain's ruling classes wrote:

"Three centuries of error and pain have weighed us down. How could it have been legitimate for us to so frivolously claim that we had nothing to do with this sorrow?"

The expulsions of 1492 and 1609

The crusading nature of the Re-conquest, the quest for national unity, the religious vision of Santiago de Compostela, the struggle of Spain to maintain an empire that included the Low countries and Sicily. Its vigilance against the threat of the infidel Turks as well as the new heretical Protestant powers of England and Holland, all added their weight to the suspicions and fears of Spain's monarchs and the powerful Catholic Church. Together, these two institutions created a nation imbued with religious fervour and a homogeneous but impoverished society. ●

Are there any remnants of Franco and the Falange?

uring the latter part of General Franco's long 35-year rule, more and more speculation revolved around the question of who or exactly what would succeed him. Unlike Hitler and Mussolini, Franco survived World War II as well as the isolation of his country by the Allies, who at first considered him a remnant of the Fascist states aligned with the Axis powers.

Franco, however, was a military man whose career in the army and arch-conservative views propelled him to lead the uprising against the Republic, but he did not establish a political party nor did he express open support for any of the various Catholic, conservative, Monarchist and Fascist parties who rallied to his cause.

His supporters, moreover, were divided between those who saw a return to the monarchy, rival wings of the Bourbon dynasty, and the Fascists. The Fascist but anti-monarchist forces of the *Falange*, which had been founded by the extremely popular (and handsome) "martyred leader" Jose Antonio Primo de Rivera (son of the *dictator* who ruled the country following World War I), wanted a republic modelled after Mussolini's Fascist Italy, and claimed to be the hero of Spain's poor and dispossessed.

During the Civil War, Franco, who had assumed the status of Commander-in-Chief (*Generalissimo*), adopted the title of *Caudillo* (leader) and merged the rival groups of the Nationalist coalition into a "National Movement" with the extraordinarily long title of *Falange Española Tradicionalista y de las Juntas de Ofensiva Nacional-Sindicalista* (abbreviated as La FET de la JONS), or simply *El Movimiento Nacional*. The National Movement became the only legal political entity in Spain during the remainder of Franco's rule until his death in 1975.

All the groups maintained their identity, however, but unreservedly supported the slogans of *España Una, Grande y Libre* (One Great and Free Spain) opposed to any separatism by the recalcitrant regions of Cataluña, the Basque Country and Galicia. Franco tiptoed among these groups, assigning them influence and posts in his cabinet according to his mood at the time, with the intention of balancing them so as to leave everyone in doubt where he stood on a successor to the regime.

It was, however, the Falangists who exercised the most influence and even caused concern to the Church and well-to-do supporters of a return to the monarchy. The Falange had modelled itself as a popular Fascist movement, complete with a uniform (blue shirts) for street demonstrations and its youth movement that taught respect for all the traditional virtues and values of Spanish civilization.

It aspired to a return to Spain's glorious status as a world power. Readers of Spanish are referred to the memoirs of Luis Olero, whose book *Al Paso Alegre de la Paz* (On the Happy Road of Peace) is a satirical tragic-comical look at the pedagogical "truths" and heroic, almost supernatural, virtues of General Franco and "Jose Antonio," inculcated by the Falangist youth movement in his native Galicia.

The Franco regime endured thanks in part to food supplied by Argentina's General Perón, and managed to get through the extremely difficult first post-war years. To diminish Spain's fascist image, the Falange was accorded somewhat less influence in the government, but its economic policies still prevailed, with priority given to rural development and self-sufficiency, coupled with the stern morality of a nineteenth century and ultra-Catholic view of parent-child and male-female relationships. In spite of a "tight-lid", these very conventional attitudes were weakened by a growing flood of migrants from rural Spain to its big cities, that continued unabated from the mid-1950s.

Economic realities, continued urbanization, a growing realization that a Fascist Spain would be totally out of place in Western Europe and that Spain would benefit enormously from membership in NATO and the European Community, led Franco to further moderation of his tight political, economic and social controls. Real prosperity resulting from amazing economic growth throughout the 1960s and 1970s led to increasing unrest and further pressure to remove Spain from its self-imposed isolation and to change the unreal view of itself as a great power with a noble imperial past.

Following the restoration of the monarchy under King Juan Carlos in 1975 and a new democratic constitutional form of government, dissatisfaction in army circles with what appeared to them to be growing instability resulting from the reforms, a plot was hatched by conservative army officers in February 1981, led by a Lieutenant-Colonel in the Civil Guard, Antonio Tejera Molino, to attempt a *coup*.

The King immediately disassociated himself from the coup attempt, which failed. It is, however, noteworthy that although some of the army officers involved had started their careers in the Franco period, the Falange as a political movement was not involved. The internal tensions between the different elements that had supported the Franco regime, especially between monarchists, conservative Catholics and the army on one hand and the Falange on the other, were constant – and it was clearly the Falange that had lost out during the latter part of the Franco years. The fall of the Axis powers at the end of World War II left the Falange without any allies and increasingly isolated as a factor in Spanish politics.

Are Franco, Francoism and the Falange "just history" now? Judging from the change in many street names and the removal or neglect of statues and monuments to the *Generalísimo*, José Antonio (always referred to by his supporters by his first names) and the Falange, the answer is yes.

However, the Falange remains a political party (it has even split into two factions). The inability of successive governments to halt the campaign of terror carried on by the Basque separatist movement ETA and the recent friction with Morocco over a host of issues, as well as the presence of half a million Muslims in the country, some of whom are sympathetic to extremist views, have led to a reaction that may benefit the Falange. Older Spaniards who grew up in the Franco era may not look back with nostalgia on many aspects of the regime but are certainly growing increasingly uneasy over what appears to be Spain's susceptibility to terrorism and humiliation by the use of appeasement tactics.

El Valle de los Caidos is a monument erected by Franco outside Madrid for the combatants of both sides in the Civil War. Although built in part with the equivalent of slave labour by Republican prisoners and prominently displaying the tombs of both Franco and Jose Antonio, no one in Spain realistically would think today of trying to somehow tamper with it by removing Franco's body (as has been done with Stalin). Approximately 40,000 combatants, equally divided between the Republican and Nationalist sides, are buried there.

There is a National Association to Preserve the Legacy of General Franco (*Fundación Nacional Francisco Franco*) that publishes a bulletin and tries to influence public policy by emphasizing the *Generalísimo*'s many achievements. It stresses his anti-Communism, active alliance within NATO, aid to refugees including many Jews fleeing Nazi Europe, his social policies on behalf of the poor, such as the *menú del día* (requirement for most restaurants to offer a several-course meal including beverage and dessert for a specially reduced price), providing adequate government sponsored housing, price controls and wise leadership in preparing a transition to democracy. Most critics would dispute all these claims and believe that the government has been remiss in not having officially censured the entire Franco period starting with the 1936 uprising.

The People's Party (*Partido Popular*) was founded by a former Franco minister, Manuel Fraga Iribarne, and has blocked several attempts by parliament in recent years to explicitly condemn the 1936 military rebellion. It did, however, approve a parliamentary motion officially recognising the existence of victims of "repression of the Francoist dictatorship" and denounced "the violent imposition of ideologies".

This measure allowed local authorities the freedom to spend money to help recover the bodies of several thousand victims of Nationalist civil war death squads that are believed to be in mass graves around Spain. Estimates of the number of Republican prisoners who were executed after the Civil War range up to 200,000.

The successful transition to democracy that followed Franco's death in 1975 was based partially on what has become known as "the pact of forgetting". Both Left and Right agreed that no attempt would be made to open old wounds by seeking revenge or "justice" for past wrongs. The parties on the Left are aware that Republican forces also committed occasional atrocities and there was mob violence against the Church, but a recent flood of revelations depicting the brutality of the Franco regime and its treatment of prisoners has whipped up emotions again.

The Falange rejects any "apologies" and condemns any attempt to portray Franco as some kind of Spanish Hitler. It also surprises many observers by its "populist" position on many issues. It calls itself an anti-capitalist workers' party, demanding worker participation in the economy. It demonstrates on the First of May because this is the workers´ holiday.

It criticized the pro-American government of Prime Minister Aznar for its arrogance and described the electoral victory of the Spanish Socialist Party candidate Zapatero as justified. It supported the withdrawal of Spanish troops from Iraq, yet it calls for a massive NO not only to the Basque separatists but to Islamic terrorists as well.

It rejects homosexuality and abortion, and what it calls "secularism" that it defines as a "civil religion" in competition with the teachings of the Church, and demands strict controls on immigration and censorship measures to limit the excessive pornography and cheap popular culture on television. It rejects the new government's decisions to grant increased regional autonomy and demands an active defence of all Spanish interests.

It would fight Islamic terrorists but not as part of an "American war". The Falange has a major problem in any attempt at restoring the regime. It apparently cannot recreate Francoism without another Franco. Franco's daughter has written fondly of her father and is widely respected but is not a political figure. There is no other natural "heir apparent" with which to restore the regime.

The splinter Falange group, calling itself "authentic" or "independent," maintains that it alone carries on the program and ideals of Jose Antonio that were perverted and neutralized under the Franco dictatorship. No less than the parties of the Left, the "authentic Falangists", believe that they were victims of the Franco dictatorship and that they alone represent the true interests of the workers in a corrupt capitalist society. They have no sympathy for either the Church or the Monarchy. Neither Falange party managed to get even one percent of the popular vote in the last general parliamentary elections in March 2004. ●

correos
ESPAÑA *Picasso* **200**
PTA
GUERNICA PABLO RUIZ PICASSO

The refugees and the Republican Government-in-exile

The Spanish Civil War led to the flight and exile of hundreds of thousands of men, women and children, who were hurtled towards an uncertain future existence. Many abandoned their native soil never to return. Others sought to enlist in the Allied armies or represent the Republican Lobby in Mexico, France, Cuba, Argentina, the United States and England, to continue the international fight against Fascism. Many found a new homeland from which to carry on and rebuild their lives and careers, most notably in Mexico. For more than a generation, much of Spain's intellectual and artistic life was dispersed abroad in a great Diaspora extending into the New World.

For decades, the cause of the Spanish Republic stood high on the emotional list of the political Left in many countries and was celebrated in the songs of the International Brigade. It is a chapter in recent history that many in Europe and the United States preferred to forget. Thousands of Spanish Republicans fled Spain to fight in the French Foreign Legion, the British and American forces and even in the Red Army.

By and large they were not accorded the status of veterans and even denied the privilege of parading on V-E Day and flying the Republican flag. Even more shameful was the vindictiveness of local communist parties loyal to Stalin, especially in France and Argentina, who labelled left-wing but non-communist or anti-Stalinist Spanish exiles as Trotskyites, renegades, spies and CIA or MI-5 agents.

As early as 1936, a special committee to "Save the Spanish children" was established in France and approximately 30,000 were evacuated to France, Belgium, the U.S.S.R., the U.K., Switzerland, the Netherlands, Denmark and Mexico, where adoptive parents and sponsoring agencies had been found. Some were never reunited with their parents.

The camps in France

The war refugees arrived in France in three major waves. The first was from the Basque region and the closure of the Spanish-French frontier under the control of Franco's forces in June, 1937. The second occurred during the final weeks of the war from Cataluña (January to April, 1939). The third and last wave was by sea during the final days of the war from the last ports under Republican control, Cartagena and Alicante. Their heart wrenching stories have been told many times. Some parents were separated from children and many waited in vain for ships that never came.

In a short space of time, an unprepared France was inundated by approximately a half million Spanish refugees and had to find accommodations for them in a small area with only half that population. Many of the men voluntarily joined the French Foreign Legion or served in the regular French armed forces, and those with families were transferred to French North Africa. The remainder were gradually dispersed, but the camps were poorly staffed and administered and conditions remained inadequate.

Emigration to Mexico and America

Mexico, under the leadership of the sympathetic Socialist President Lázaro Cardenas, offered the most generous hospitality, accepting more than 20,000 Spanish refugees in 1939-40, the majority either with resources of their own or aided by funds made available from the assets (including a substantial amount of gold) that the Republicans managed to send abroad during the last days of the war. Many of these prominent Spaniards had occupied senior positions in the arts, sciences and government in Republican Spain and the aged among them were clearly aware that their choice was not a temporary exile but the right to "die in dignity".

Several hundred university professors, writers, philosophers, film producers, scientists, doctors, lawyers, artists, musicians, mathematicians, football players and poets were by and large quite successful at integrating within Mexican society. There were, however, many displaced persons, orphans and children whose parents were never able to join them and each one of these had a tragic history.

Every April 14th (the day of the founding of the Spanish Republic in 1931) was dutifully celebrated by the exiles in Mexico. Nevertheless, there was considerable antagonism among the new immigrants and older Spanish residents who had been living in Mexico for many years, a number of whom were pro-Franco, and who labelled the newcomers as "Reds" or "criminals".

Other Latin American countries were motivated less by idealistic concerns and only about 2,000 Spaniards managed to settle there. The Dominican Republic was anxious to settle European whites in the rural areas of the country. The large Basque community in Argentina was active in adding the Basques among the refugees but, in general, pro-German Argentina was very selective and anxious to avoid Left-wing intellectuals.

The government in exile

Political and ethnic divisiveness marred the functioning of a representative Republican government in exile. The biggest split was between the last government with its very strong Communist participation, headed by Juan Negrín, who arrived in Mexico City from Paris. He was opposed by the Socialist Party under the leadership of Indalecio Prieto and, with the support of a majority of the members of the last *Cortes* (Parliament), it managed to gain control of most of the assets. A strong anarchist group (most of its members remained in France) and the Basque and Catalan delegations struggled to maintain their independent identity.

Diplomatic defeat

In spite of the clearly logical and correct argument that the Republic's democratically elected government in the 1936 elections had been violently overthrown by a coup and military revolt and was officially recognized as the legal representative of Spain in Mexico, the Nationalist side under Franco had already won recognition from the British, the French and the Vatican.

Even more galling was the attitude of the Soviet government, which refused to recognize the Republican government in exile in Mexico City for the simple reason that such recognition would provide a legal justification for the Spanish to demand the return of much of the country's gold reserves that had been shipped to the Soviet Union for "protection" shortly after the outbreak of the Civil War.

World War II

Although the war with American and Soviet participation on the Allied side greatly raised Spanish Republican hopes, and Spaniards in exile volunteered and bravely fought in every theatre of war on all fronts from Northern Norway to the steppes of Russia and the Saharan desert in British, French, and Russian uniforms or as members of the resistance in France, they were to suffer disappointment after disappointment.

Moreover, approximately 10,000 Spaniards with a "suspicious background" and wanted by Franco, who were serving with the French or in the resistance in occupied France, were deported to the German extermination camps of Mathausen, Buchenwald, Dachau and Auschwitz as *Rotspaniers* (Red Spaniards, i.e. communists). They wore the prison uniform of the camps with a blue triangle marked by the letter "S". Only about 2,000 of the 10,000 prisoners survived the camps. On 5 May 1945, the Spanish survivors of the biggest camp in Mauthausen were liberated by the American Army.

The Soviet refuge

About 3,500 high ranking Spanish communists, and those who had worked closely with Russian technicians and military advisors during the Civil War, preferred to escape to the Soviet Union, but most of them soon became painfully aware of the true nature of the regime. They had little choice, although some were lucky simply because Stalin preferred to have them work in factories rather than sent to the front. Among those who were, Rubén Ruiz, son of the famous Basque woman communist deputy in the *Cortes*, Dolores Ibárruri (*La Pasionaria*), fell fighting heroically against the Germans and was awarded the medal of Hero of the Soviet Union.

The Republicans and the Spanish Government in exile in London

Although operating for a time in London, many Spanish Republican refugees felt handicapped by British policy towards Franco. Even Churchill, the hero of the British people, symbol of their resistance to Nazism and a leader even willing to make the best deal possible with Stalin, was reluctant to become involved in a dispute with Franco and remained anxious to maintain Spanish neutrality.

Given this policy, many Spaniards felt embittered and disappointed again. Many Spanish doctors rendered valuable assistance to the victims of the Blitz bombing and others were active in many intellectual and artistic walks of life. However, they were convinced at the end of the war that only America held out hope for an anti-Franco policy that would restore them to their homeland and end their exile. Michael Portillo, a Minister in the government of Margaret Thatcher and now a TV personality, is the son of a Spanish doctor who came to the UK as an exile and received an academic position, but never returned to Spain.

The final disappointments

Buoyed by the anti-Franco resolution in the United Nations in 1945, urging a diplomatic and economic boycott against Spain and specifically labelling Spain as a Fascist country and former ally of the Axis powers, many exiles pinned their last hopes on American foreign policy and a robust United Nations. The government in exile of the Basque autonomous region transferred its seat to New York City and tried to take advantage of the good will and links it had with American security agencies.

This was the result of expected gratitude for the assistance provided by the Basque resistance to downed American fliers who had been secretly escorted into Spain after escaping from German occupied France. The Spanish Socialist Party (PSOE) even believed it could negotiate with the monarchist pretender to the throne at the time (1946) to present a joint front against Franco. The British Labour Party ostensibly gave its blessing but the Republicans were disappointed by both of them, who preferred to compromise with Franco rather than force a change of the regime.

In November 1950, the anti-Franco resolution requiring a diplomatic boycott of Spain was withdrawn with the help of Franco's new-found allies in the Arab world and Latin America. By 1953, the American government began to change its policy toward Spain by requesting the establishment of airbases in the country and with the hope of encouraging

167

Spain to eventually join NATO. These security considerations outweighed the propaganda activities of distinguished Spanish artists and writers living in exile in the United States or visits by anti-Franco Spanish intellectuals urging the US to maintain its previous anti-Franco policy.

By 1960, the only countries officially recognizing the Spanish government in exile were Mexico and Yugoslavia. It was becoming clear that Franco would not be overthrown and that the best hope would be a gradual transition to democracy. Although these hopes were eventually realized, and some Republican exiles returned, others have accepted that, although Spain has a King today, it is a monarchy with Republican values. A few may still hope that one day the Republic and its flag will be restored. In the last elections there were no nationwide political parties advocating a return to the Republic. The strongest Republican grouping is the *ERC (Esquerra Republicana de Cataluña),* which is limited to Cataluña.

The poet, León Felipe, expressed what Republicans felt during the long bitter years of exile. Nationalist Spain had all the material resources but Republican Spain kept alive the spirit and culture of the country:

Franco, tuya es la hacienda,
la casa,
el caballo
y la pistola.
Mía es la voz antigua de la tierra.
Tú te quedas con todo y
me dejas desnudo
y errante por el mundo.   .
Mas yo te dejo mudo…mudo!
Y como vas a recoger el trigo,
y a alimentar el fuego,
si yo me llevo la canción?

Franco, yours is the household,
the home,
the horse
and the gun.
Mine is the ancient voice of the land.
You remain with everything
and you leave me naked
and wandering across the world.
But I leave you mute… mute !

And how are you going to harvest the wheat,
and feed the fire
if I carry the song?

Picasso and his powerful painting *Guernica*

Among those Republican exiles who sang the Republic's song referred
to in Felipe's poem was Pablo Picasso, Spain's foremost artist and the
spokesman for "modern art" in much of Europe from the 1930s to the
1970s. He was sympathetic to the Republic and had reached a crisis
stage in his work when the Civil War broke out. He was searching for
new inspiration after a decade of frustration in his personal life,
dissatisfaction with his work and depressed by the political situation in
his homeland.

Since the turn of the century, he had been living in Paris, the "artist's
capital of the world". Representatives of the new democratic government
and fellow artists came to Picasso in Paris to ask him to paint a mural
to depict the plight of the Republic at the forthcoming Paris Exhibition
to celebrate modern technology. Organizers hoped this vision of a bright
future would jolt the nations out of the economic depression and social
unrest of the thirties.

On 27 April 1937, Guernica, a little Basque village in northern
Spain and the historical site of the Basque *fueros* (traditional rights
guaranteed to them by Spanish monarchs) was mercilessly bombed by
the German volunteer air-force in the service of General Franco's
nationalist forces. At that time it was the worst bombing from the air of
a civilian population in history. Sixteen hundred civilians were killed
or wounded and the town burned for three days. News of the massacre
reached Paris immediately and by May 1st more than a million
protesters floodedthe streets to express outrage in the largest May Day
demonstration in the city's history.

Picasso was shocked and outraged by the still photographs and
the newsreels and immediately rushed home to sketch the first images
of his mural that would become the twentieth century's most powerful
statement on canvas of the horrors of war and his personal statement
of the obscenity of Nazi barbarity. The central figures are a woman with
outstretched arms, a bull, and a horse in agony. The painting *Guernica*
was delivered to the Spanish Pavilion at the Exhibition already in
progress. It soon became the most visited attraction and, in the course
of a few years, a constant reminder of what had engulfed the entire
world.

The initial critical reaction was unfavorable and labelled by "experts" from Germany, Italy and even the Soviet Union as "a hodgepodge of body parts that a four-year-old child could have painted." The Soviet response was surprising in the light of its anti-Fascist stance in the Spanish Civil War, but according to Stalin and "Marxist-Leninist principles," only "social realism" as an art form was acceptable for the masses. Stalin's view prevailed on any question of art or music.

After the Paris Exhibition, *Guernica* toured Europe and North America to raise awareness of the threat of Fascism and in support of the Republic. It was housed in the Museum of Modern Art in New York, and was loaned to great art museums after the war – except to Spain itself.

Picasso had dedicated it to the Spanish People and specified that it would only be allowed to travel to Spain when the country enjoys "public liberties and democratic institutions." Picasso died in 1973 and Franco in 1975. On the centenary of Picasso's birth, 25 October 1981, Spain's new King and the government celebrated the event by transferring the painting to Spain, and it is now housed in the *Reina Sofía*, Spain's national museum of modern art in Madrid. It has long been acclaimed as a masterpiece and for many years represented the artistic and intellectual opposition to the Franco regime.

Attempts at reconciliation

Although accused by the political Left in Spain as being founded by ex-Franco ministers and associates, the centre-right *Partido Popular* approved by a unanimous vote a measure, with Communist support, to help erase the wounds of the past by extending Spanish citizenship to those surviving members of the International Brigades who had volunteered to fight in the Civil War in order to save the Republic.

This generous act was without precedent. Nevertheless, some die-hard political figures among the older generation of the far Right called the move an "historical lie" and maintained that most, if not all, of the volunteers were communists or other subversives. They were "war criminals" and had, in fact, acted as "a Soviet force in Spain".

The veterans of the International Brigade are now few in number. Many of them, after returning from Spain, fought in the Allied armies in the hope that, with the victory in Europe, Spain would be liberated from "Fascist rule". There were also some die-hard communists who were deaf, dumb and blind to the revelations of veterans of the conflict on the political Left such as Arthur Koestler (*Darkness at*

Noon, Thieves in the Night) and George Orwell (*Homage to Cataluña, and 1984*).

These two great authors realized that Stalin's first intention was not to save the Republic but establish a communist bridgehead in Europe. They spoke out against the communist attempt to subvert the Republican cause and were ostracized by many "fellow-travellers" in Britain and America. Obviously, for some, on both sides of the political aisle, the wounds will never be healed.

The Republican flight in 1939 in the light of the expulsions of 1492 and 1609

Those who do not learn from history are doomed to repeat it. Contemporary accounts of the expulsions of the Jews in 1492, the *Moriscos* in 1609 and the mass flight of Spanish Republicans in 1939 are remarkably similar in their accounts of Spaniards deprived of their homeland and reduced to a wretched mass of human misery.

This tale of woe has been repeated three times in Spanish history and each time it left Spain worse off than the refugees. Franco, just as Ferdinand and Isabella and Felipe II, rejected any compromise that would have allowed some of the country's most creative and productive citizens to stay and contribute to a Spain they continued to love in exile. Each of these rulers contributed to depriving their country of some of its most valuable economic resources and cultural creativity.

The cultural wasteland of Franco's Spain from 1939-1975 was obvious. Garcia Lorca, Unamuno, Picasso, Dalí, Miró, Machado, De Falla, Segovia, Casals, Buñuel and the great sculptor Victorio Macho read like an honour roll of victims and exiles. Looking at these names of some of the world's greatest artists, writers, musicians, and composers, one may gain some idea of what Spain lost and understand how Spain crippled itself with the tragic expulsions of 1492 and 1609. ●

Culture, Art, Language, Music and Literature

Civil War propaganda posters that are now art

Propaganda posters produced during the Spanish Civil War represent one of the most effective historic uses of art in the service of politics. Barcelona and Valencia were the chief centres of graphic art and poster production in Spain in the 1930s. During the Spanish Civil War (1936-39), these two cities remained firmly in Republican hands and turned out hundreds of political posters that proclaimed the message of the Republic's fight for its life, and influenced public opinion throughout the world.

Although originally conceived as a propaganda tool, scores of these posters have become admired collectors' items as socially significant art. Several very expensive massive volumes of Civil War posters have been issued and the artists who created them have left us with the most graphic and striking portrayal of the dramatic events of that time. Not

175

only artists but writers, actors and film producers were organized in a collective, whose task it was to bring art and the theatre to Republican audiences throughout the country.

The poster artists – Josep Renau, Helios Gómez, Eduardo Vicente, Carlos Fontseré, Siwe, Laurenzo Goñi, Monleón, Cominguez Clavé, Dominguez, Josep Subirats, Martis Bas, Evarist Morá, Rafael Tona, Ricard Obiols, Bardasano, Alex Hinsberger, Oliva Perotes and Michael Adam are not as well known as Goya, Velazquez, Picasso or Miró, but their contributions to the cause of Republican Spain, Catalan and Basque autonomy, equal rights for women, and the struggle for economic and social benefits for the working class, struck a responsive chord in the hearts and minds of many observers of the Spanish scene – much as did George Orwell and Ernest Hemingway with their pens.

Of course, the Nationalists also produced their share of political posters but they were simply outclassed by the fact that most artists in this genre who resided in Cataluña and Valencia were politically sympathetic to the Left wing, were members of the artists union, or had experience designing covers for such distinguished liberal magazines such as *La Iberia* and *Campanyera*.

As early as July 1936, the antipathy of many anti-Nazi Spaniards to the Olympic games scheduled for Berlin led to the sponsoring of "A People's Olympics" to be held in Barcelona as a popular protest

against the discrimination of the German authorities shown in the accommodation and training facilities provided for Jewish and Black American athletes. The anti-Berlin Olympics received the support of the *Generalitat de Cataluña* and were scheduled to take place in the Estadio de Montjuich.

The first poster, following the victory of the Popular Front in the 1936 elections and which heralded the Republican struggle, demonstratively portrayed the Catalan colours and symbolized portraits of black, yellow and red athletes bearing aloft a rival

Olympic banner. Some of the 2,000 participating athletes were caught up in the street fighting and joined the various militia forces defending Barcelona against the military uprising.

The differences between the traditional Nationalist posters and the Republican side with its more modern format, caricatures, and lettering are immediately apparent. Even a brief glance at the many Republican posters with their confusing array of languages and abbreviations (*PSO, PCC. USC. PCP, JEREC, POUM* etc.) is convincing proof of the many groups, unions, Left-wing parties and regionalist forces that made up its supporters.

The favourite targets of Republican propaganda were General Franco, the Church, German and Italian interventionist forces (often symbolized by a claw grasping at a map of Spain). Quite naturally the most hated symbols were the Nazi swastika, the eagle representing the monarchy and Arab headdress or a crescent moon representing the Army of Africa's Moorish troops that Franco brought from Morocco.

The Nationalists made effective use of such traditional symbols as the Cross, the uplifted fascist right-arm salute, the arrows and yoke of the Falangist movement, the royal eagle and doves promising the advent of peace. Their most effective artist, Carlos Sáenz de Tejada, developed a heroic style using El Greco type figures glorifying the Spanish family and the Nationalist slogan *Arriba España*.

On the Republican side, Bardasano was a Madrid artist who eschewed the currents of modern art prevalent in many Republican posters. He sought to emphasize traditional Spanish themes and his work has been compared to Goya's. His most famous poster shows the parallel of a Spanish patriot fighting against the Napoleonic-French occupiers at the beginning of the nineteenth century, with the modern resistance of an anonymous Republican soldier in grey. The Slogan *Fuera El Invasor* (Out with the Invader) highlights this patriotism to expel the foreign German and Italian forces supporting Franco and the generals on the Right. The July 18 date recalls the first anniversary of the attempted uprising.

Other Republican posters emphasize social and cultural themes such as the struggle for women's rights, a campaign to increase literacy, the rejection of fashion and adaptation of simple dress (workers' overalls), the intensification of industrial and agricultural production, the protection of civil rights, the cultural creativity of the theatre, poets and writers working for the Republic, campaigns against alcoholism and "idleness", for sharing one's home and food with refugees displaced by the fighting in other regions, the need for land reform and increased productivity, collectivisation of agriculture, autonomy for the Catalan and Basque regions and the participation of all the sectarian Left-wing militias in one "Popular Army".

A difficult task for the Republic was in bringing a unified message to the countryside. Republican territory contained the major cities and the rural population was divided in outlook by contrasting views towards the policy of collectivisation. Many farmers preferred to sell to the "free market" but were hindered in doing so by government policy.

One of the most imaginative posters vividly portrays the dangers of the free market and speculation by portraying agricultural production symbolized by young children being guided through a dangerous forest by their parents – the farmers who are threatened on all sides by wolves representing speculators.

Although many fewer in number, and only under Republican control for a short period of time, the Basque Country had more than its share of

talented artists, who produced effective and striking posters emphasizing the necessity of fighting to defend one's family and home. They are also quite different in that there was no communist, socialist or other left-wing influence with the ubiquitous symbols of the political Left, most notably the hammer and sickle.

The fall of *Euzkadi* (the Basque Country) to Franco's forces led to an exodus of many of the region's artists, who continued their work in exile from Cataluña. Several of their most prominent posters called upon the Republic to launch a new offensive to recover the region and liberate it from Fascism. Extensive use of the Basque flag (known as the *ikurriñ*a, with its white and green crosses on a red field) is featured.

These posters were produced by the umbrella organization of refugee Basques in Cataluña (*Delegació General D'Euzkadi a Cataluña*) and express the deep appreciation of the Basques towards their Catalan hosts and allies. The prominence of these two regions in the Civil War produced a pathological disgust by Franco for any hint of separatism or cultivation of their local languages. Any public or even private display of either flag was tantamount to treason in nationalist Spain under Franco for more than a generation following the end of the war.

Many posters made brilliant use of similar imaginative, metaphorical images such as a red hand and powerful hammer striking the tough nut of Fascism, an evil serpent representing Fascism, a blindfold around the eyes of a Republican soldier symbolizing illiteracy, a soldier lancing his bayonet through a calendar marked with many red-letter dates representing previous holidays which the Republic abolished to intensify production, marked with the slogan "Down with the Holidays – Impose a War Calendar", and a simple table set with wine and bread and an empty chair for war refugees. In spite of the trauma of the war, many Republican posters uplifted spirits with a positive message.

One of the most powerful yet brilliantly understated posters by Hinzburger shows a simple couple with the man's arm around the woman's shoulder facing a rising sun with the slogan at the top, in elegant slender block capitals, *"El Que Sabe La Grandeza de Nuestro Mañana"* – and below in thick italics the refrain *"No cae el pesimismo"* ("Whoever is familiar with the Greatness of our Tomorrow will not allow Pessimism to take hold"). Equally striking are those posters portraying the ugliness of such vices as sloth and drunkenness.

Instead of the many messages promoted by Republican posters, the Nationalists stressed the early end to suffering a victory would bring, the traditional values of the Church and established order, the depraved nature of the Communist enemy and the promise of victory. A Baroque-style homage to *El Caudillo,* General Franco, as the Great National Leader (a Spanish "Cult of the Personality") grew less pronounced after the war. The enemy was usually referred to as The Red Army (*El Ejército Rojo*).

Although in the early days of the revolt, the nationalist forces under Franco continued to use the Republican tricolour flag, an about-face was soon made and only the previous imperial flag of the monarchy was revived. Many other symbols of the old order were also popular as well, such as the crown, the Lion and Castles of Old Castilla, the traditional colours, the Cross of St. Andres, the Fascist symbol of arrows, the yoke and the *fasces* (originally a Roman symbol of authority), a bundle of rods tied together about an axe with the blade projecting. The frequent use of the slogans *Arriba España* (Spain Arise!), *Viva España* (Long live Spain!) and *España – Una, Grande y Libre* (One Great United and Free Spain) and general appeals to *Dios, Patria, Rey* were characteristic of many nationalist posters.

The nationalist posters are nowhere as imaginative, colourful or experimental as the Republican side produced. The message is limited primarily to defeating the barbaric and anti-Christian enemy portrayed as advocating atheism and leading to chaos, supported by international communism. The nationalist side was also careful not to draw attention to the various elements in their coalition of forces that included monarchists of different stripes supporting rivals to the throne, fascists and even some traditionalists who did not favour a return to the monarchy.

An exhibition of posters and other propaganda material from the Civil War was held in Salamanca as part of the European Capital of Culture programme and attracted large crowds. The exhibition successfully combined history with art in revealing the power of words and pictures in the epic Spanish ideological struggle of the 1930s.

Readers interested in learning more about the Spanish Civil War are referred to the one-volume *The Spanish Civil War* by Anthony Beevor, Cassell Military Paperbacks, London, 1999, and the monumental 6-volume work of the same title *The Spanish Civil War*, by Hugh Thomas, London, 1977. ●

Why is Don Quixote so popular?

No foreigner who has been in Spain for more than a few days will fail to recognize Don Quixote and Sancho Panza, even if he or she has never read the book. After the Bible, and the fairy tales of Danish writer Hans Christian Andersen, Don Quixote is probably the most widely translated literary work in history. The duo are everywhere. Don Quixote and Sancho Panza bars, cafes, book stores, laundromats, restaurants, travel agencies, mini-markets, souvenir gift shops, and yes... even brothels bear their names!

What does a sixteenth-century Spanish novel about an unattractive odd couple who might be mistaken at first glance for Oscar and Felix, the two contrasting characters in Neil Simon's play of the same name, or the film comics Laurel and Hardy, tell us of lasting value? What is the enduring heritage of Don Quixote for modern Spain and the world?

Cervantes and Unamuno

It is a literary-intellectual-moral heritage no less powerful than Shakespeare's words, re-echoed by Churchill during World War II to rouse the British people. Spain's greatest twentieth-century intellectual philosopher, the Basque-born Miguel de Unamuno, saw in Don Quixote a modern version of Jesus – a lonely hero in a cruel world, who could not persuade others to follow his unselfish example except for the very naive, such as Sancho Panza.

181

Unamuno, who held the post of Rector at Spain's greatest university, Salamanca, had been rescued from prison in the Canary Islands, where he had been sent by the new Republic. Unamuno was too individualistic to identify with the Generation of 98 Spanish writers who welcomed the new Republic in the 1930s. He had initially favoured the Franco uprising and openly admired leaders of the Falange party.

Nevertheless, he quickly realised his mistake and termed Franco's brutal war and stifling of all dissent as "an epidemic of madness." He had unsuccessfully pleaded with the *Generalísimo* to release several of his friends who had been imprisoned, and then found himself in charge of a reception at the university in 1936, several months after the outbreak of the Civil War, to celebrate Spain's national holiday, then known as "The Day of the Race" (October twelfth; also known as Columbus Day in America).

Present were the Archbishop of Salamanca who had called the Fascist rebellion a "Christian Crusade", Franco's wife Doña Carmen, and prominent Fascists and military leaders. These included the one-eyed, one-armed Commander of Spain's Foreign Legion, José Millán Astray, who called the Basques and Catalans "cancers in the body of the nation" and roused his supporters with the Legionnaire's slogan *Viva la muerte* (Long live death!).

Unamuno shocked and dumbfounded the audience by pointing out that the Archbishop was a Catalan and he himself was a Basque who had devoted his life to the Spanish language and that the absurd death-wish cry of "Long Live Death" was an insult. He told Astray to his face that although a war invalid, crippled like Cervantes, he totally lacked the author's spiritual greatness. Unamuno warned that this senseless morbid cry would inevitably lead to many tens of thousands more crippled and dead Spaniards.

Millan Astray was outraged at the elderly philosopher. Unamuno finished by telling his angered audience that "You will win because you have more than enough brute force but you will never convince". It is then no wonder that Don Quixote and Sancho Panza have become immortal and no coincidence that Spain's official international cultural relations agency promoting the teaching of Spanish is called the *Instituto Cervantes.*

Cervantes – a Spanish Shakespeare

The author of Don Quixote, Miguel de Cervantes Saavedra, is recognised today as Spain's greatest literary figure – a Spanish

Shakespeare who encompassed all the futile strivings of the human condition in a single book and unmercifully mocked the quest for glory that has often been their cause. Don Quixote is, however, redeemed by his essential dignity in the face of all adversity. It is this last characteristic that also emerge so strongly in the hit songs of *Man of La Mancha* and what makes the book into something much greater than just a farce.

Statues of Don Quixote and Sancho Panza are landmarks that abound in many Spanish towns. Their portraits and poses are likely to stare out at you from tiled murals on the walls of schools, museums and cultural centres. The familiar figures of the tall, lanky, and gaunt knight-errant with his rusty sword, crooked lance and broken helmet, perched on his emaciated old plough horse turned charger, *Rocinante*, towers over the stocky peasant Sancho Panza sitting astride his mule.

Why have these two figures achieved such fame? This book, considered by many as the first true novel, has gained world-wide renown and contributed words and metaphors to many languages including such English terms as "Quixotic", "Tilting at Windmills", "Putting all your eggs in one basket", "Judging people by the company they keep", "The lance has never blunted the pen", and "An honest man's word is his bond".

Don Quixote is the subject of a successful Broadway musical called *Man of La Mancha* with its hit song "The Impossible Dream", a Russian ballet, posters by Picasso, a modern opera by the composer Cristóbal Halffter, which opened in Madrid a few years ago, and great musical works by Richard Strauss and Bedrich Smetana. It is the name of an American left-wing political forum with its own web-site, a Latin-American institute for social justice and greater involvement of the Catholic Church on behalf of the poor as well as a high risk mutual investment firm – apparently for people with their own special "impossible dream."

The Strange Duo

At first glance, the popularity of the novel seems quite straightforward. It is an expression of sarcastic comment on well-meaning people with noble idealistic motives who have their heads in the clouds and only bring disaster upon themselves and everyone round them. Time and time again it is the uneducated, crude peon, Sancho Panza, with his physical appetites and feet firmly on the ground, who speaks up as the voice of sanity to prevent even greater misfortune.

Yet the two – this dynamic duo of classical misfits – set out to right wrongs, aid the weak and downtrodden, and correct the injustices of a venal and corrupt society. Don Quixote seeks to do great deeds without wavering from devotion to the ideals of chivalry, bravery, modesty, self-sacrifice, fair play and devotion to his lady, the noble and beautiful Dulcinea, who is actually an ugly, stupid peasant girl who takes care of swine.

Cervantes used a literary format that was far ahead of his time and it is this technique that makes the book so sophisticated and contemporary to modern readers. The text is divided into two parts. In the first (completed in 1605 and spanning 52 chapters), Don Quixote and Sancho are the laughing stock of all whose path they cross – haughty noblemen, simple peasants, learned scholars, rogues and criminals, sanctimonious priests, the insane, wronged women and jealous men, crass prostitutes and inn-keepers. Don Quixote roams around his native Castilla and the Sierra Morena, suffering mockery and injury in his quest for chivalry.

In the second part (completed in 1615 and containing 74 chapters), however, the characters they meet are portrayed as having actually already read the accounts of the first part of the book (which became a best-seller) and are aware of the duo's absurd quest.

All the world's a stage

These characters intentionally provoke Don Quixote and Sancho in order to amuse themselves and show by their own perverse behaviour that it is society that is absurd. This is what Shakespeare meant by "All the world's a stage". They are acting a part rather than reacting naturally as they did in the first half of the book.

In the end, they drive Don Quixote back towards sanity and teach both Sancho and him that the human condition consists of learning to cope with earthly reality, whilst still being able to soar to the heavens on the wings of imagination and idealism. Towards the end of the book, Sancho also becomes more a friend and companion than an exploited servant.

Cervantes is also the first author to mock his country's quest for imperial grandeur. He had taken part in many campaigns, was wounded at the battle of Lepanto where he lost the use of his left hand, spent five years in Turkish captivity, observed the disastrous defeat of the Invincible Armada in 1588, and was refused permission to emigrate to the colonies and start a new life in America.

In Part II, chapter VII, Samson Carrasco, a poet and bachelor of arts and the friend of Don Quixote's niece, is asked by her to restrain her mad uncle. He cannot resist the temptation to mock and addresses Don Quixote as the "refulgent glory of arms, living honour, and mirror of our Spanish nation" and even volunteers to serve as Don Quixote's squire. In so doing, he provokes Sancho Panza into a jealous rage and to volunteer his services to his master again and give up his modest request to be paid a fixed   salary.

Sancho had only just managed to win this promise for a fixed wage instead of the fanciful promise to become governor of an island to be won in some future act of chivalry. On his deathbed, a much-chastened Don Quixote writes his will, admits his madness and recognises the debt he owes to Sancho Panza for his integrity and faithfulness.

Don Quixote's view of the world has changed, too. "There is nothing but ups and downs in this world", and "He that is cast down today may be a cock-a-hoop tomorrow. I was mad but I am now in my senses; I was once Don Quixote de la Mancha but am now, as I said before, the plain Alonso Quixano, and I hope the sincerity of my words and my repentance may restore me to the same esteem you had for me before".

Swift and Voltaire

There is, moreover, a debt that has never been explicitly recognised, shared between Don Quixote and two other great classics of French and English literature – Voltaire's *Candide* (1759) and Swift's *Gulliver's Travels* (1726). All three novels demonstrated an early use of black humour – the clever use of vivid exaggeration, ironic understatement and grotesque humour to express the paradox, cruelty and insensitivity of the world. The same black humour can be observed in the avant-garde theatre of such works as *Waiting for Godot* and *Rosencranz and Guildenstern* or novels such as *Catch-22*.

Cervantes, Swift and Voltaire directed their satirical attacks on the absurd and hypocritical notions maintained by respectable society regarding patriotism, religion and the established social order. Candide's mentor, Master Pangloss, who taught *metaphysico-theologo-cosmo-lonigology*, was another Don Quixote in the role of philosopher who, like his Spanish knight-errant predecessor, confused cause and effect and could always explain that everything that happens, no matter how cruel, degrading, senseless and unjust, had a higher purpose and was part of the design for the "best of all possible worlds".

Candide and Cunegonde are no less an odd couple than Don Quixote and Sancho Panza. Their irreconcilable differences are glossed over and lead to the most laughable situations immortalised in the song *Oh*

Happy We from Leonard Bernstein's comic operetta *Candide*. Candide sings of his vision of the future in a "modest little farm in a sweet Westphalian home while they sit beside the fire" and Pangloss "tutors them in Latin and Greek surrounded by faithful dogs".

At the same time, Cunegonde pines to live in the lap of luxury bedecked with jewels in their mansions… "all will be pink champagne and gold, we'll live in Paris when we're not in Rome, surrounded by faithful servants." After worldwide travels and harrowing adventures, Candide comes to the same realisation as Don Quixote, that the only recipe for a happy life is to abandon the quest for great acts of noble heroism or chivalry and the vain quest for fame, glory and riches, and to settle down to "make one's own garden grow".

Gulliver's Travels has a less obvious connection since Gulliver travels alone and does not have a partner to challenge and confront him. Yet Swift was undoubtedly indebted to Cervantes for the bitter satire encompassed in his hero's observations of mankind, disguised as the follies of four mythical kingdoms ruled by miniature beings, giants, mad philosophers and human-like horses.

Whereas Cervantes uses Don Quixote as a lunatic who comes to his sense to understand how mad the world is, Swift transferred the notion of a degenerate European society to a world of alien creatures, much like an eighteenth-century forerunner of the cinema's *Planet of the Apes*.

Ideologies lampooned

All three works lampoon ideologies that come before common sense and pity. Swift mimicked the religious intolerance and fratricidal conflicts that had torn Europe apart in the Thirty Years War between Catholics and Protestants by describing the great schism between the Lilliputians and their arch-enemy the Blefuscans, who had been split over the great issue of whether to crack eggs from the big end or the small end.

In *Candide*, Voltaire mocks religion, patriotism and loyalty to kings as excuses for greed, plunder and rape. Cervantes uses Don Quixote to demonstrate how noble ideas such as freeing the galley slaves (Book I, Chapter VIII) are often the whim and excuse of a madman to serve his own ends. Don Quixote insists that the freed slaves put on their chains again and carry them a great distance to do homage and impress his noble lady.

A hidden plea for tolerance?

Cervantes – in much the same way as Shakespeare had inserted a plea for tolerance and against anti-Semitism in his *Merchant of Venice* monologue ("Hath not a Jew eyes?") – included a story that was camouflaged so as not to offend the Inquisition but could be "read between the lines" as a defence of the exiled religious communities.

It can be found in the second book, Chapter LXIII: "Of Sancho's Misfortune on board the Galleys with the strange adventures of the beautiful *Morisca*". The *Moriscos* (see vignette 16) were the Moors who had been forced to convert to Christianity but maintained their Arabic language and other customs and traditions but eventually proved too divisive and offensive to the Church which finally forced them into exile in 1609, following the example of the Jews.

It is the story of Ana Felix, a *Morisca* whose parents were forced into exile and took her with them, although she fervently desired to remain true to Catholicism. However, she was simply not permitted to demonstrate her loyalty and she speaks of Spain as "my country". She poses as a boy and thus is already practicing a form of concealment. Cervantes puts these words in her mouth: "All I have to beg is that I may die a Christian, since I am innocent of the crimes of which my unhappy nation is accused."

For the more sophisticated reader, there is the inference that if she is not guilty of the crimes which the Moors had been collectively accused of, might others have also been unjustly banished? Might the same also have been the case with the Jews? Cervantes probably went as far as he could go without provoking the Church and, like Shakespeare, he was not a prisoner of ideologies and dogmas. ●

Spain's greatest composers

The Spanish passion for love and beauty has been expressed in all its many musical varieties that include *Flamenco*, the *Habaneras*, the *Pasodoble* (bullring music), *Boleros, Sevillanas*, the *Sardena* (a Catalan folk dance in a ring formation), *Malagueña, Jota, Chato* and *Muñeira.*

Many Spaniards have a profound love for opera and it is no coincidence that there are today so many renowned Spanish-born stars – Plácido Domingo, Josep Carreras, Montserrat Caballé, Joan Pons (by the way, "Joan" is a man and the name is the Catalan form of Juan), Jaume Aragall and Teresa Berganza. There is also a special Spanish variety of music-hall light opera known as *Zarzuela*, an art form many foreigners have fallen in love with after a short stay in Spain.

For serious music fans, there is the classical guitar of Andrés Segovia, the cello of Pablo Casals and the stirring music of world-famous Spanish composers such as Isaac Albéniz (1860-1909), Enrique Granados (1867-1916), Manuel de Falla (1876-1946), and Joaquín Rodrigo (b.1901). They all drew heavily upon popular and regional Spanish music for their inspiration.

This enormous wealth of musical talent often surprises the newcomer, but if any of the above names of singers, composers, musicians and song and dance forms are unfamiliar, then you have a treat in store. Just as Spain's food and wine have long been dwarfed by French dishes in the field of fine cuisine, it too had often had to play "second fiddle" to the prominence of Italy in the area of classical music and opera until the mid eighteenth century.

Spaniards are justifiably proud of the accomplishments of their countrymen and women in the field of music. All the above opera stars appeared on the stage to sing a selection of arias at the opening ceremonies of the 1992 Olympic Games in Barcelona. There could have been no more fitting venue for the event. Of those six performers, four are Catalans (only Domingo and Teresa are not).

By the mid-nineteenth century, Spanish composers began to adopt the new wave of "nationalistic" music free of Italian, French and German influences. The examples of Scandinavian, Russian, Polish, Hungarian, Finnish, Bohemian classical music, utilising nationalist themes and folk music, was propagated by Felipe Pedrell (1841-1922), a native of Barcelona.

He investigated the archives of libraries, monasteries and court chronicles to discover and catalogue the many rich musical traditions of the past, and travelled throughout Spain to observe the living folk traditions in song and dance. His work gained recognition and he devoted himself to the production of a trilogy in the spirit of the new nationalist music. The prologue of this work, entitled *Los Pirineos,* had its debut in Venice in 1897, and the full composition was performed in Barcelona in 1905.

Although not successful in his own right, he had the initiative and possessed the enthusiasm to motivate greater talents than himself to pursue a course of finding the harmony and counterpoint necessary to capture the folk character of Spanish classical music without destroying its original purity.

Isaac Albéniz, a Catalan from Girona, was the first great Spanish composer to popularise the new nationalist music on an international scale. Many Spaniards believed him to be from Andalucía, due to the character of much of the music he composed based on folklore. He achieved his initial fame thanks to more than 200 piano concertos starting with *la Suite Española* (1886) and in a major work entitled *Iberia* (1905-1909).

Enric Granados (1841-1922) was also a Catalan who derived much of his musical inspiration from another region – Madrid and Castilla, where he studied under Pedrell. Like Albéniz, Granados specialized in works for the piano. His most popular works are *Goyescas*, inspired by the life and work of the Spanish artist Goya, which he later turned into a full opera (first performed in New York in 1916) and *Danzas Españolas.* His success in New York led to an invitation to the White House but, upon his return to Europe shortly after the opening of the opera, he was killed in a German submarine attack that sank the passenger ship he was travelling on.

Pedrell's last and most famous disciple was the composer Manuel de Falla (1876-1946), a native of Andalucía. His best-known works all derived from the melodies and rhythms of Spanish folklore. They include the ballets *El amor brujo*, based on an episode from Don Quijote and performed with singers and marionettes, and *El sombrero de los tres picos* (1919), still performed the world over in the repertoire of the great opera companies, *Noches en las Jardines de España* (Nights in the Gardens of Spain), *Fantasia Bética* (1919), *Soneta a Córdoba* (1927), the opera *El Retablo de Maese Pedro* (1923) and the suite *Homenajes* (1924-1939), a homage to Pedrell. De Falla fled from Spain during the Civil War and went into exile in Argentina, where he composed the opera *La Atlantida*. He died before its completion and it was finished by his pupil Ernesto Halffter.

Last but not least is Joaquín Rodrigo (1902-1999), born in Sagunto near Valencia to a wealthy landowning family and blinded at the age of three by diphtheria. In spite of this terrible handicap, he became Spain's pre-eminent composer during the latter part of the twentieth century. As a child, he learned to play piano and violin with the help of Braille. Later, he invented a special instrument to read musical notes for the blind, which is displayed at the Museum of Art in Valencia.

By his early twenties, he was an accomplished pianist and budding composer. His first orchestral work, *Juglares*, had its premiere in 1924 in Valencia. He moved to Paris in 1927, where he met the well-known Spanish composer Manuel de Falla, whom he befriended. During a tour of Turkey, he met his lifetime partner, the pianist Victoria Kamhi, from a distinguished *Sepharadi*-Jewish family, and the couple married in 1933.

It was in Paris in 1939 that Joaquín Rodrigo composed his popular *Concierto de Aranjuez* for guitar, shortly before returning to Spain. This haunting, melodic composition is named after a town about 30 miles south-east of Madrid, dominated by a royal summer palace and lush gardens. It was first performed in Barcelona in 1940. A fellow composer, Xavier Montsalvatge, who attended the 1940 debut in Barcelona, wrote after Rodrigo's death that "the work even then made a great impression for the originality of being one of the first concertos for guitar and orchestra, and for its great beauty."

It has subsequently inspired dozens of interpretations worldwide, including a jazz version by Miles Davis in his 1959 album *Sketches of*

Spain. Rodrigo took a teaching position in 1940 at Madrid's Royal Higher Conservatory of Music. In the 1940's, he also worked as a music critic for various Madrid newspapers and was musical adviser for Spain's National Radio.

Rodrigo wrote 26 works for the guitar and helped to move the instrument to centre stage in concert halls. In 1958, Rodrigo's *Fantasía Para un Gentilhombre* ("Fantasy for a Gentleman"), written for Andrés Segovia, premiered in San Francisco, with the San Francisco Symphony Orchestra and Segovia as soloist. Rodrigo wrote more than 200 works for ballet, movies, light operas, and for voice, piano and full orchestra.

The noted Spanish poet, Gerardo Diego, said of Rodrigo that he "created acoustical landscapes". His style always mixed happiness with a touch of melancholy. Spanish Culture Minister Mariano Rajoy called Rodrigo "one of the most relevant figures in Spanish music". In 1991, King Juan Carlos granted Rodrigo the royal title of Marquis of the Aranjuez Gardens and the city named its concert hall after him.

Although sometimes expressing a certain regret that he had become so universally associated with one particular work, he said that his *Concierto de Aranjuez* was about "looking for the roots, the most traditional and authentic Spanish things." And he admitted that he "liked to be an ambassador for Spain."

Two great Spanish string instrumentalists: Segovia and Casals

Andrés Segovia (1893-1987) practically single-handedly transformed the guitar from a folk instrument into a respected part of the repertoire of classical music. He made his first professional appearance at age sixteen in Madrid and became a recognized celebrity within a few years, even attracting the attention of famous composers such as Rodriguez, Villa-Lobos and Tárrega, who wrote works based on Spanish and Brazilian music especially for his guitar. He was also a composer in his own right and developed the modern nylon strings for his instrument that produced louder tones. Segovia remained opposed to Franco, returning to Spain only after the dictator's death.

Pablo Casals (1877-1974) achieved lasting fame as the master of the cello. His father was an organist in the local church and gave the boy lessons in piano, violin, and organ, but the young Pablo dedicated himself to the cello after first hearing it played when only eleven years old by a group of travelling musicians in his native Cataluña. He gave a solo recital in Barcelona at the age of fourteen. He graduated from the Barcelona Academy of Music with honours two years later.

In 1893, the great Albéniz heard him playing in a café and was so impressed he arranged for a royal recital at the palace. He was appointed principal cellist in the orchestra of the Liceu, Barcelona's famed opera house, and went on to make several international tours, including royal recitals for Queen Victoria and President Theodore Roosevelt.

Casals was devoted to the Spanish Republic and, upon its defeat, vowed never to return to Spain until the restoration of democracy. He went on to live in Switzerland and France, settling later in 1956 in Puerto Rico. His opposition to the Franco regime was notorious and he even declined to appear in those countries that recognized the nationalist government with one notable exception, a special appearance for President Kennedy in the White House in 1961. From 1956 onwards he resided in Puerto Rico. He died in 1974 at the age of 96. He died before Franco but was posthumously honoured by the Spanish government and by King Juan Carlos I.

The popular *Zarzuela*

Zarzuela is a Spanish light or comic opera in the tradition of the music hall and is often compared by Brits living in Spain to Gilbert and Sullivan or a West End staged musical play. It is sung, spoken, acted and danced. The name derives from the Spanish word *zarzas* (brambles) that grew in one of the favourite hunting lodges of King Felipe IV near his Royal Palace, El Prado. The lodge was called *La Zarzuela*.

In 1657, the King attended the first performance of a musical comedy by the great writer Pedro Calderón de la Barca. Since then, this genre has grown in popularity with audiences who favour slapstick comedy and popular songs more than the traditions of Grand Opera. For some time, the Zarzuela was looked down upon by the more "educated classes", who considered Italian opera the only true serious art form combining music and the theatre.

The Golden Age – the nineteenth century

By the middle of the nineteenth century, after the loss of empire, *Zarzuela* began to enjoy a renewal of popularity. Writers appealed to the masses by shortening the length of the play, making the dialogue more realistic and colloquial, setting the plots in familiar lower-class urban neighbourhoods, especially in Madrid, and employed greater ingenuity in creating entertaining plots.

The great composers of *Zarzuela* placed more emphasis on the vitality, theatricality and sophisticated style of the play rather than the originality of the music. Much of the music makes generous use of traditional folk melodies such as *tonadillas, fandangos* and *habaneras.* Just as Sir Arthur Sullivan achieved immortal fame through his operettas in cooperation with Gilbert, the *Zarzuela* composers are all better remembered for their *zarzuelas* than their more serious church, operatic and concert compositions

The twentieth century

The popularity of the *Zarzuela* continued during the first two decades of the twentieth century and the subject matter was extended to include more diverse themes and settings (especially Cataluña and Cuba) and serious issues. One *zarzuela, El Niño Judío* (The Jewish Boy), by Pedro Luna, even raises the issue of Spanish anti-Semitism and prejudice in general. It is also very much in the Gilbert and Sullivan tradition of mistaken identities as in *The Pirates of Penzance* when the Captain and Rick Rackstraw discover that Little Buttercup had mixed them up at birth.

The same composer, Pedro Luna, based another *zarzuela, El asombro de Damasco* ("The Wonder of Damascus") on a tale from the Arabian Nights. The story line is a virtuous woman under siege by powerful suitors and the libretto moves from lightweight comedy situations to satire and deeper passion. Here, too, Gilbert and Sullivan fans will recognize much that is familiar from *The Mikado.*

This *zarzuela* was so popular that it was performed in English in London's West End theatre district on 10 November 1924 under the title "The First Kiss". With the approach of the Civil War, few composers were interested in the *zarzuela* format any longer.

The genre itself, that had elevated working class types into heroic roles, was even somewhat suspect in Francoist Spain. The Basque composer, Pablo Sorazábel, had even set his *zarzuela Katiusha* in the Soviet Union and portrayed a commissar torn between his love of a young peasant girl and his communist duties! He was the last active composer of the genre and died in 1988.

Zarzuela fans love the old favourites and *El Teatro de la Zarzuela* in Madrid is as important to the *Zarzuela* art form as the Savoy Theatre in London was important as the home of the D'Oyle Carte Company for the performances of the Gilbert and Sullivan repertoire.

Happy Listening! ●

Spain's languages and regional diversity

Anyone looking at Spanish-produced food items in a supermarket anywhere in Spain will find the wrappers, cans and bottles crowded with the ingredients and instructions in all four official languages! Yes, there are no less than four (See annex, page 279). In today's Spain, the Constitution grants the autonomous regions of Cataluña, Galicia and the Basque country (*El País Vasco,* also known as *Euzkadi*) control over their own languages, cultural identity and education. The result is that there are four "Spanish languages"– all recognized as official in different parts of Spain, alongside of Castilian, which is what foreigners recognize simply as "Spanish". The minority languages are recognized by the local administration and courts as absolutely equal to Castilian. Since both Cataluña and the Basque Country are developed industrial regions that have attracted a lot of migrants from other parts of Spain, there has been a growing tendency for their children to acquire the regional languages that are taught from the first year of primary school.

The graffiti plague

The difficulties of this multilingualism are legion. Spanish officials, policemen, military officers, soldiers, teachers and ordinary citizens face serious problems of integration and the education of their children when contemplating a transfer to a different region, in spite of the supposed universal acceptance of *Castellano.*

Even tourists can judge the harsh feelings evoked by the language controversy by the frequent graffiti on thousands of official public notices as well as on road and street signs, bearing the name of a locality that was designed as bilingual, with diverse spellings, but now have one variant effaced in the autonomous regions (almost always the *Castellano* spelling).

How Castilian became the national language of Spain

We know that Latin was introduced and widely used in Spain sometime during the second century BC. Prior to that time, various Iberian languages and Basque were spoken and, although there are many written records that have been preserved on a variety of materials (stone, bronze, lead, papyrus, cloth, ceramics), it has not been possible to decipher them. The emergence and eventual domination of Castilian as the major language of the Peninsula is a matter of historical and linguistic geography. The native population of the Peninsula began to speak the "vulgar" Latin they heard from the Roman soldiers with the local pronunciation as a result of their previous language. To this was added the Germanic speech of the invading Visigoths, who crossed the Pyrenees in the fifth century upon the collapse of the Empire.

By the eighth century, most of the Peninsula was under domination of the Arabic and Berber speaking Muslim invaders. The languages of the western half of the Peninsula in Galicia and León resembled Portuguese and had a certain Celtic influence, whereas those in the eastern half in Aragón and Cataluña were closest to Rome. Between the two were the Christian remnants who had been pushed north by the Muslims and may originally have been Basque speakers.

We know that common to Basque, Arabic and Castilian Spanish are the harsh "j" and "ch" sounds that are absent from both *Gallego* and *Catalan*, and several words such as *perro* for dog and *izquierdo* for left that are not of Latin origin but are related to Basque words. The distinctive "ñ" also occurs in Basque as well as the Iberian languages, but is absent in Latin and Arabic.

At the beginning of the twentieth century, several outstanding Spanish scholars interpreted a manuscript (referred to as number 60) that had been found in the monastery of San Millán de la Cogolla in the Rio Alta region (La Rioja) and has come to be known as the *Glosas de San Millán* of the *Codice Emilianense.* It is dated to the year 980. The distinguishing characteristics written in the margin of this document are the earliest clearly distinguished forms that can be identified as Castilian. This manuscript is commemorated on a Spanish stamp recalling the one-thousandth anniversary of the Castilian language.

At the time, La Rioja was close to the frontier with Muslim Spain. It was absorbed by an ambitious new dynasty that set out to expand further south and repopulate the territory abandoned by the Muslims. Much of the new territory was secured by the construction of a series of castles that gave the name Castilla to the region. Under populated and located on the flat central tableland of Spain, the region, Castilla, formed an expanding wedge between the two coasts and their respective language groups.

The domination of Castilla owed as much to its military prowess as to successful diplomacy and dynastic marriages. In addition, the earliest great literary epics proclaiming the holy mission of the Re-conquest – *Cantar de Mio Cid* and a biography of Santo Domingo de Silos written by the monk Gonzalo de Berdeo, that appeared in the twelfth century – were written in Castilian, a language that apparently was also easier for Arabic-speakers to pronounce than either of the western or eastern varieties.

It became the lingua franca of this borderland and then, with ever increasing Castilian power, the rest of the Peninsula. The Muslims learned Castilian readily and even gave Castilian names to their children, just as several of the Christian rulers of Castilla dressed in Arab costume during the many generations of coexistence and reciprocal influences until the fall of Granada in 1492.

"Thetheo" or "seseo" ?

The most significant dialectal-regional variation in Castilian Spanish is a north-south division that has been apparent for many centuries. It runs roughly in a line that divided Christian and Moslem Spain in the eleventh to the thirteenth centuries, north of Badajoz near the Portuguese border to the south of Toledo. North of the line, the letter "s" in front of the vowels "i" and "e" and the letter "z" in front of the vowel "a" have a "th" pronunciation as in the English word "think".

South of the line, these letters are pronounced as "s". The "th" sound also extends to a final "d" in some words, especially place names such as "Madrid" (Madrith). This peculiarity also served as a marker of upper-class speech by those trying to imitate the language of the powerful court and nobility in Madrid. In some plays, the use of the "th" pronunciation is a marker of effeminate or ultra-refined speech.

Due to the fact that a majority of the conquerors and early settlers in the Spanish possessions of the New World originated in Andalucía and Extremadura, this "th" sound is absent in much of the popular speech of the Hispano-American countries. The imaginary word *"ceceo"* would thus be pronounced *"seseo"* in Mexico, Argentina, Perú, etc.

The regional languages

Many tourists and casual observers who encounter Catalan and Galician (*Gallego*) for the first time immediately see the close similarity with the dominant language of Spain – Castilian Spanish (*Castellano)* – and leap to the conclusion that these are only regional dialects, blending it with French and Portuguese respectively. Nothing is calculated more to infuriate their speakers, who point out that they are official Spanish languages, so designated by law and on an equal footing with Castilian. In Spain, all languages but Castilian were once regarded as regional variants or even looked down on as dialects, such as *Catalán*, *Gallego* and *Valenciano*.

The local "minority" languages have only recently been accorded official status as regional languages in the educational systems, courts and mass media. In these areas, there is still a considerable debate over whether a distinctive language is synonymous with a distinctive sense of nationhood. For a textbook in a subject like English to qualify for use in the Spanish school system, it must include a vocabulary list in the back with the equivalent words in all four Spanish languages (*Castellano, Catalán, Gallego* and Basque).

Spain's diverse regions

Historians, cultural anthropologists and many political scientists view the language controversies in today's Spain as the outcome of much deeper cultural, historical-psychological and political differences, that are masked by the perception abroad that Spain is a country that has enjoyed existence as a unified state for more than 500 years. Such unity, however, has been imposed, and the issue has continually re-emerged at critical points in history, most recently during the bloody Civil War (1936-39).

Today's regional and social diversity is the outcome of Spain's historical division into four great cultural and religious traditions. The Castilian heart of the Spanish state most accurately reflects the values of Medieval Christianity and devout Catholicism – the haughty pride and exaggerated sense of honour and disdain for manual labour exemplified by the quest of Don Quixote to achieve the status of a knight errant and create a just world, but one in which everyone knows his place.

The opposite pole is represented by Cataluña, which is said to have absorbed a respect for industriousness and initiative and is oriented towards finance, international trade, sobriety, literacy, and ambition. These values were often held in contempt by the wealthy land-owning class in Castilla. The third region of the northwest, modern Galicia, reflects an older Celtic and Gothic mystical past in much the same way as Scotland and Ireland within the UK, complete with a German fondness for story-telling and a Celtic love of nature and bagpipes. The fourth distinctive area is the Basque country.

Spain has always been and remains a multi-lingual country – the largest in Europe. It is today subject to continual controversies over the language issue, even as the Castilian language abroad continues its rapid growth, and probably has already overtaken English as the language with the greatest number of native speakers (after Mandarin Chinese).

For all Castilians and many speakers abroad, the terms Castilian and Spanish are synonymous. For part of the population in the autonomous communities of Cataluña, Galicia, Valencia and the Basque country, their native language or mother tongue is not Castilian, which practically all understand and speak but regard as only one of Spain's national languages.

The Spanish example is more complicated than other countries torn by distinct ethnic or regional rivalries such as Belgium or Canada. Most Catalans and Galicians would not challenge the appellation of "Spaniards" when applied to themselves. Many Basques do. Spain liberated itself from Arab-Moslem rule largely through the efforts of the kingdoms of León-Asturias, Castilla and Aragón-Cataluña. Castilla in the central upland was better situated to dominate the liberated lands and first absorbed León and then, through dynastic marriage (1476), was united with Aragón.

The Catholic Sovereigns, Ferdinand of Aragón and Isabella of Castilla, were not only joint rulers of Spain but also the separate rulers of their respective kingdoms. Not until 1707 did Spain become a totally centralized state. Before then, the honorary title King of the Spains (*Rey de las Españas*) was used to indicate (much like the title "Czar of all the Russias") royal dominion over several associated lands.

This tension between a centralized state and autonomous regions led in the past to conflicts over the degree of local autonomy permitted. The present Spanish constitution is the most liberal since the formal unification in the fifteenth century. It accords a large measure of autonomy to the local *communidades* (autonomous communities) and, in the case of Cataluña, Galicia, the Basque Country and Valencia, special privileges designed to enhance their cultural identity.

Both Spanish and English share the distinction of being the most widely distributed languages in the world. Both have close to 400 million native speakers and each is the official or widely spoken language in more than two dozen independent states spread across Europe, the Americas, Africa and the Far East – yet both are also not entirely sovereign in the United Kingdom and Spain. Each must recognize the aspirations of speakers of other languages who claim priority in their own regional homelands, most notably Wales in the UK and Cataluña, Galicia and the Basque Country *(País Vasco)* in Spain.

It is worth repeating that both Catalan and Galician lack the rough guttural "ch" sound of Castilian marked by the letters "j" or "x" (as in Don Quixote) and derived from Arabic – and by contrast share the soft "zh" sound found in French and in an English word like "pleasure". Basque with its multiple "z's" and "k's" looks out of this world (see annex 1). It galls many Catalan and Basque nationalists that the word "España" appears solely in the Castilian form! Such sensitivies are still aggravated by the slightest grievance or oversight, even if unintentional.

Catalan

Catalans justifiably point out that more people speak Catalan as their native language (at least 6,500,000) than Danish, yet their language is not accorded the same respect and official status outside of Spain. Within the country, they have had to pursue a long campaign to gain equality in their own homeland with Castilian Spanish. Catalan is more distinctly different from Spanish than is Portuguese, yet the language was derisively labelled as a dialect by supporters of a strong centralist government based in Madrid, who believed that Castilian was a major unifying force in Spain.

In Cataluña, there is considerable tension over the issue of language and there is a constant struggle to ensure that Catalan receives priority in every sphere of public life, including official actions that many Castilian speakers believe threaten their identity and civil rights.

The law has made Catalan the language of instruction in all state primary and secondary public schools. Other laws guarantee the equality of Castilian and Catalan within Cataluña, but which in fact favour Catalan. These have been modelled after the laws passed in Quebec to favour French in education and public places. They have similarly provoked indignation, anger and protests by local Castilian speakers who have pushed for their case to be taken up by the European Community's Court of Justice and other bodies to protect human rights.

Although shop windows and some public services often post bilingual signs, the passer-by is well advised to be able to read Catalan as it is often the only language used to warn the public of nasty fines for traffic violations and illegal parking and forbidding smoking on the metro!

The government, local authorities and public institutions as well as utilities conduct all their business in Catalan. Although the citizen or consumer is guaranteed to have the right to correspond in Castilian Spanish, this requires a special request that is sometimes honoured only if written in Catalan (catch-22!). Delays resulting in fines are the lot of many Castilian speakers who have tried to utilize these theoretical equal rights.

It is undeniable that Catalan has witnessed a remarkable flourishing and is in the best of health but, like the French speakers in Quebec, there is considerable resentment that the "majority" (i.e. English speakers in Canada and Castilian speakers in the rest of Spain) make little effort to learn it unless forced to do so in Cataluña – and that, outside the region, the utility of the language is very limited.

Whereas bilingualism is normally considered a very desirable skill, there are aggrieved nationalists who resent that few Catalan speakers can get by exclusively using Catalan. As in Quebec, there is legislation that provides generous subsidies for Catalan language films, books, choirs, lectures, radio and television programmes, etc. Moreover, there are rigorous quotas for the exact minimal proportion of artistic endeavours that must be performed in Catalan.

Many Catalans, even those who consider themselves well-integrated Spaniards, often bear a repressed animosity towards the dominance of Castilian Spanish and the quite natural function of Spain as the acknowledged leader of the Castilian-speaking world, a force of hundreds of millions of people in more than 20 diverse independent countries.

Some Catalans believe the "eccentricities of Castilian" and its deviance from Latin in pronunciation and vocabulary is due to the influence of Basque and Arabic. It is no accident that the international language Esperanto enjoyed considerable popularity in Cataluña and that Catalan Esperantists still maintain a separate federation from the rest of Spain. For much of the 1950s and 1960s, when Catalan was still frowned upon by the regime in Spain, the Catalan Esperanto Federation was suspected of being a "front" organization for Catalan nationalists parading as international Esperanto speakers. Compare for example the following common words:

Castilian	Catalan	Esperanto	Latin
ventana (window)	*finestra*	*fenestro*	*fenestra*
mesa (table)	*tavla*	*tablo*	*mensa*
cerdo (pig)	*porc*	*porko*	*porcus*
hijo (son)	*fill*	*filo*	*filius*
azul (blue)	*blau*	*bluo*	*cærulus*
llave (key)	*clave*	*klavo*	*clavis*
ojo (eye)	*ull*	*okulo*	*oculus*
noche (night)	*nit*	*nokto*	*nox*
primo (cousin)	*cosí*	*kuzino*	*sobrinus*
caballo (horse)	*cavall*	*cevalo*	*equus*
abuelo (grandfather)	*avi*	*avo*	*avus*

Many Catalans are aware and proud of the fact that their language more closely resembles Latin in the spelling of most words than other Romance languages. This "more international" (compare *Catalán* and Castilian vs. Latin and Esperanto) vocabulary and the greater age of its literature makes some Catalans haughty, resenting the role of Castilian as a world language that superseded Catalan late in the amalgamation of the Kingdom of Aragón with Castilla.

As early as the twelfth century, Catalan balladeer-poets, known as troubadours, wandered through the region and northward in Provence, in what is today the south-east of France, at a time when the language spoken there was almost identical to Catalan. This vibrant poetic tradition and the use of Catalan by philosophers and historians – including King Jaime I, conqueror of Valencia, who enabled the Castilians to throw off the Muslim yoke – are recalled by those who regard the subsequent dominance of Castilla as a disaster that led directly to the decline and eventual persecution of their beloved language.

There are differences, too, in pronunciation, grammar and syntax between Catalán and Castilian. Catalán has a greater variety of vowel sounds, and several consonantal combinations like the hard "g" in the word "general" and the "zh" as in the word "pleasure". There are many fewer words of Arabic origin and more of Greek origin than in Castilian. The most politically incorrect remark one can make is to call the language a dialect of Spanish!

Cataluña has always been distinct from Castilla and, although merged in a united Spain by the Catholic monarchs in 1492, preserved its distinct laws, customs and traditions. As early as 1640-1652, Cataluña tried to follow the example of Portugal and resist Castilian control, provoking a civil war. In spite of defeat, the region conserved much of its own limited sovereignty. The situation was different during the War of Spanish Succession (1699-1702), in which the Catalans supported the losing Habsburg dynasty.

The victorious Bourbon monarch, King Felipe V, was determined to punish the region and abolished the peculiar institutions that remained, as well as the use of the Catalan language in official matters. Nevertheless, the attempt of the Kings to centralize the monarchy in Castilla much in the same way as Paris had dominated France, was doomed to failure.

The Catalans made a transition to a modern economy and became the dynamo of Spain, outdistancing economic activity in the rest of the country. During this time, Barcelona grew much faster than any other city in Spain. Industry in the manufacture of paper, iron, wool, leather, textiles and processed fish, as well as the export of wine and cotton to the colonies, and the resultant prosperity, led to a new sense of self-confidence and to exploitation by Madrid. Unlike in France, where Paris reorganized the country and wiped out old feudal privileges and distinctive laws and customs, Spain remained a pluralistic nation.

Starting in the mid-nineteenth century, Barcelona rather than Madrid became the engine of progress, change, industrialisation, workers' unions, the first railways and the first opera. It pioneered its own way rather than follow that of Madrid. In Castilla, the old prejudices against merchants and working with one's hands still prevailed among an elite that was out of touch with the new developments.

This sense of deprivation and exploitation felt by many Catalans was further aggravated by the disastrous wars forced on them in order to maintain the remnants of the empire in the Philippines, Cuba and Morocco, all ending in Spanish defeats. The Catalans may stop short of demanding independence but they will never yield their sense of identity and distinctiveness as being more industrious, ambitious, sober, progressive and hard working within a united Spain.

Galician *(Gallego)*

How and why Galicia came to be part of Spain rather than Portugal proves that the long cherished ideal of so many poets, patriots and philosophers that "language is the heart and soul of the nation" is not necessarily so. If it were, then Galicia would have been part of Portugal, not Spain. At one time in the Middle Ages, Galician and Portuguese were identical and have only diverged slightly after many centuries.

There are many similarities to Portuguese vocabulary (the definite article "o" instead of "el", *rua* instead of *calle* and *boa noite* instead of *buenas noches*, etc.) but without the presence of so many nasal dipthongs (the "ow" sound, spelt "ão", the ending on many Portuguese abstract nouns).

Galicia was liberated from Moorish rule with the help of nearby Asturias-León before the independence of Portugal. The early development of the great pilgrimage centre in Santiago de Compostela tied Galicia to other parts of Spain, even though the original language was basically Portuguese. A great lyrical-poetic tradition developed in Galicia and spread to other parts of Spain, including Castilla where Galician even became the accepted vehicle for court poetry.

After a long decline, a renaissance of Galician took place in the nineteenth century and competitions were held for poetry and serious literary works, modelled on the movement to revive and promote Catalan. During the last decades of the nineteenth century, a great deal of work was done to devise modern grammars and dictionaries to standardize the language. Galicia remained a poor region and suffered considerable emigration abroad, provoking a further effort to preserve the language lest it die out.

In 1931, when the Republic was established, Galician was proclaimed as the "official language of Galicia". As Galicia fell quite early in the Civil War to Nationalist forces, Franco took a more relaxed attitude towards what was simply considered a dialect of the poor semi-literate rural population, all of whom also spoke Castilian. A new revival got underway in the mid-1950's and some progress has been made to develop a wider vocabulary to meet modern needs and literary expression. Today, about 2,100,000 Galicians out of a total of 2,700,000 speak the language along with Castilian, and are essentially bilingual, but few use it for purposes outside the home.

Many Spaniards have no difficulty at all understanding *Gallego*. Television comedy and drama productions can be received outside the region. Most Galician artists, actors and writers are adept at speaking and writing the language with a maximum of clarity, so that Castilian speakers can readily understand more than 95 percent of any dialogue.

The language controversy is much calmer in Galicia than elsewhere. Most Spaniards interested in a resolution of language issues would prefer to see the Galician system used as a model. The only requirement for teachers in the state school system is to take a two-year course in Gallego, and the only enforced requirement of pupils is that they study at least two subjects in the regional language.

Basque *(Euskera)*

The language issue is emotionally tied to the demand for Basque Independence (see vignette 10). Many Basque adults have had to go to special schools *(ikastolak)* to learn the rudiments of the language that their grandparents had stopped using a century ago. This includes the present *lehendekari* (Basque Prime Minister). Few migrants from other areas in Spain see any point in trying to learn it unless under pressure to do so at their workplace.

While both Catalan and *Gallego* are so close to Spanish that most Castilian speakers can easily read and understand texts in both minority languages, the Basque language *(Euskera)* presents a totally different case. It dates back to the stone age and is the oldest surviving language in Europe without any known relatives. Of the more than two million Basques in Spain, all use Castilian Spanish but probably no more than 40 percent speak Basque, many of them infrequently, only about 25 percent read it and no more than 10 percent write it.

Basque nationalism

Although all Basques in Spain are fluent Spanish speakers and many Basques have made notable contributions to the country's commercial, intellectual and artistic creativity, their full integration within society was postponed due to their peripheral location and involvement mostly in primary industries such as agriculture and fishing.

Few Spaniards were attracted to settle in the Basque country until the development of modern industry in the nineteenth century. These new immigrants posed a challenge to the earlier self-contained existence of many Basques in a cocoon-like environment. Traditionally the Basques had been allowed a degree of autonomy under their old customs and laws known as the *fueros,* but the new liberal forces seeking to promote national unity, economic development and limit the power of the King and the Church met strong resistance from arch-conservative Basques.

Even more than Catalan, Basque and the nationalist government were brutally suppressed during the Franco era. Modern Basque nationalism which seeks to re-integrate the entire Basque country, including the provinces under French control, into an independent state, traces its origin to a remarkable and eccentric leader, Sabino Arana.

Arana provided an ideology of nationalism, a history of the Basque nation in which Basque contributions to Spain, Spanish culture and the Castilian language were reinterpreted as mistaken, misguided or the result of Spanish deception and intrigue. He designed the Basque flag and also helped modernize the language by supplying the missing vocabulary where there were few words for abstract concepts, such as nation, homeland and patriotism.

Arana and the new Basque nationalism seized upon racist ideas that all intermixing of Basque blood with "foreigners" (i.e. Spanish or French) was a threat to the "purity" of the Basque people and anathema. Spain's defeat and loss of territory (Cuba, Puerto Rico and the Philippines) in the Spanish-American war added fuel to the fire of Basque nationalism.

For a thorough history of the Basques, see *The Basque History of the World* by Mark Kurlansky. Random House, New York, 1999).

The Basques were living proof that Franco's propaganda about an atheist, anti-clerical and pro-Communist Republican conspiracy at the very outset of the Civil War was a lie. A majority of the Basques supported the Republic, although most were devoutly Catholic and conservative, in return for the willingness of the government to accord a maximum of local autonomy, including official recognition of the Basque language and local use of the Basque flag, both rejected by Franco who believed strongly in a centralized Castilian dominated state.

During the brief period of Republican Spain before the outbreak of the war (1931-36), there was a flowering of Basque cultural expression through *Euskera* in literature, poetry, the theatre, dance, singing, and traditional sports. In the post-war period, the Franco regime tried to woo traditionalist and conservative opinion in the Basque country by permitting an expression of cultural activity, but deep suspicion remained of any attempt to develop literature or make semi-official use of the language. Increased migration of workers from all parts of Spain to work in industry in the Basque region made most Basques uneasy. They feared their language would be further neglected and eventually disappear.

In 1957, the Israeli Cultural Attaché in Paris, S. Levine, received a confidential letter mailed from France from a group of Basque intellectuals in Spain, asking advice on how to implement a programme of instruction in Basque modelled after the successful Israeli methods to teach Hebrew to new immigrants. Forced underground by Franco's oppression at the end of the Civil War, the Basque language was cultivated in secret. Since the 1960s and particularly after the end of the Franco regime, folk songs, theatre productions, a daily press, the celebration of traditional sports and festivals are all now a visible expression of Basque cultural creativity.

The local government, police and the educational system of the autonomous *communidad* have been controlled by the Basque Nationalist Party for many years. In 1975, when Franco died, almost 40 percent of the population in the Basque provinces were migrants or their children, with no Basque parent. Considerable progress has been made in the adaptation of a standard literary language to overcome the numerous regional dialects.

In the last twenty years, a working knowledge of Basque has been acquired by 75 percent of teachers in the state sector, compared to 5 percent at the outset. New legislation is designed to eliminate teachers without knowledge of the language from the entire elementary school system. Basque is the language of instruction in some schools and is a required subject, whereas Spanish has become a second language,

This has meant that today practically 90% of pupils in the elementary schools in the region study bilingually or wholly in *Euskera,* but the percentage drops sharply to less than 40 percent for those completing high school and studying for entrance to a university.

Valenciano

In the *Comunidad* of Valencia and the Balearic Islands, a variety of Catalán is spoken which local nationalists insist qualifies as a language and they reject the label of "dialect". The locals have an historic grievance against the arrogance of Catalán authorities who resettled the region after its conquest from the Muslims. South of a line near the city of Alicante, Castilian is used for all official purposes. In the northernmost two-thirds, "Valenciano" is the language of instruction in public schools.

The Judeo-Spanish language

The Jewish exiles from Spain and Portugal took their language with them to the new lands of dispersion in Turkey, Greece, the Balkans and Northern Europe and remained faithful to sixteenth century Spanish, Catalan and Portuguese. Spanish visitors to these areas, most notably in Salonika (Thessaloniki in present day Greece) were amazed to find that most of the port workers, including stevedores, spoke their language, albeit in a somewhat antiquated form.

The language, most commonly called *Judeo-español,* (Judeo-Spanish), or *Judezmo*, colloquially known as *Spanyolit,* followed the literary norms of the sixteenth century, but came to be influenced by the languages of their new neighbours, especially Greek, Turkish, Bulgarian and Serbian.

Here is an old folk-saying in modern Castilian Spanish and two varieties of Judeo-Spanish (JS):

My mother-in-law hates me because I took her son.

Spanish: *Mi suegra me aborrece porque (le) tomé a su hijo.*

Eastern JS: *Mi esxuegra me aborrese por ke le tomi a su fizhu.*

Western JS: *Mi sfuegra me aborrese por ke le tomi a su izho.*

The term *"Ladino"* has also often been popularly applied to these languages, but restricted by linguists to apply only to the liturgical "mirror-image" or literal translation of the Hebrew Bible. This unusual hybrid was the product of a word-to-word translation following Hebrew grammar and syntax by authors who felt that this was necessary to preserve the holiness of God's sacred word.

Today, four universities in Israel have special programmes for the study of JS: Bar Ilan University in Ramat Gan, the Hebrew University in Jerusalem, Ben-Gurion University in Beer Sheva, and Tel Aviv University. Although "JS" is still used by the older generation in Israel – where there are several small circulation newspapers and journals and the Israeli national radio *Kol Israel* (The Voice of Israel) broadcasts daily in JS – most linguists believe that the language is in danger of extinction for the simple reason that the youngest "native-speakers" are now at least 60 years old. With their death, the last living vestige of the Sepharadi heritage, testifying to more than a thousand years of Jewish presence in Spain, will soon disappear. Those who love the language, just as strongly as Jews devoted to *Yiddish* (Judaeo-German), believe that it will endure. ●

La Dama de Elche

Ifirst saw her when I was a 16-year-old student at high school in New York and became instantly infatuated. She seemed to me a unique combination of mysticism and eroticism, elegance, beauty and sophistication, other-wordliness and an earth mother. *La Dama de Elche* has captivated me ever since.

When I saw her, I knew I made the right choice to have selected high school Spanish rather than French or German. I now live less than 45 minutes away from where she was found in 1897 but, unfortunately, the Spanish fondness for centralizing objects of art in Madrid has made a visit to honour her more time consuming.

This bust of local limestone is testimony to the wonder and splendour of the remote pre-Roman and pre-Christian Iberian past. In 1948, the Spanish Central Bank used the Iberian sculpture to illustrate the first one-peseta banknote. The archaeologists who found her on 18 August 1897 on the eastern outskirts of Elche in Alicante province believed that the statue had been removed from a more central location in town for protection against vandals and looting. The bust stands 56cm. high and may originally have been part of a full-length, life-size statue. It still bears traces of some of the original red colour on the lips and parts of the elaborate clothing. It is believed that the statue was produced in the fourth century BC as part of what is called the Iberian culture

The Lady's most astounding feature is an elaborate and very complex headdress reminiscent of a *mantilla* (the lace scarf over a high comb embedded in the hair) traditionally worn by Spanish women, but attached with enormous shell shaped coils over her ears. Who was she? The mystery has never been answered. She looks too individual and real to have only been a goddess. Was she a queen? A cavity or compartment located on her back was used to deposit something – perhaps an offering or the ashes or bones of the dead. It could have been an urn used in Iberian funerary rituals.

It is her captivating expression and beautiful features that make her so enchanting. Next to her, the *Mona Lisa* looks like a dowdy grandmother studying for the nunnery. Her fine facial features, almond shaped eyes, heavy eyebrows, gaunt cheeks, round chin, and downcast eyelids retain an air of absolute serenity.

Pierre Paris, a French archaeologist, bought the sculpture on 18 August 1897, only two weeks after its discovery, for a measly 4,000 French Francs and had it shipped from Alicante harbour to France. Nobody in the Spanish government or art circles paid any attention. It was put on display at the Louvre (not too close to the *Mona Lisa*) and given the name *La Dama de Elche* (The Lady of Elche). In 1939, during World War II, it was moved for security reasons to Montaudau Castle near Toulouse (southern France) in an area that became part of unoccupied France after the surrender in 1940.

The Spanish government under the leadership of General Franco, on excellent terms with the Axis powers, saw an opportunity to make a move that would win approval from all Spaniards by urging the return of *La Dama* to Spain. Negotiations for the return of the sculpture were undertaken with the French Vichy government of Marshall Petain and, in 1941, permission was obtained to reclaim the statue.

It reached Spain on 8 February 1941 and was placed in the Museo del Prado in Madrid. It was then moved to its present home in Madrid's National Archaeological Museum. Many copies are found all over Elche and the vicinity at local restaurants, meeting halls, public buildings, the best of which is in the entrance hall of the City's Archaeological Museum (Palace of Altamira).

Far-out views of "The Lady"

Her tunic, necklaces – and most especially the elaborate headdress with enormous coils – have provoked intense speculation. Among those with a strong penchant for belief in contact with beings from outer space, *La Dama* has been hailed as either a survivor of the lost civilization of Atlantis or an alien from another planet.

The coils are obviously part of her intergalactic communications system or an ancient mobile phone. A Spanish historian, Jorge Alonso, has recently advanced the controversial theory that she spoke *Euskera* –

the Basque language. This is a matter of intense controversy, due to the strange unrelated nature of that language to any of the major language families. Various theories have attempted to explain Basque origins.

Many archaeologists believe that inscriptions found from the Iberian period probably are a very early written form of the Basque language that was once more widely spoken throughout the peninsular. This is indeed controversial because there are no written records in Basque until quite recent times. The subject has been made all the murkier due to extreme claims by Basque nationalists that their language is the oldest in the world going back to the stone age. The Basques are renowned for having a peculiarly high proportion of type O blood, which is likewise considered a trait of unbroken ancestry going pack to prehistoric times (see vignette 10: The Basque Conundrum).

Perhaps Alonso, too, had a crush on *The Lady* and could not resist adding to her mystery, fame and glory. He believes that the earliest recognizable civilizations in Spain date back to the Iberians and Etruscans, who probably migrated from North Africa and further East in Asia. Although this is speculative, the Lady of Elche has made such a great impression that the prestigious *Atlas of Ancient Worlds – A Pictorial Atlas of Past Civilizations* (Dorling Kindersley, 1994 by Dr. Anne Millard) uses an enormous illustration of the Lady superimposed on Spain to represent the ancient pre-Roman Iberian and Phoenician civilizations.

The return of the Lady of Elche

Just before the centenary anniversary of the find in 1997, a campaign was mounted by local enthusiasts to return The Lady to her original home in Elche. Supporters were urged to sign petitions in the town and on the internet stating: "I request the *Dama de Elche* be returned to her home in Elche." Following the failure of this campaign, new hope has been generated by an exact 3D copy of the bust, using the latest in digital scanning technology providing an "authentic replica" to be displayed at the Museo Arqueológico Provincial de Alicante, not far from Elche. The claim is that it cannot be distinguished from the original.

Art forgery and nose job?

Like any beautiful and mysterious woman, *The Lady*'s reputation has been challenged. *Art Forgery – The Lady From Elche* is the title of a book written by John Moffitt that has attempted to demolish the legend, mystery and beauty by claiming that the Lady is nothing more than a forgery. This book has also appeared in Spanish, *La Dama de Elche: Crónica de una leyenda* (Barcelona: Destino, 1997) and, as might be expected, created a furore in the Spanish media. It had one immediate consequence: The Lady of Elche was withdrawn from an exhibition of ancient Iberian art in Paris in 1997. Further results, including requests for serious scientific examination of the bust, are still being awaited and debated.

In the meantime, Professor Moffitt, a respected art historian at New Mexico State University, claims that *The Lady*'s nose and eyes are too delicate to have been carved in pre-Christian Spain. He argues that differences in colour between the exterior an interior of the statue, revealed by x-ray, are not natural. According to him, the white exterior is too pristine to be so old.

Until Moffitt's thesis, most experts agreed that the bust represented the finest example of early Iberian civilization and dates from the late fifth century BC. This was confirmed by specialists at the Louvre museum in Paris, which owned the statue until 1941 and was never troubled by doubts of the bust's authenticity. The claim has, of course, infuriated the people and mayor of Elche.

The site of La Alcudia, only a mile from the town, has long been researched and excavations have taken place for more than a century. Other finds there show similar differences in colour, so critics of the critics believe that some "experts" are motivated by sour grapes because they themselves hadn't discovered the most beautiful object of Iberian civilization.

The rival ugly cousin – *La Dama de Baza*

A similar funerary, full-length statue of a seated woman goddess known as *La Dama de Baza* was discovered in 1971 in the locality of Baza near Granada. Like her cousin in Elche, it is assumed that this statue also served as the repository of the remains of either a warrior or priestess. Various weapons and tools were found at the feet of the statue. It, too, was originally painted in red and has traces of brown, blue and black with a similar space for ashes or bones in the back.

The throne is decorated with wings and the lady wears a diadem and has huge earrings but nowhere near the size of the coiled shells of *La Dama de Elche*. In general, her facial features are nothing like as delicate. This reasoning has been used as ammunition by those attacking the authenticity of *La Dama de Elche* supporting the accusation that her features are too fine and beautiful to be authentic.

The political tug of war with Madrid

There is a campaign underway to celebrate the two-thousandth anniversary of the town, and the inhabitants are again petitioning Madrid to let *The Lady* come back home. The snub from Madrid has become an issue of not just local but also regional pride. The town councils of Alicante, Benidorm, Santa Pola and other nearby cities have passed resolutions supporting Elche's request. Christmas cards bearing the statue's picture have been distributed by local political and civic groups and a local poet has composed a song in *The Lady*'s honour that is sung at festive occasions.

A government commission has argued that the precious bust is too fragile to make the 250-mile journey from its home in the National Museum of Archaeology in Madrid to Elche in south-eastern Spain. Some museum officials said the government had refused for political reasons. Elche's demand and Madrid's refusal are typical of the tug of war between the central and regional authorities in Spain.

This dispute is by no means limited to those *comunidades* (autonomous regions) such as Cataluña, Galicia and the Basque country, which have had their regional languages recognized in full or in part as the language of instruction in local schools. Madrid has gradually relaxed its hold and granted more and more local autonomy to the 17 regions on many issues such as taxes and education, but more and more conservatives fear that decentralization may go too far, pulling Spain apart.

A major concern is that the country's artistic treasures may be dispersed and not properly cared for under local authorities. Barcelona is asking for the transfer of the historic archives of Cataluña, which are kept outside the region. The Basque city of Bilbao has asked Madrid to send it Picasso's *Guernica*, which depicts an air raid on the city near Bilbao.

Rafael Ramos, director of Elche's archaeology museum, says: "It's preposterous to say that it's unsafe to transport the statue. Far more delicate works of art travel around the world all the time," and recalls that *The Lady* has already been to Elche once on a previous visit, about 30 years ago.

Well, like every beautiful lady, *La Dama de Elche* must be smiling even more today, knowing that she has become the subject of so much competition, envy and gossip. ●

Spain's Poet Laureate; Federico García Lorca

There is little disagreement with the claim to fame of García Lorca as the most deeply respected and widely known poet and playwright, not only in Spain, but in the entire Spanish speaking world. Born on 5 June 1898 in Fuente Vaqueros, Granada, he was murdered by the Nationalists at the start of the Spanish civil war as a result of his political sympathies.

On 9 August 1936, Falangist soldiers dragged him into a field and shot him, tossing the body into an unmarked grave. Franco's government tried to obliterate his memory, his books were prohibited, and even mention of his name was risky. It might be said that he was the most famous casualty of the Spanish Civil War. This undoubtedly solidified his status as a cultural martyr and symbol of the liberal and humanitarian values he embodied.

For this reason, too, García Lorca, even after his death, became a *persona non grata* for the Franco regime. Critics were found to denigrate his work and martyr status. They had no trouble finding ammunition. They claimed the quality of his work was greatly exaggerated and that much of his popularity was due to his good looks, engaging smile and dark complexion, combined with his political rhetoric, homosexuality and the range of his interests.

The central themes of his poems and plays are love, pride, passion and violent death, which is also how his own life ended. García Lorca was indeed a renaissance man who was a talented painter and musician

213

as well as playwright and poet. His fascinating personality as well as his talent earned him countless friends among artists and writers in Spain and abroad.

What was the poet's childhood like? Lorca describes his childhood as carefree, happy and imbued with the love of the surrounding countryside and an immense appreciation for music, the arts and writing which he acquired from his mother. His personality was formed by a naïve happiness and unquenchable optimism. Only a year before his death, in speaking about his famous smile, he told a journalist, "My smile of today is my smile of yesterday, my smile of always until I die".

He had a generosity for the poor and disenfranchised that was apparent when a young boy. One of his earliest memories was fetching the largest loaf of bread he could find in the pantry to give to some gypsy beggars who had come to the door. Also readily apparent was his fertile imagination with which he endowed every animal and insect in the fields, as well as flowers and objects in the home, with their own personality. His Aunt Isabel taught him to play the guitar, which considerably influenced his poetry and for which he was eternally grateful.

As a dramatist, García Lorca wrote for public theatres. His work reflected his social concerns and he was very quickly labelled a Left-wing artist. *Mariana Pineda*, a historical drama of a Spanish heroine (Madrid, 1928; tr. J. Graham-Lujan & R. L. O'Connell in *Collected Plays*, London, 1976) and *La zapatera prodigiosa* (first performed 1930, amplified 1935, pub. Buenos Aires, 1938; *The Shoemaker's Prodigious Wife* in *Collected Plays*) established him as a major playwright.

His greatest achievements in the theatre form a trilogy of folk tragedies; *Bodas de sangre* (Madrid, 1935; *Blood Wedding*), *Yerma* (Buenos Aires, 1937) and *La casa de Bernarda Alba* (Buenos Aires, 1940; *The House of Bernarda Alba)*. All three were translated into English by J. Graham-Lujan and R. L. O'Connell, in *III Tragedies*, NY, 1959, incorporated into *Collected Plays*.

The crucial moment in Lorca's literary career was ironically a music festival, the *Fiesta de Cante Jondo* in 1922. Here he presented work that sprung from Andalucian traditions of folk and gypsy music. *Poema del Cante Jondo* (Deep Song), made García Lorca known as *the* poet of Andalusia and its gypsy subculture.

He used old ballads and mythology to express his tragic vision of life. The dramas and poems deal with dark forces so common in the folklore traditions of Andalucía and its Arab-Moorish past – earth, blood, sex, water, fertility/infertility, death, horses, fish, and the moon. The following example is a personal favourite:

Song of the Horseman	*Canción del Jinete*
Córdoba,	*Córdoba,*
distant and alone.	*Lejana y sola*
Black pony, big moon,	*Jaca negra, luna grande*
olives in my saddlebag	*aceitunas en mi alforja*
Although I may know these roads,	*Aunque sepa los caminos*
I'll never reach Córdoba.	*yo nunca llegaré a Córdoba*
Through the plains, through wind,	*Por el llano, por el viento*
black pony, red moon,	*jaca negra, luna roja*
with death watching me	*La muerte me está mirando*
from Córdoba's towers	*Desde las torres de Córdoba.*
Ay! What a long road	*Ay que camino tan largo!*
Ay! My brave pony	*Ay, mi jaca valerosa*
Ay, death awaits me	*Ay, que la muerte me espera*
before arriving at Córdoba!	*antes de llegar a Córdoba!*
distant and alone.	*lejana y sola.*

Lorca lived in Granada and studied law at the University of Granada until he moved to Madrid in 1919. He would return on holidays and often stayed at the family home for months at a time. He both loved the city that, in his words, "had opened the vein of its lyrical secret to me," yet hated it, too, and realized that if he stayed he would be suffocated by it.

In the 1920s, García Lorca collaborated with the great Spanish composer, Manuel de Falla, becoming an expert pianist and guitar player. Upon moving to Madrid, he lived at the *Residencia de Estudiantes*, an important centre of cultural exchange, where he came in touch with many like-minded artists, including the painter Salvador Dalí (with whom it is said he had a homosexual affair) and the film producer Luis Buñuel.

His roots go back deep in his native Andalucía, its myths, superstitions and landscapes, from which he drew much inspiration. As a poet, his early reputation was achieved by an accomplished rhythmic beauty demonstrated in *Romancero gitano* (Madrid, 1928; tr. R. Humphries, *The Gypsy Ballads of García Lorca*, Bloomington, 1953), the poems of *Poema del Cante Jondo* (Madrid, 1931), and *Llanto por Ignacio Sánchez*

Mejías (Madrid, 1935; tr. A. L. Lloyd, in *Lament for the Death of a Bullfighter, and Other Poems*, London, 1937).

His visit to New York City in 1929 brought a change in style that shifted to the surrealism and dissonance that became his trademark. *Poeta en Nueva York* expresses his horror at American industrial and urban society with its violence and its lack of roots and impersonality. They were published in Mexico following his death; *Poeta en Nueva York* (Mexico City, 1940; translated into English by B. Belitt, *Poet in New York*, London, 1955).

After writing several successful plays, Lorca made a grand tour of Argentina and Uruguay in 1933-34 and was very favourably received. Other well-known poems such as *Sonetos del amor oscuro*, written during a stay in New England, are much more personal and show a desperate and erotic side to his nature. His *Llanto por Ignacio Sánchez Mejías*, 1935, is an elegy composed upon the death of a famous bullfighter and friend of many of the poets of his generation (known by the sobriquet "The Generation of '27").

The poetic images representing primeval forces appear in his poems and manipulate the characters in such plays as *Bodas de sangre* and *Yerma*. *La casa de Bernarda Alba* is more prosaic and interpreted as social criticism with political undertones. The forces at work here are the frustration of female sexuality, intensified by the need to wait for an acceptable match, the stultifying effects of convention and mourning customs. *Yerma* is the mother of five daughters whom she tyrannizes. All his plays combine powerful dialogue with striking stage effects.

People began speaking publicly about Lorca again in the late 1940's, and one of his plays, *The House of Barnardo Alba,* was finally allowed to be presented publicly in Spain once more in 1950. Nevertheless a ban on staging other more controversial works was still in effect during the last years of the Franco regime.

Anyone unfamiliar with his poems may still get a strong sense of their expressive power, rhythm and musicality by listening to how they have been set to music. The brilliant cassette produced by the CBS recording company in 1986 presents poems drawn from his visit to New York, set to music and sung by a variety of great artists including Leonard Cohen, Lluis Llach, Raimundo Fagner, George Moustaki, Manfred Maurenbrecher, David Broza, Angelo Branduardi, Víctor Manuel, Paco and Pepe de Lucía – in Spanish, Catalan, Portuguese, Italian, English, German, Greek and Hebrew. Nothing better illustrates his international appeal and musicality. ●

Gaudí and Dalí – two eccentric Catalan artists

Two eccentric Catalan artists, Antonio Gaudí and Salvador Dalí, created a revolution in their respective fields of architecture and art – and exemplified with their magnificent work the Catalan genius for non-conformism and innovation. These characteristics among many other behavioural traits set the Catalans apart and explain why they are so insistent on maintaining a separate identity from the Castilians and other segments of Spanish society.

The works of Gaudí and Dalí were highly original. Although architects speak of the turn of the century "Art Nouveau" form and Dali is often referred to as a "surrealist" in art circles, both were "one of a kind" artists. Nevertheless they were for a time ridiculed by their contemporaries for their daring ingenuity.

Antoni Gaudí (1852-1926)
Antoni Gaudi created buildings that lived, breathed and moved. He transformed the "modernist movement" of architecture at the end of the nineteenth century into a stunning art form admired throughout the world.

No other architect has set his individual mark so clearly upon a city as Gaudí did with Barcelona.

He was born near Tarragona and began his working life as a blacksmith's apprentice. This experience made him familiar with working with iron, which became an important element in designing his renowned intricate ironwork balconies. He studied architecture and was inspired by the revival of Catalan culture, to which he devoted his life in spite of the abuse and ridicule he received from colleagues and Barcelona's self-styled intellectuals.

After finishing his studies in 1878 at the age of 26 and following several successful commissions for private home owners, he was put in charge of the planning and development of what had been the suburb of Gracia. At the time, Barcelona was a city of about 350,000 people and had only knocked down its medieval walls 20 years earlier. The new city had ambitious plans for expansion and the inclusion of all the latest technical developments, such as electricity, sewage systems, lifts, running water and gas. The city fathers wanted a new city that would rival, if not excel, Madrid, especially in view of the forthcoming World Exposition to be held in Barcelona in 1888.

They were willing to accept the daring and unconventional views of the young architect. Pride in their city, its development, its new industrial prosperity and the renaissance of the Catalan language, all coincided to give expression to their national reawakening of *Catalanismo.* The period from 1880 to the end of World War I witnessed a renaissance of Catalan culture *(La Renaixença,)* expressed by a flair for innovation and inventiveness, and a desire to make Barcelona a different city than Madrid.

Gaudí was able to take full advantage of these trends and maximize his daring. His notorious buildings, such as Casa Milá and Casa Battló along the Passeig de Gracia, the elegant street in the fashionable Eixample quarter of Barcelona, departed completely from the accepted principles and standards of the architecture of his time.

Gaudí departed from the straight line. His balconies, the walls, staircases and roofs all "flow" like the sea. The "roofscapes" make chimneys and vents into abstract sculptures and geomorphic forms vaguely resembling birds. He was ahead of his time by decades and designed houses with their own parking spaces for the newly introduced automobile.

He disdained the straight line. None of his houses had regular straight lines. He imitated trees, flowers, beetles, ancient Mexican and Hindu gods, leaves, shells, reptiles, rocks and the landscape of the nearby Montserrat dolomite mountains. All these can best be seen in the magnificent Guell Park in the city. He achieved an amazing synthesis though his combination of glass, wrought iron, wood and stone.

Spain remained neutral during World War I, and the prosperous war years increased Spanish self-esteem and confidence, allowing more daring experimentation in art and architecture. His freedom and individuality appealed to a few wealthy businessmen, mostly textile millionaires, without whose support he would have remained the outcast individual immortalized in the novel *The Fountainhead* by Ayn Rand.

Her hero, a non-conformist architect following Gaudí's precepts and life style, battles the prevailing ideologies of socialism, collectivism and community. He champions egoism over altruism and defends reason as the supreme guide to conduct. *The Fountainhead* was turned into a brilliant motion picture starring Gary Cooper that offended the Hollywood left-wing establishment.

Gaudí's *Sagrada Familia* Cathedral is certainly Europe's most unconventional. It became his life's work, as well as his undoing, and remains unfinished to this day. He lived like a recluse on the building site and was run over by a tram while in deep thought over how to raise more money to keep the project going. He is buried in the crypt and the entire city turned out for his funeral.

Salvador Dalí (1904-1989)

Like Picasso, Dalí felt it was necessary to relocate to Paris to launch a meaningful career in art. In Paris, he joined the Surrealist group of painters and sculptors. The content of his work, reflected in shocking paintings dealing with erotic themes and echoing many of Freud's theories, such as *The Great Masturbator, The Spectre of Sex Appeal, The Lugubrious Game* and *The Persistence of Memory* (soft watches), created a sensation. His "soft watches" was a brilliant artistic interpretation of Einstein's *Theory of Relativity,* and made the public aware of the links between art and science on the one hand and art and the subconscious on the other.

In 1956, Dalí would paint *Nature Morte Vivante,* showing the spiral of the DNA molecule and a mathematical grid within a cauliflower. Another combination of art, history and science is *The Discovery of America,* showing Columbus's voyage as the prelude to the landing on the moon.

His hallucinatory images were way ahead of his time. Even in the political field, Dalí was perhaps the most prescient painter in Europe. His ominous *Horseman of Death,* painted in 1935, portrays a gruesome skeleton on horseback with his arm extended in a Nazi-like salute.

In 1929, he met a young Russian girl, Helena Diakonova, known by her nickname of Gala, who would from that time on become his model and girlfriend. She was born in 1894 in Kazan, Russia. She had been sent by her parents to the Swiss sanatorium in Clavadel to be cured of tuberculosis. There she met the French poet Paul Éluard. They married in 1917 and, under the influence of her husband and his friends, she entered the *avant garde* Parisian Surrealist movement.

In the summer of 1929, Gala and her husband, together with some other friends, visited the young painter Salvador Dalí in his Portlligat studio. During that short stay, Gala and Dalí fell in love and she took a firm decision: "We will never again be apart."

At the start of World War II, Dalí and Gala settled in the United States, where his realistic yet dreamlike work met with growing success. He wrote *The Secret Life of Salvador Dalí* and also worked for the cinema, theatre, opera and ballet. His work during the war included *Soft Self Portrait with Fried Bacon*, *Basket of Bread*, *Rather Death than Shame*, *Leda Atomica* and *The Madonna of Portlligat*.

By the end of the war, Dalí was recognized as one of the most famous painters of his time. Unlike Picasso, he had not taken a political position on the Spanish Civil War and was thus allowed to return to Spain after the war. He spent much time at his home and studio workshop in Portlligat near Barcelona.

His interests turned to religion, history and science during the 1950s and 1960s, and he used very large canvasses to complete such works as *Christ of St. John*, *Galatea of the Spheres*, *Corpus Hypercubus*, *The Discovery of America by Christopher Columbus* and *The Last Supper*.

During the 1970s, the Dalí Theatre-Museum was inaugurated. It remains Spain's most visited museum. It houses a large collection of his works, from his earliest days and his Surrealist creations through to the works produced in the last years of his life. After having lived for many years in Portlligat, the artist moved to a new home in Figueres, near the Dalí Theatre-Museum, where his wife Gala died. He is buried close by.

In 1983, he created the Gala-Salvador Dalí Foundation to manage, protect and promote his artistic and intellectual legacy. The most comprehensive collection of his paintings, however, is to be found in Saint Petersburg, Florida, at the Salvador Dalí Museum.

An Ohio businessman, Reynolds Morse, and his wife first met Dalí during his American stay in 1943. After having seen several of his paintings at an exhibition, Morse became fascinated with the eccentric artist with the odd upside-down pencil-thin handlebar moustache, and began to buy up his work.

The collection spans 95 original oil paintings, more than 100 watercolours and drawings and other objects from 1914 to the 1970's. It has been estimated that Morse's purchases of Dali's paintings cost him about $5 million. Their market value today would be close to $400 million! ●

En un lugar de la
Mancha, de cuyo nombre
no quiero
acordarme....

The Economy

Spanish wines and cheeses

Many Brits, Germans, Dutch and Scandinavians have discovered after only a brief stay in Spain that they had been brought up on the mistaken belief that France was the last word in fine wines and quality cheeses. "Why haven't we heard more about these excellent Spanish products" is a common refrain – as well as the realization that the best quality Spanish wines and cheeses are considerably cheaper than French products and are now very desirable exports. My favourite Spanish song *Como en España Ni Hablar* boasts of *"las mujeres, el vino, y el cantar que nadie puede igular"* (the songs, women and wine that no one else can equal)

Spanish wines

This is not a connoisseur's guide to Spanish wine but the briefest introduction to learning what a novice should know in shopping or ordering wine in a restaurant in Spain. For the truly devoted, there are adult education courses in *enología* (Oeneology – the science of wine appreciation).

Spain is a world-class producer of wines, both in quality and quantity. Wine and vineyards have always held a special place in Spaniards' hearts. Spain has more acreage planted than any other country. Just as

225

champagne, to be labelled and recognized properly, must come from the Champagne region in France, so there are four Spanish wines that are universally recognized as being produced only in Spain. They are *Rioja, Cava, Jerez* (Sherry) and *Málaga* .

1. Rioja is a region in Spain with a long, glorious history of wine production that is older than the Roman occupation of the country. The autonomous region of La Rioja is the smallest on the Spanish mainland. It is located between the Basque country and Navarra. The red wine of Rioja is the most well known, but there is also a white and rosé version. Anything from the Rioja region in general is labelled *Rioja Calificada*. The wines of the region are further divided into three sub-regions called *Alavesa, Alta* and *Baja* – and reflect the altitude at which the vineyards are located. The leading grape variety is the large red *Tempranillo* variety.

2. *Cava*, a fine sparkling wine, is produced in the northwest of Spain and uses similar methods and bottling techniques as Champagne. The different land the grapes grow on affects the flavour to give *Cava* a distinctive taste. Traditionally, *Cava* is made from *Macabeo, Xarello* and *Parellada* grapes and comes in white and rosé versions.

3. *Málaga* is a deep brown, rich, resiny fortified wine from the Andalucía region of Spain – the same region where Sherry originated. *Málaga* began with the Greeks, who developed it about 600 BC. It was originally called *Xarabal Malaguii*, (Malaga Syrup) and is very sweet. Spain now produces 5.8 million gallons of Málaga a year. There are several main types. The most common are:

Lágrima - very sweet and free run (i.e. not pressed)

Moscatel - sweet, aromatic, using the muscatel grapes only

Pedro Ximenez - sweet, using the *Pedro Ximenez* grapes only

Solera - coming from a dated *"solera"*

4. Sherry refers to the fortified wine made in Jerez de la Frontera. Most types are sweet but there are a few that are dry, such as *La Ina*. Production was begun by the Phoenicians around 1100 BC and continued by the Romans. The EU ruled in the mid 1990s that all member states recognize that sherry can only come from this region in Spain. Almost 20 million gallons are made each year, following a complicated method of production. The name "sherry" is actually a corruption of *Jerez.*

Sherry is aged for five years by a blending method know as *solera.* The sherry is first "laid down" in a cask. The next year, a similar tasting sherry is added on top. Some sherry (about a third) is then removed from the bottom cask and replaced with liquid from the cask above – and so on. The series of casks is called a *criadera,* and the cascade method is called "running the scales". In this way, the sherry maintains a consistent taste. Sherries are labelled with the date that the *solera* was first started.

There are forty recognized wine regions in Spain and, of course, one year's vintage varies from another, depending on the growing season's condition that year. In time, people come to depend on their favourite wines and vintage years.

Pay attention to the label!

To avoid problems at the checkout counter, take a careful look at the label. Every real quality wine must bear a label with a serial number testifying to its *Denominación de Origen* and to its type – *crianza, reserva or gran reserva*. The differences in price are substantial and foreigners can be confused by glancing at the shelf price label but not carefully reading to determine if the price is for the ordinary *joven* type or one of the more select varieties. The label will also specify the principal grape type and the year of harvest.

The wines of three other regions are also much sought after. They are the Ribera del Duero, along the Miño river in Galicia, near the Portuguese border; Valdepeñas in central Spain, 190 kilometres south of Madrid in Castilla-La Mancha; and Penedès in Cataluña, south of Barcelona. Penedès is the traditional home of *Cava* and also produces fine reds and whites based on the French grape variety Cabernet Sauvignon. There are also fans of Jumilla, the region of hilly vineyards north of Alicante, where the leading grape variety is the black *Monastrell* and the main output is a strong sometimes-sweet wine. It is popular, too, because of its generally lower price in comparison with other types.

The following designations are also helpful. They are in ascending order of price:

Vino de mesa: table wine, in restaurants often referred to as *vino de la casa* (the house wine).

Vino joven: young wine, usually from a qualified region, with a short ageing period, but not enough to be a *crianza.*

Crianza: aged for two years, at least six months in oak casks.

Reserva: quality wine made from top vintages, normally aged at least three years – at least one year in oak cask and two years in the bottle.

Gran Reserva: quality wine made from exceptional vintages, aged at least two years in oak, plus three years in the bottle.

Basic wine types

The basic wine types are: *tinto* – red wine; *rosado* – rosé wine; *clarete* – light red wine; *blanco* – white wine; and c*ava,* sparkling wine made by the champagne method. Sweetness levels for whites, sherries and *cavas* are: *dulce* – sweet; *seco* – dry; *semi-seco* – medium-dry; and *brut* – very dry.

Sherries are subdivided into the following categories in order of increasing sweetness:

Manzanilla – very dry sherry from Sanlucar

Fino – light dry sherry

Amontillado – an aged *fino*

Palo cortado – dark, superior grade sherry (or *Montilla*)

Oloroso – dark, full-bodied sherry

Pedro Ximenez – a dark, sweet sherry (or *Montilla*)

Cremoso (Cream) – very sweet sherry

Other useful Spanish terms are: *bodega* (winery), *añejo* (aged), *cepa* (vine or name of grape), and c*osecha* (vintage year).

Wine idioms in Spanish

The label specifies the region where the grapes were grown and is referred to as *Denominación de Orígen*. A glass of wine (i.e. a glass with a long stem) is a *copa*. Quite a few idioms and songs make use of the term such as *tomar una copa* (to have or drink a glass of wine); *estar de copas* (to be out drinking); *convidar a una copa* (to invite out for a drink); *llevar una copa de más* (to have had one drink too many); *apurar la copa de dolor* or *ahogar las penas en vino* (to drown one's sorrow in wine); *bautizar el vino* (to water down the wine); *tiene el vino triste* (he gets sad when he drinks too much wine); *tiene el vino alegre* (he gets happy when he has too much wine); *tiene mal vino* (he gets nasty when he has too much wine to drink).

Spanish cheeses

Cheese has long been one of the most important elements in providing nutrition for a large part of the population in Spain. The country's bio-geographic diversity and the extensive herds of cows, sheep and goats, combined with the traditions developed by generations of artisans in thousands of villages, have resulted in an enormous variety of types that have been produced over the centuries and become some of the world's most outstanding cheeses. Archaeologists believe that cheese making in the Iberian Peninsula probably began in the Neolithic (New Stone Age), several thousands years ago.

Several hundred distinct types varying in taste, size, shape, fat content, freshness, methods of curing and texture, must – just like wines – bear a *Denominación de Origen* label, and must meet exacting standards. Making fine cheeses is no longer simply a village industry and, during the past twenty years, more than 40 new cheeses have been created and already achieved fame. Another important aspect of consumption is whether the cheese is intended to accompany drinks as an appetizer, as a desert or by itself.

The Romans further elaborated and extended the manufacture of cheese throughout the empire, including Hispania. Both the Visigoths and the Muslims added their own preferences but, for most of the Middle Ages, production was on a purely subsistence economy of local scale in the countryside and in monasteries. Cheese was an important ingredient in some hot dishes of fried bacon that were sweetened, and in stews.

Later during the eighteenth century, considerable advances were made in the manufacture of cured "mature" cheeses and in the production of much larger quantities using new industrial techniques. It was, however, the bacteriological research pioneered by Louis Pasteur in the nineteenth century that converted cheese making into a modern industry.

Continued improvements in technology, transportation, and a much greater commercial awareness of both the public and the food industry led to the introduction of the *Denominación de Origen,* as with wine, and hence to identifiable types and standards of cheese quality. Unfortunately, this late start hindered the progress of the industry and enabled such cheese producing nations as France, Italy and the Netherlands to take an early lead.

Just as wine is dependent on the type of grape, the quality and characteristics of cheese ultimately depend on the quality and nutritional value of the pasture consumed by cows, sheep and goats in their different habitats, which vary according to soil type, climate, altitude and water. Cheeses also vary according to the methods and time employed to cure them. All cheese is produced by the separation of whey after the coagulation of milk and cream.

In the most general terms, cheeses produced from cow's milk are more common and popular in the mountainous north of Spain and on the Balearic islands. Most cheese made from sheep's milk comes from the central plain (*Meseta*) of Castilla-León and Castilla-La Mancha, Extremadura and a section of the Pyrenees in Navarra and the Basque country.

The generally drier climate in these regions accounts for a more pronounced or sharper, acidic or saltier taste than the smoother or blander cow-derived cheeses of the north. Some of the sheep varieties in the central areas also give less milk but with a high fat content and a somewhat bitter taste.

Goat's cheese is the type that many North Europeans are suspicious of, particularly for those who have ever tried to drink goat's milk! It is most likely the type of cheese that was produced earliest by herdsmen for their own consumption and only much later for the market. The areas where goats prevail are much more difficult for cows or sheep to derive adequate nutrition, due to a more severe climate and steeper or rockier terrain.

These areas are a large part of the dry interior of Extremadura and Andalucía, the Mediterranean (Levante) coast and the mountainous regions of Asturias, León and La Rioja, and on the higher elevations of the Canary islands. These cheeses are mostly fresh with a smooth creamy texture and a bland or aromatic but agreeable taste. Most cheeses are fresh or only cured for a week or two.

More than half the cheeses produced in Spain are "mixtures" that combine the three animal types – the exact combinations that determine the taste, texture and consistency vary. In such mixtures, the cows lend acidity; the sheep, a higher fat content; and the goats, 20 percent, the white colour. Spain is the only European country that produces all three types throughout the entire year, due to its great biodiversity. It also accounts for the greater variety and mixtures.

The "mixtures" are classified into three groups called *Queso Hispánico, Ibérico* and *Mesta*. The best advice to further educate one's palate is to pay attention to these terms when you buy cheese and begin to sort out the types you like from those you don't. It also means carefully checking the information provided on the wrapper. It may be a long process but well worth the effort.

The best wine-cheese marriages

The great danger the novice faces is overwhelming the flavour of the chosen wine with the wrong cheese and vice-versa. The general rule is to combine strongly flavoured cheeses with young wines and delicate cheeses with finer quality *reserva* wines. Many people like to order or serve a tray of several cheeses and here the rule is to select a young red or rosè *Rioja, Penedés, Rueda* or *Ribera del Duero* wine. Aged or mouldy un-sliced white cheeses harmonize best with slightly fruity reds, such as *Ribera del Duero, Bierzo* and *Valdepeñas*, whilst creamy and tasty cheeses go best with more vigorous *Rioja* and *Navarra* reds.

Young and "dry" *Rueda* or *Penedés* white wines, sherry and *cava* are the preferred accompaniment to goat cheeses. "Blue" cheese demands a strong-bodied *crianza, Ribera del Duero, Jumilla* red or *moscatel*. *Manchego* sheep cheeses require a full-bodied dry red or white from any of the recognized regions.

The real gourmets also have a decided preference for types of bread to choose from and follow various rules for choosing between wheat, rye or corn derived flour. There are also a number of delicious combination dishes with cheese, the most well- known probably being *membrillo* and *queso manchego. Membrillo* (quince jelly) is a delightful Spanish delicacy easy to find in supermarkets, etc., but not well known by foreigners. The combination of the (sweet) *membrillo* and the *Manchego* cheese is a delicious appetiser or dessert.

Famous names of cheese types worth trying

Not being a gourmet, I will not attempt to recommend any particular variety but simply mention several of the names you are most likely to see or hear discussed by people who love Spanish cheeses. As space only allows a mention of a few, there will undoubtedly be gourmets who will claim that I omitted their favourite. My apologies to them.

The adventurous and curious will no doubt like to try them all by buying a small section of the wheel and sampling them with a variety of wine. Most of the hard cheeses are produced in varying cylindrical shapes or wheels weighing between half a kilogram and three kilograms! Remember, after slicing out a section of cheese, wrap the remainder to prevent the exposed part from drying up.

Topping the list has to be:

1. *Manchego* (from La Mancha) which, of course, features Don Quixote on many labels. It is produced from the milk of sheep from La Mancha and fermented in a special way. The best known variety has a fat content of at least 50 percent, is quite dry, is shaped into cylindrical blocks, has a hard rind and a chestnut or yellow colour, and is quite firm and compact. The Arabic term *manya* meaning "without water" supposedly was the origin of the name La Mancha, covering the area of the central plain between the cities of Ciudad Real, Toledo and Albacete.

2. *Cantabria* (from the region by that name in the North) is also a fatty cheese and made from cow's milk. It is creamy and has a yellow

colour with a smooth taste and smells like butter.

3. The strange-sounding *Idiazábel* (from the Basque country and Navarra) is one of the most special cheeses and is made from sheep's milk, which requires a longer period of time to cure. It is creamy, slightly sharp, with a white or amber colour. It is also fatty and is smoked using beech or cherry wood that gives it a delightful aroma and taste. It is my favourite.

All of the above are hard cheeses with a rind. The soft or fresh cheeses such as *Burgos* are probably familiar or similar to the type of breakfast cheese most North Europeans know from home. These are all very white and milky in taste. They vary considerably in saltiness. After trying these few varieties, one can easily begin to select others based on an appreciation of which ingredients and tastes are most appealing – and then looking for other types that match these characteristics. ●

Spain's rich fishing industry

With its more than 8,000 kilometres of coastline, Spain is the number one fishing nation in Europe). Moreover, it has the largest fleet in Europe, with 18,000 vessels, of which 2,000 are modern deep-sea ships capable of plying waters far from home – and accounts for the largest catch in Europe (over one million tons annually).

Spain, likewise, takes first place in the largest per capita consumption of fish and the most people directly employed both onboard ship (80,000) and in the allied industries of canning, processing, storage, transport and marketing (close to half a million). Another important source is aquaculture, the products of Spain's own inland freshwater lakes and rivers. Big game sports fishing is also an important tourist attraction in the Canary Islands.

More than one embarrassed tourist has been caught trying to order meat in typical Spanish fish restaurants, apparently unaware of the possibility that a restaurant could be so specialized as to serve only fish and seafood. I have observed this several times at the two well-known fish restaurants on the shore of Santiago de La Ribera, where I live. Spain's location along both Mediterranean and the Atlantic (based in

233

the Galician ports of Vigo, and La Coruña) provides environments for a wide diversity of fish. The quality and quantity of Spanish seafood is indeed something to write home about.

The fish wars

Spain's long-distance fishing fleet, which reaches as far as the territorial waters of Morocco, the UK, Iceland and Canada, brings home an abundant variety of seafood, but has also involved the country in numerous disputes referred to as "wars" over halibut with Canada, tuna with France, sardines and anchovies with Morocco – and with the UK over access to the waters around Gibraltar.

Efforts to support the UK fishing industry created a major dispute over Spanish boats fishing in the territorial waters of the United Kingdom. On several occasions, pressure from MPs to send British Navy gun-ships to Gibraltar to prohibit fishing by Spanish vessels escalated tensions. The result was the filing of formal complaints in Brussels over what both the Spanish and the British termed "unacceptable threatening behaviour". The Spanish government has, in the past, threatened retaliatory measures such as banning flights leaving Gibraltar from flying into Spanish airspace, as well as refusing to accept Gibraltar driving licences as valid.

Before Spain's entry into the European Community, it was frequently at odds with other member states over fishing rights. The importance of fish in the Spanish diet and economy can hardly be exaggerated and every Spanish government, whatever its political make-up, is sure to defend Spain's right to fish all its traditional grounds and defend the industry from the threat of ecological dangers and in political disputes with other countries.

The fishing issue in the European Union

Spain is also intent on maintaining its current standing within the European Union regarding the need to modernize its fishing fleet, for which it has received generous subsidies in the past. This financing has occurred through *FIFG* (Financial Instrument for Fishing Guidance).

Spain is busily engaged in a programme of modernizing and restructuring its fishing industry, covering all aspects of port and ship modernization, hygiene and more efficient production, processing, transport, storage and marketing, while at the same time ensuring observation and close monitoring of conservation measures.

European Community conservation measures designed to protect fish stocks from over-fishing have meant a drastic downsizing of the industry. These measures are a potential threat for Spain greater than for any other member state. Agriculture and Fisheries Minister Miguel Arias Cañete told reporters after an emergency meeting with fishing industry leaders that "We will use all the means at our disposal" to fight the proposals.

A day after the EU proposed cutting national fleets by up to 60 percent over four years, a major political crisis developed. The British, Dutch, Germans and Scandinavians claimed they would have to make the biggest cuts in annual catches. Spain protested that it had already halved its national fishing fleet since the country's 1986 entry into the EU, but this made little impression on the northern countries who charged Spain with maintaining its enormous catch by the progressive use of larger ships and more modern equipment.

Since 1983, the European Union has managed a Common Fisheries Policy (CFP) to conserve the decreasing stocks of fish for its member states. This policy hopes to conserve stocks and has primarily taken the shape of fish quotas called Total Allowable Catches (TACs), which member states can bring to port. Other measures are aimed at decreasing and decommissioning a part of the EU's fishing fleets.

Member states realize that it is in their common interest to reduce the size of their catches but, in the short-term, most of them are constantly fighting for a bigger share. Large Spanish boats ply waters as far as the Pacific and Indian oceans to provide the home market with its accustomed consumption of fish. It is no wonder that the Spanish fishermen fear that EU regulations will reduce their catches and further limit their activities in the North and Baltic Seas.

Spain also found itself in conflict with France over fishing rights upon entering the EU, and demanded that France open up its waters for white fish catches. The other European Community states had to adjust to Spain's entry and its prominence as the sixth-largest fishing fleet in the world. All quotas had to be adjusted. A Spanish fleet of over 250 boats sailed along the coastal regions of the Franco-Spanish border for three days to demand greater access to French waters as a means of exerting pressure

This dispute was a taste of things to come, demonstrating that, with decreasing quotas, there are entirely too many ships for too few fish. An increasingly bitter issue in the UK is the purchase by Spanish companies of UK fishing boat licences within the UK quota, with the result that supposedly British fishing boats are operating in UK waters but with crews who are entirely Spanish.

Although the EU is a net importer, several countries such as Spain are significant exporters of fish and fish products. Part of the difficulty in the debate about over-fishing is monitoring and enforcing quotas and other regulations such as net sizes at sea in waters that are hard to define into exact geographic zones. The fish do not recognize any boundaries. Threats of over-fishing have led many countries to expand their territorial waters (three or six miles traditionally) into extensive 200 mile "exclusive economic zones". This is the current extent of Morocco's claim and has involved Spain in a major dispute.

Spain and Morocco and the fishing issue

Spain has concluded numerous agreements with Morocco, allowing Spanish ships to fish off the coast of its North African neighbour in return for various benefits, primarily monetary to purchase fishing licences and fees. The volatility of Spanish-Moroccan relations involving other questions (illegal immigration and the status of the Spanish *plazas* of Ceuta and Melilla, see vignette no.11) make the issues particularly complicated. This is still a hungry planet and, for Morocco, fish represent the largest proportion of animal protein in the local diet.

Since 1992, Morocco has several times threatened to withdraw all permits for Spanish fishing boats and has reacted emotionally whenever the European Union made critical remarks about Morocco's alleged disregard for human rights. Loss of rights in Moroccan waters would immediately put 10,000 Spanish fishermen on the dole.

In 1995, Morocco's Prime Minister, Abd-al-Latif Filali, said that "the best accord would be if there is no accord" – only to relent when Morocco's subsidies were substantially increased.

The ecological threats

Fishing is especially important in Galicia (which accounts for almost half the fishing fleet), Andalucía, the Basque country and the Balearics. Fish dishes are particularly popular in these regions. Basque fishing activities, navigation and ship-building contributed substantially to Spain's historical role as a naval power, and the culinary delights of such humble creatures as the octopus, eel, elvers (baby eel), mussels, spider crab, squid cod, and whale became world famous.

The last speciality has, of course, disappeared due to the extraordinary success of Basque whale hunters who were in great demand by all European maritime nations until the beginning of the twentieth century, when electricity replaced whale oil as the principal fuel for lighting. Salted and dried fat-free cod, perfected by the Basques after having been copied from the Vikings, sustained long distance expeditions that enabled the Spanish and Portuguese to circumnavigate the globe.

The ecological disaster two years ago along the northwest coast of Spain resulting from the break-up of the oil tanker "Prestige" has focused attention on Spain's fishing industry. The Greek-operated vessel was carrying more than 20 million gallons of fuel oil – about twice as much as spilled on Alaska's shores from the Exxon Valdeez in 1989.

The nearby Galician shoreline was covered with oil, killing wildlife, spoiling sandy beaches and endangering a fishing industry that is the main source of income for tens of thousands of people in the rugged northwest of Spain. Environmentalists feared that currents would draw the oil south and pollute one of the world's largest mussel beds.

About 30,000 southern Galician families rely on the bed for their livelihoods. Much beloved by both Spaniards and tourists, fresh mussels are one of the most appealing items on the menu of fish restaurants. Spain is the world's second largest producer of mussels – behind only China – and its nearly 290,000 tons of mussels harvested in 1999 accounted for more than 15 percent of the world supply. Fortunately, the damage was not as severe as feared.

Mussel growing is a special form of fishing. In the numerous rich inlets of the Galician coast, thousands of floating rafts can be observed. These are platforms from which mussels are suspended and grown in what is considered to be one of the top quality areas in the world. Harvesters pull up ropes on which clusters of black mussels grow; the larger ones are plucked and the smaller ones left behind to mature. Fear of another environmental disaster is so great that many local politicians claim that many Galicians would be forced to emigrate to Latin America, as in the past.

Morocco used the ecological crisis of the "Prestige" to make a goodwill gesture to Spain, allowing about half the Galician fishing fleet to fish in Moroccan coastal waters. The price of most seafood, especially shellfish, rose immediately after the oil spill by more than 50 percent. It is not only the Galician coast, however, that is threatened. The risk to Spain's supply of fish is especially severe in the waters around the strait of Gibraltar. Approximately 90 percent of the world's supply of crude oil exported by sea passes through this narrow stretch of water. About 90 super tankers pass through the strait each day and, during the last twenty years, there have been at least 40 spills that have caused ecological damage. This makes the Gibraltar question and its political status particularly sensitive.

Favourite fish and seafood dishes

Practically every Spaniard and tourist has his or her own special favourite fish and seafood dish. The most renowned regional specialities are Gallegan octopus, Basque *pil pil* (*bacalao,* a Cod dish); *angulas* (elvers), *truchas* (trout) *vieras de Santiago* (scallops), mussels, lobsters, *percebes* (black barnacles) from Galicia; grilled *mariscos* (shellfish) and "*Suquet*" (a fish and shellfish stew) from Cataluña; seafood *paellas* from everywhere; *Cachorrenas* (a fish soup), *fritura de pescado* (a fried squid and fish dish) and *pescado a la sal* (several types of fish baked whole in salt) from Andalucía and the south; and *Langosta a la parrilla* (grilled lobster) from the Balearic Islands.

Vegetarians who eat fish need never worry about not getting a delicious and nutritious meal in Spain. However, the near extinction of whales is a clear historical warning that Spain must be careful in managing its rich fishing resources to avoid a catastrophe in the future. ●

Spain's great water diversion project

L
ike so many other arid countries, Spain has a water problem. Its very large size (second only to France in Europe) and varied geography create a number of intriguing possibilities to bring water via pipelines from the quite humid and temperate mountainous regions of the north to where it is needed most – along the Mediterranean in the more arid southern part of the country.

This seems all the more logical, given that the Mediterranean coastal region has attracted enormous revenues spurring overall development in the country. These incomes have been generated through tourism and the settlement of many north European immigrants, who have come to that area to enjoy their retirement.

The enormous needs generated by this development make it essential to provide more water to the south. However, ecological and political factors have turned the Water Transfer plan, colloquially known as *El Trasvase* (The Transfer), into a political football.

For and against

There is little doubt in any of the debates on this question that more water is needed in the south – for both agriculture and increases in population

239

that far exceed population growth in the north. Hundreds of thousands of Spaniards have demonstrated on behalf of the National Water Plan (NWP, and officially referred to in Spanish as *El Plan Hidrológico Nacional*), and even more against it.

The plan was adopted by the previous government of the Partido Popular in July 2001. The massive turnouts of pro-demonstrators have been most obvious in cities in the two southern provinces (autonomous communities as they are known officially) of Valencia and Murcia.

Opponents of the plan were able to mobilize 400,000 people in Zaragoza, in Aragón, one of the largest demonstration ever held in Spain. Carrying placards to protect "our River Ebro", the "anti" forces pictured their water being used to keep golf courses green, fill swimming pools for tourists and supply amusement parks while "others die of thirst and neglect".

The NWP, prepared by the Ministry of Environment, is a legislative text. It includes a list of 863 "investments" or "interventions", affecting water resources and works to be carried out for the whole of the Spanish territory, and has a series of annexes containing different supporting documents, such as an analysis of the water systems, the identification and allocation of resources in shared aquifers, and an economic study of the planned interventions.

The largest single element in the plan is the massive construction of dams and canals to bring water from the Ebro River basin to the coastal regions of Murcia, Valencia, and the area around Almería in Andalucía. A second much smaller project envisages bringing water from the Rhone River basin shared with France to Barcelona.

"Our region needs water" is a familiar cry of the supporters who fear that, without the plan, much of the region's agriculture and industry will be put in danger of economic collapse. The NHP foresees the construction of about 120 dams and the transfer of 100,000 million litres of water annually. Such a plan would, of course, have massive ecological consequences. The debate, in progress since the plan's adoption until its demise, revolved around what the actual pay-off would be in benefits and probable damaging effects.

The political football

Naturally, such statements regarding the need for water benefited the *Partido Popular* in Murcia and Valencia and aroused considerable opposition along the Ebro basin in the region of Aragón and Castilla, where the party suffered a loss of support. The Spanish Socialist Party

(*PSOE*) found valid objections to the plan and proposed various alternatives. As the European Union is required to finance somewhere between 33 and 40 percent of the project's cost, both supporters and detractors made appeals not just to the voters in Spain, but to the entire European Community.

Opposition to the plan on ecological grounds grew and also resulted in a pick-up of electoral support for the *PSOE*. Opponents pointed out that the plan is an "excise tax" to finance dam and canal construction in one part of the country for the benefit of another part, and insisted that the problem of water scarcity in the south be solved by "ecologically responsible" means.

The economics of the project

From an economical point of view, the plan included a major expenditure of more than 4,200 million Euros for the Ebro water transfer – to be implemented in eight to ten years time - and other investments amounting to almost 8,900 million Euros for dam construction and improvement of irrigation infrastructures. Other sums were reserved for desalination, water treatment and supply (5,400 million Euros), water quality control (1,260 million Euros), flood prevention and reforestation (3,300 million Euros).

According to the Spanish Ministry of Environment's figures, the cost of the water transfer project would be 0.3 Euro per cubic meter, both in the urban and agricultural areas. The water price for the final user would cover this cost and be established using economic criteria. The territories of the Ebro watershed that provide the water would be paid 0.03 Euro per transferred cubic meter to fund hydro-environmental programmes in the Ebro area.

There are a number of realistic objections:

1. Increased Salinisation at the Delta and Intrusion of Seawater
According to many biologists, the transfer of water from the Ebro would increase the salt content of the Delta. The reduction in the volume of fresh water, as a result of the Plan, would lead to an increase in the penetration of salt water into the Ebro estuary. There is a risk that the increased salt content would gradually lead to reduced crop yields, because the rice fields and other crops in the north are irrigated with river water. Half the delta has already sunk to sea level. The Delta loses about five millimetres in height each year. In approximately 100 years, half of the Ebro plain will be a half metre below the level of the sea, leading to penetration of seawater

inland. The inflow of salt water into the estuary has increased as the volume of the Ebro has fallen, and now reaches 32 kilometres inland! Although this intrusion varies during the year, it is estimated that, as a consequence of the Water Transfer Plan, the saline water would last nine months instead of the current average of six months. The result would be severe damage to citrus fruit and other crops using well water.

2. Erosion of the Ebro Delta

As less sediment arrives at the river mouth, the coastline would continue to retreat. As it is, the Ebro no longer floods and the 60 dams constructed upstream are retaining more and more sediment. There is always a balance between erosion and deposition in a delta producing changes in its shape. The balance has already shifted in favour of erosion. The Delta is changing shape and this instability is a danger for the agricultural zones located close to the sea.

3. Contamination of the water and a decline in fishing

Water can "rot" – due to the accumulation of organic material that uses up oxygen. Salt water lies underneath the better-oxygenated fresh water and does not mix with the layer above. Water that is poor in oxygen will not support an environment rich in fish life. This factor has already been noted in the Ebro.

4. Effects upon the food chain

The reduction in the flow of Ebro water reaching the delta and the sea means that the river's normal fertilizing effect on the sea, through the contribution of nutrients (nitrogen, phosphorus), will be much reduced. This means lesser growth of plankton, the base of the marine food chain. A reduced flow will affect the plankton growth and the food chain dependent upon it, including oysters and mussels. The Plan has been criticised by much of the scientific community and created a serious social, political and regional-political conflict in Spain.

"Us and them"

Economic analyses of costs and benefits of the controversial plan are still hotly debated by both sides. The "anti" side constantly claims that the "real environmental costs" are not adequately taken into account. An additional social consequence of the plan is the growing sentiment in Spain that too much consideration has been given to "them" (the foreigners), who are mostly wealthy and elderly retirees from northern Europe, to the detriment of Spaniards, especially the young, who find themselves priced out of the housing market and believe that they are now being called upon to subsidise the "foreigners" at the expense of their own environment.

Of course, such views are much more common in the north than in the south of the country. As well as the forecast damage to the Ebro Delta ecosystem that is one of the richest areas in biodiversity in southern Europe, the plan proposes to flood beautiful inhabited Pyrenean valleys, and affect dozens of protected natural areas.

How practicable and expensive are the alternatives?

Is there then an ecologically responsible alternative that would nevertheless manage to transfer large amounts of water to the south for development and population growth? This was one of the principal issues decided in the last general election. One's point of view is very much a factor of political sympathies and geography.

The supporters of the government plan, especially in the south, feel that they deserve the "excess water" that the north "does not need" – and that this is small compensation for the tremendous rise in Spanish living standards and the prosperity generated largely by developments along the Mediterranean coast in the south. Global warming will only exacerbate the problem.

Critics believe that the diversion of the River Ebro is completely unnecessary and claim that the answer to Spain's water problems lies in "reorganizing the supply." They argue that the country is suffering from "water schizophrenia" and that taxpayers won't accept subsidizing the irrigation of crops that are already subsidized and are often produced in excessive quantities.

The reason lies in the fact that irrigation water for agriculture is very cheap, whereas the cost of water used in cities and industries is much higher. The price differential should be reduced to encourage water conservation and the growing of less water demanding crops. This would make more water available for population increases. Of course, growers are reluctant to alter their well-established crop rotations and irrigation systems or make new efforts to market different products than those they have become accustomed to.

Critics point out that Spain has more than enough experience to learn from its mistakes. It began its first major river diversion scheme in the 1960s by linking the Tagus River in the west to the Segura River in the southeast – a transfer of 600 million cubic metres of water a year.

What happened? The cultivation of maize, which demands a lot of water, increased considerably. Increased irrigation meant that underground water was drawn upon more heavily. In dry years, there is even less irrigation water available than previously. Agricultural experts have supported the "anti" forces in their charge of considerable wastage.

Forty million hectares of Spain have a Mediterranean climate and, due to the fact that the rainy season and warm weather do not coincide, there is little vegetation. Planting such crops as maize, alfalfa, potatoes and beans, all of which depend upon a lot of water, has greatly aggravated the water shortages of the south. If water were not so highly subsidized, much more land could be profitably farmed without adversely affecting city dwellers.

These critics therefore urge environmentally responsible policies of desalinisation, sustainable development and balanced land use. They believe much can be done to conserve water in private households by repairing leaky pipes. Most people prefer a simple solution if water can be cheaply brought from somewhere else. One progressive proposal borrowed from agricultural policy in California would allow efficient farmers who save water to re-sell some of it to cities that need it. Because they make money from this, they can then grow crops that need less water, even if they are less profitable.

Spaniards from all parts of the country in every region will have to live with a need to provide more water and shape the NWP to take future generations into account. The new Socialist Prime Minister Rodríguez Zapatero promised in 2004 that the south will still get the water it needs, but he faces massive scepticism and doubts that any combination of "ecologically responsible" programmes such as massive and expensive desalination plants which use much energy and pollute will adequately fill the bill. ●

La Huerta Valenciana, Spain's most famous orchard

The famous region of the Valencian *Huerta* (orchard) is immortalized in the charming song Valencia, whose melodic lyrics portray the orchards of citrus, flowers, nut and fruit trees, cotton, rice and vegetables. The song is second in popularity only to *Que Viva España*. It sings of Valencia….

Tierra de las flores, la luz y del amor
donde las mujeres, todas tienen las rosas el color
en la Huerta Valenciana te dan el corazón

Land of flowers, light and love,
the women have the colour of roses and they give you
their heart in the Valencian orchard !
As the song puts it…
Al sentir como perfuma
en tus huertas el azahar
Quisiera en la huerta valenciana
mis amores encontrar
On feeling the orange blossom perfume
of your orchards,
I would like to find my lovers
in the Valencian *Huerta*.

245

The great market garden of *La Huerta (La hort*a) in the local *Valenciano* dialect, together with the nearby freshwater lagoon called L'Albufera, offer a scenic setting combining unique natural beauty, unmatched agricultural productivity and one of the chief wetland habitats for bird-life in Europe. Although many other areas in Spain have productive irrigated regions of fruit and vegetable cultivation called *huertas*, none can compare with the *Huerta Valenciana.*

This region grew to prominence as the top producing region of citrus fruit in Europe during the latter a part of the nineteenth century, through the use of spring water and irrigation ditches (*acequias*) and the later construction of rail links to the ports of Valencia, Castellón and the smaller harbours along Spain's Eastern Levantine Coast.

Historical development

During the period from 1860 to 1920, more than 40,000 hectares of the great *huerta* region were brought under irrigation, and the difference with the surrounding dry and rocky terrain is striking. The *huerta* is very much a product of human effort and not a result of geography or nature. It needs constant maintenance and is the result of careful management and scientific research. Spain's leap into the age of modern tourism owes much to the typical images of the Valencia region – citrus orchards and the perfumed smell of orange blossoms.

The area was inhabited as far back as pre-historic times, and both the Romans and the Visigoths cultivated cereals. The much more intensive cultivation techniques of irrigated agriculture using giant water-wheels (*norias*) were introduced by the Arabs, who also brought citrus fruit, rice, sugar cane, date palms and silk.

Testimony to the Arab presence is the prevalence of many place names with the Arabic prefix *Beni* ("sons of"). Following the Christian conquest launched from the kingdoms of Aragón and Cataluña under Jaime Primero 1232-1245, new irrigation canals were dug and dams constructed along the rivers of the Júcar and Alicante.

The tragic expulsion of the *Moriscos* (Muslim converts to Christianity who were still suspected by the Church for being disloyal in 1608-1611; see vignette 16) resulted in an immediate decline in agricultural production. The area remained economically depressed and under-populated for two centuries, until the large scale cultivation of citrus fruit, wheat and American maize in the late eighteenth century.

The construction of railways and the use of fertilizer completely transformed the economy of the region. The cultivation of the *chufa* nut took off spectacularly as a result of the popularity and national demand for the popular drink called *horchata* – a summer drink composed of water, lemon, cinnamon and the nut.

Crops and yields

Yields are very high in the *huerta*. The plots are generally worked by small scale owner-operators. Almost 80 percent of orchard owners have plots of less than one hectare, another 17 percent operate plots of up to five hectares and the remaining three percent are large owners who account for about one-quarter of the total cultivated land.

Many of these are absentee-operators who employ large-scale seasonal labour. Great dams now regulate the flow of water and each owner is assured a quota of irrigation water. Another distinctive part of the landscape are the *norias*, old water wheels that still dot the landscape.

It is possible to produce two or even three crops a year for some varieties of the very intensively cultivated crops, such as tomatoes. During the progress of the seasons, the appearance of the *huerta* changes in kaleidoscopic fashion. In winter, the grey-green-white of cauliflower, artichokes, potatoes, peanuts, onions, and cotton dominate. In the summer, the more striking colours of dark red, green and yellow representing tomatoes, green beans, peppers, lettuce, flowers, melons and wheat prevail. Harvests are staggered to stretch out labour needs throughout the year.

Since the 1950s, the rural work force has declined with continuing migration to the cities, resulting in increased mechanisation and the abandonment of many small farms. Average plot size has grown. The cultivation of almond trees has increased considerably at the expense of other crops due to the smaller demands these trees make on scarce labour and water. Many farmers also keep pigs, the most important variety of livestock holding.

The human face of *la huerta*

Compared to the *huerta*, much of the rest of central and southern Spain is quite different – rocky, mountainous and quite arid. A great deal of the irrigation water is now provided by carefully maintained canals and the run-off from the mountains is carefully guided to the fields and orchards.

Typical of much of the *huerta* region is the *barraca*, a house type also mentioned in the song. Its steeply sloping thatched roofs made of sewn reeds and other aquatic plants, and whitewashed adobe walls,

247

is distinctive to the Valencia region. The house is built in two sections, each with its own roof and separated by a central passageway. One side serves as the living area of the house and the other as a stable and kitchen. Bedrooms are on the top floor and there is usually a yard for chickens. Although the typical *barraca* is becoming increasingly modernized, many families are intent on keeping the traditional shape.

The region has progressed, due to new industrial techniques that spread beyond the *Huerta* to the rest of the Valencia region in the nineteenth century – textiles, shoes, ceramics, fruit processing, paper production, the chemical and iron and steel industries. The last two have been made possible by the use of modern dams generating hydroelectric power.

For anyone thinking of visiting Valencia, Spain's third largest city, it is certainly worthwhile planning a trip that does not bypass the *Huerta* and the Albufera lagoon. The lagoon is one of the most important areas covered by the "Ramsar Convention", an international agreement aimed at preserving the world's wetland and bird sanctuaries.

The last summit meeting of representatives from the countries that have signed this agreement was held in Valencia in 2002. Politicians of all political parties in the Valencia region are committed to policies that will preserve the ecological well-being and productivity of *La Huerta Valenciana,* as well as its tourist appeal. ●

Spain's weekly outdoor markets – *los mercadillos*

"**I**f it's Monday, this must be San Pedro." In the *Mar Menor* area of southeastern Spain where I live, the local residents have learned to think of the days of the week in terms of the weekly outdoor markets (*mercadillos*). Spanish dictionaries list *Mercado* as "market" – but here in Spain, *mercadillo* is the special term used to denote the weekly outdoor version, which has a special attraction for those who enjoy the more leisurely stroll and social atmosphere of shopping without the necessity of driving and looking for parking.

The *mercadillo* is a recognized form of retail business for a great variety of merchandise and is regulated by local municipal and national Spanish laws. It dates back to the Middle Ages when local peddlers (*buhoneros*) realized that they could perform an important function serving urban areas with agricultural produce by acting as an itinerant middleman. In this way, they did not need the large investment, inventory and overhead of a shop, and could reach a much larger clientele.

The older indoor markets that still exist in many Spanish towns are distinguished by their imposing architecture, often with classical pillars, and are open during the regular workweek. Some of them go back many centuries and originally incorporated warehouses and attracted wholesalers. This type of market existed for centuries in London in Covent Garden and Billingsgate or *Les Halles Centrales* in Paris. A few of these indoor markets also functioned as stock-markets for the trading of currencies, bonds, shares and commodities

Many of the indoor markets (*mercados*) in Spain are located in or very near the central Spanish plaza. In the past they became gathering places for prostitutes and pickpockets, who were eventually banished and sought new clients in the outdoor *mercadillos*.

Although merchants pay a fee to the municipality for the use of public space according to the area of their stalls, there is still a certain amount of unregistered or illegal goods, even though all merchants are required to prominently display their licences to carry on trade. This licence must be renewed every year and brings in considerable revenue to the municipalities. On a non-market day, you will be able to see areas marked off with numbers for the stalls.

All Spanish towns have local ordinances regulating what is called *venta ambulante* (travelling sales) that control retail activity outside permanent commercial establishments. In most towns, these markets are weekly, in a few they are once a fortnight. In a town like Cartagena (population 62,000), 650 mobile merchants are licensed to sell in the 18 weekly markets selling produce and an array of goods.

In addition there are a number of seasonal markets tied to specific festivals. During processions and parades at Christmas, Easter (*Semana Santa*) and *Carnaval,* some of these vendors become even more ambulant as they march together with the procession selling souvenirs and balloons.

Traditionally, the licences are granted under the following conditions:

· The licence is personal and"non-transferable to avoid sub-letting to third parties. This protects the public against fraud and inferior quality goods.

· The license must be produced for the police or municipal inspector on demand.

· The site of the stand must be cleared of all goods and items and left in excellent sanitary and hygienic conditions at the end of the market time allotted.

· Exceeding the number of violations permitted will result in the revocation of the merchant's licence.

Of course, an essential precondition for the efficient functioning of the weekly *mercadillos* is that the state of the roads, access roads and nearby parking facilities be adequate. The flow of traffic and necessary loading and unloading must take place at the appropriate times without interfering with normal business activities. In many towns, these pre-requirements necessitate major investment to bring the facilities up to   the required standard. Often, roads have to be re-paved to accommodate the necessary traffic.

Many of the stalls have been owned by the same family for generations. The *mercadillos* are for pedestrians. Once a week, you can see a procession of people towing their shopping carts during the morning hours in the towns holding a weekly *mercadillo*. An important non-economic feature is the opportunity for social contact, a chat with neighbours, enjoying the rainbow colours of seasonal fruit and vegetables, relaxing over a coffee break amidst the fragrance of newly plucked oranges, spices and herbs or fresh-cut flowers without the interruption of noisy cars.

Many of the vendors have a fixed clientele but are always on the lookout for new customers and enjoy advertising their wares. Often the vendors call customers by pet nicknames – the most popular for women being *guapa* (beautiful). I have even heard a client addressed as *gorda* (fatty), which suggests she must be a particularly good humoured and easy going lady.

I like to go to a vendor who sells fruit and vegetables and always calls me *moreno (*darky). Quite a few have a cute sense of humour and like to entertain by singing out a jingle or slogan. My favourite is the owner of a clothing stall in La Ribera who calls out to passers-by, advertising himself as the "Bargain Basement of El Corte Inglés".

It is much easier to recognize friends and spot typical characters among the vendors and customers in a *mercadillo* than in a supermarket, simply because people relate to each other in a more personal way. Perhaps this was also so because originally there was much bargaining or haggling over price.

The *mercadillos* are more prominent than in any other member state of the European Community, with the exception of Italy. It is estimated that there are 8,000 outdoor markets on a weekly or more infrequent basis in Spain, almost as many as the number of villages and towns.

Various studies indicate that more than one-quarter of the Spanish population regularly does part of their shopping in a weekly *mercadillo*, more in the south of the country (Andalucía and Extremadura) than in the north. One reason for this greater geographical concentration is the mild weather. Another reason is the local presence of a large gypsy (*gitano*) population, who own many stalls and work in the *mercadillos,* setting them up and taking them down.

The *mercadillos* annually account for almost 2,000 million Euros in sales! It is also generally true that most seasonal products are at least 20 percent cheaper in the *mercadillos* than in supermarkets and small shops, but are open only during morning hours until about one in the afternoon. It is usually housewives or the retired population who make up the great majority of shoppers.

Although all *mercadillos* sell fruit and vegetables, meat and cheese, nuts and dried beans, quite a few also sell clothes, shoes, household products and handicrafts, such as leather goods and pottery. Many have recently added tourist souvenirs! The sale of many processed durable goods has sometimes caused resentment among shop-owners in town, whose high overhead costs require them to sell at a much higher price. Even today it is a fact that prices for many products are cheaper in towns where there is a *mercadillo* that offer competition.

In the Mar Menor area of south-eastern Spain where I live, Monday is the day of the *mercadillo* in San Pedro del Pinatar, a short distance from the townhall. It is a very large one and has a huge parking area on site. On Tuesdays, the *mercadillo* of *Los Alcazares* (site of the Airforce Academy) offers more than 100 stands of merchandise along three very long streets. Tuesday is also the turn of *Mil Palmeras* in the afternoon. On Wednesday, La Ribera's *mercadillo* stretches out for more than a kilometre. On Thursday it is the turn of San Javier. On Saturdays, Torre Pacheco and Los Narejos, which offer products that are generally a bit cheaper due to their inland location in Murcia province.

Even Sunday is no longer a day of rest and, if you missed out during the week, you can go a bit further to Cabo de Palos and Campo Verde. A major urban area, Torrevieja, has a Friday market. Readers can map out their own weekly schedule of local *mercadillos* to keep handy if friends or relatives arrive and would like to tag along for the shopping.

A word to the wise is in order to escape "parking traps" and other risks. If you come by car, be sure to park it in a legal area with a clear sign indicating that parking is permitted. In some municipalities there are streets close by the *mercadillo* with no yellow lines or signs prohibiting parking but in fact are normal roads and not areas for parking. You will pay dearly if you have to recover your car after it has been towed away. It is also a good idea to keep an eye on your money and documents since another time-honoured "tradition" of the *mercadillos* is the pickpocket, who doesn't have to worry about store alarms.

Of course, the main enemy of the *mercadillos* is bad weather, which both reduces the flow of customers and makes the work of setting-up and dismantling the stalls more difficult. Most foreigners I know look forward to the *mercadillo* as a welcome break in routine – a chance to get out of the house, enjoy the local milieu and practise one's Spanish. ●

254

Festivals and Pageants

Carthaginians vs. Romans festival – and Cartagena's heritage

In much of Spain, the annual Moors and Christians festivals (see vignette 32), with their colourful, costumed processions, recall an important part of modern Spain's heritage that culminated in the victory over the Moors in 1492 in Granada and unified the country.

There is, however, another epic conflict that is immortalized and is no less important. It will be familiar to those readers who studied Latin. For those of you who did not, it was the distinguished elderly Roman Senator, Cato, who closed every speech of his in compulsive fashion with the words: *Ceterum censeo Carthginem esse delendam* ("Besides this, it is my belief that Carthage must be destroyed").

This bit of very ancient history is relived on the streets of Spain's south-eastern port city and naval base of Cartagena every September. Spain and much of Mediterranean Europe would be an entirely different place today had the outcome of the conflict between Romans and Carthaginians been different.

257

Cartagena bay provides a natural harbour, making it an excellent commercial and naval port. The city was founded by the Carthaginians in 227 BC and was called Carthago Nova (New Carthage) after their capital in Carthage – in what is today Tunisia. The Romans conquered it in 209 BC, defeating their African rival for domination of the Mediterranean.

The town played a decisive role in the great rivalry with Rome, and the outcome of the Punic Wars was to make Rome master of the entire Mediterranean. Cartagena pays tribute to these events and its own unique history. This is the reason for the festival sponsored by the city and the regional authorities in the province of Murcia.

What might have happened if the Carthaginians had won?

We are all aware of the great Roman contribution to our laws, languages, architecture, civil engineering and history – but the heritage left by Carthage is not well appreciated or even known. It survives today in two other centres of civilization with distinctive languages and cultures, Israel and Malta.

The Carthaginians were descendents of the Phoenicians, who set out from their coast in what is today Lebanon and established bases and colonies in Malta and later in Carthage. They reached Malta in the eighth century BC, and called the island *Malat*, meaning "safe harbour" in their language. There they built many temples and statues to their goddess Astarte.

The modern states of Israel and Malta can both claim a distinctive part of the Carthaginian heritage and a pre-Christian, pre-Roman identity. Carthaginian sailors, explorers, merchants, mining engineers and then settlers developed the southeastern coast of Spain. Their original language was Phoenician later transformed into Punic, a Semitic tongue similar to ancient Hebrew. Phoenician and later Carthaginian mariners crossed the Mediterranean and established colonies along both the Spanish and African coasts. By 500 BC, there existed a Hebrew-Phoenician-Punic speaking world extending from Lebanon to Malta, Sicily, Corsica, Sardinia, the Balearic Islands and Spain.

Cartagena was originally named *Qart-Hadasht* (New City). Speakers of modern Hebrew will instantly recognize the similarity of the name to its equivalent in their language – *Kiriya Hadasha*. The early Phoenicians were allies of the ancient Kings of Israel and Judah.

Today's Maltese look upon their island home as the remnant of a widespread maritime empire mentioned in the Bible, and a reminder of the alliance between King Hiram of Tyre and King Solomon. This viewpoint was utilised in the 1930s by Maltese nationalists, who sought to cultivate their distinctive language and combat Mussolini's expansionist plans that envisioned the annexation of the island.

The Maltese people, under British domination from Napoleonic times until the 1930s, struggled to create a sense of national unity, based on their language and history. Before that time, a small elitist minority of Italian speakers dominated Maltese society. All education, law, and government administration was in Italian, a language the great majority of the people did not speak or understand. Maltese was referred to as an embarrassing reminder of "Black Africa" and Malta's "dark past" when ruled by Muslims in the Middle Ages.

During their height of power in the eighth century BC, the Phoenician city-states of Tyre and Sidon, in alliance with ancient Israel, were linked by a Semitic civilization owing nothing to the Arabs or the Romans. All the small states mentioned in the Bible – the Canaanite tribes, Tyre and Sidon, Moab, Edom, Amon, Israel and Judea – shared a similar language and a common alphabet that was later borrowed and modified by the Greeks and then the Romans.

If Hannibal had been the victor in the Punic Wars against Rome, Spain and perhaps all of Western Europe might have inherited a Semitic language and civilization unrelated to the Arabs, Islam, the desert, the Greeks or the Romans. Hannibal is still considered a national hero in Malta, the site of his traditional birthplace. Had he been able to move a few more elephants across the Alps and defeat the Romans, Europe today might possibly have a Judaic heritage rather than Latin and Christian. The defeated Carthaginians maintained a hatred of the Romans, who came to be identified with Christianity and the Catholic Church in Rome.

The famous Israeli author, Amos Kenan, had this to say of the Carthaginian heritage in the Israeli newspaper *Yediot Ahronot* (18 June 1982):

Tyre and Sidon, and Jerusalem were two axes of one culture – the spiritual one of Jerusalem and the material one of Carthage. In those days, when the prophets of Israel tried to create a universal code of morality, the seamen of Tyre established their colonies. Why shouldn't we feel a sense of pride in our proximity to that ancient contemporary of ours who stamped his image on the area, gave the alphabet to the world and once sent his elephants across the Alps under Hannibal's leadership and momentarily brought mighty Rome itself in danger of destruction?

Rome and Carthage came to a temporary understanding. The Carthaginians retained control of the Iberian Peninsula south of the Ebro River and were able to exploit the rich mineral wealth (especially tin and silver) around the site of present day Cartagena. The Romans gradually expanded into northern Spain. A showdown was inevitable.

Spear and slingshot-throwing units recruited by Hannibal among the local Iberian population provided important additions to the Carthaginian army. Hannibal's father Hamilcar landed in Spain in 237 BC to extend Carthaginian influence throughout the peninsula – and took his young son, Hannibal, with him to learn the art of war. The Carthaginians quickly expanded their control over Spain through an effective combination of military force and diplomacy. Hamilcar died in 229 BC, but had already arranged the marriage of young Hannibal to a local Spanish princess, so as to win local support.

Hannibal trained his army well, utilizing his Spanish base, and marched against a number of small city-states allied with Rome, resulting in the renewed war. He crossed the Ebro River with his army to complete the conquest of the Iberian Peninsula, thus provoking Rome into a declaration of war (The Second Punic War 218-201 BC). The Romans' intention was to totally destroy Carthage and its base of power in Spain. Rome was vastly superior in numbers of troops and resources and could more easily absorb defeats.

Hannibal was a military genius and highly unconventional. He launched a bold attack into Italy from the north in 219 BC, beginning with his famous crossing of the Alps in winter with 37 elephants. The Gauls of the Po River valley flocked to join Hannibal's army, while Rome hurried to respond to the threat from northern Italy.

Hannibal soundly defeated three Roman armies (218-216 BC) and tried to provoke the southern Italian city-states to rebel. Eventually, Hannibal was out-manoeuvred by the Romans after waiting too long to follow up his great victory at Cannae in Italy near the east coast between Bari and Foggia,.where a Roman army was annihilated.

He eventually had to sue for peace after a series of reverses and the fall of Cartagena, in a surprise attack by the illustrious Publius Scipio. The Carthaginians agreed to surrender their fleet and remaining territories in Spain. This end to the Punic Wars is replayed in Cartagena each year. In spite of his failure, Hannibal is remembered as one of history's greatest generals, both for his brilliant victories and the ability to maintain a multinational, multilingual army for many years.

Very few local residents of Cartagena are aware of the real historical significance of their pageant and regard it only as an excuse to put on a local colourful alternative to the Moors vs. Christian festivals in other parts of Spain. The city stages a spectacle with costumes and weapons worthy of the most sophisticated Hollywood movie sets. The various units of the Carthaginian and Roman armies with their commanders are duplicated with complete accuracy.

The Carthaginians put on displays designed to represent the founding of the city, Hannibal's wedding, the disembarkation of troops from North Africa, and Hannibal's expedition to Italy. The Roman forces stage the declaration of war, the speeches of the Roman Senators, the taking of the city, and homage to their fallen soldiers. For us, it is a look at an unfamiliar but important event that shaped the history and culture of Spain, no less than the battles between the Christians and the Moors.

Cartagena's individuality and liberal traditions

Walking around Cartagena today, one may spot quite a few cars that bear an adhesive label with the letters "CAR". Yet the city is not the capital of an autonomous region. The auto sticker is part of a campaign to detach the city and region from the rest of Murcia province.

It may well be that the participation of the *Comunidad Autónoma de Murcia* (one of Spain's 17 autonomous regions) in the festival is due in part to a guilty conscience or an attempt to placate local Cartagena patriots. The citizens of Cartagena are proud of their non-conformist past. Following the overthrow of the corrupt regime of Queen Isabella II in 1868, the country was plunged into a period of chaos for six years, including civil war and the proclamation of the first Spanish Republic.

The city of Cartagena was among the first to join the anti-monarchist coalition in 1873 and welcomed the establishment of the first Spanish Republic (it lasted 11 months). The city, however, quickly proclaimed itself as an autonomous canton.

The First Spanish Republic was a radical departure from everything Spanish tradition had sanctioned in the past. It was recognized only by the United States, Switzerland, Costa Rica and Guatemala. Even though committed to federalist principles, it was resisted with suspicions in many parts of the country, following Cartagena's attempt to become independent.

Efforts of the central government to restore order in Cartagena and suppress the "canton" by sending naval units, were frustrated when the sailors joined the rebels. Following the fall of the first Republic, the newly restored monarchy considered the city a hotbed of radicalism. The experience with Republicanism, however, did not burn the fingers of the *Cartageneros*.

During the Civil War (1936-39), the city was the chief base of the Republican Navy. The leaders of the Republic fled from Cartagena in the closing days of the war and it was the last Republican bastion to fall to Franco, who then took a particularly hostile view of the city and made it suffer under his regime. Could it be that these events in recent history have their origins in the remote Carthaginian past – or is it perhaps a penchant for always joining the losing side? ●

The Moors and Christians – and *Las Tres Culturas* in Murcia

A nyone living in Spain for at least a year will be aware that nothing pleases the Spaniards more than a parade with music, costumes, fireworks, religious statuary or icons – and fun. Apparently, Spain's national day, Carnival, The Burial of the Sardine in Murcia, the *Fallas* in Valencia and the religious processions of *Semana Santa* weren't enough.

Some bright promoter in the 1970s got the idea that since so many municipalities in Castilla, Andalucía, Murcia and Valencia celebrated the "liberation" of their town from Muslim rule during the Reconquest, with a special service in the local church and a procession, it would be a more entertaining spectacle to recreate the events of the Re-conquest by dressing up as Moors and Christians and staging re-enactments of the victory over the enemy. The Reconquest with its battles of the Moors and Christians has been featured on many Spanish stamps.

By the mid-1970s, there was a visible and growing presence of Muslims in a number of Spanish cities and so the reenactment could be staged and portrayed as an act of "reconciliation". Nobody bothered to ask any Muslim representatives whether they agreed, but the idea caught on and spread like wildfire.

Anyone familiar with the Shriners Organization in the United States or has seen any number of Hollywood films such as *Sinbad the Sailor*, *The Arabian Nights* or *Aladdin and his Magic Lamp* will immediately recognize the costumes, music and weapons of *Moros y Cristianos*. This is also the name of a popular dish of black beans and rice, so it won immediate acceptance as if it were a traditional fiesta.

In its organization, it is very much like *Semana Santa* and the *cofradías* (see vignette 33). Local organizations compete with each other and provide a social framework for an entire year's activities and planning to put on an even more spectacular show than in previous years. Awards are given for all sorts of different categories of events.

Moreover, it is supposed to be "educational" and youngsters can participate in this event as "living history". Since it is celebrated on the feast day of a local saint to commemorate a historic victory over the Moors, it takes place throughout the year in different localities.

Research in the archives of various municipalities shows that between 1570 and 1609, the year in which most *Moriscos* were expelled (see vignette 16), fiestas and mock battles and a solemn mass at the local church, depicting the triumph of the Christian forces, were held in numerous Spanish cities to commemorate the victory over the traditional enemy.

This event appears to be less popular in the north of Spain, where Moorish rule was limited to less than two centuries. The enactments in Andalucía, Murcia, and Valencia include attacks by "Berber Pirates", an historical event that recalls the continued rivalry between Christians and Moors long after the expulsion of the last *Moriscos.*

Women participate equally and are festively dressed in the appropriate harem attire. A custom has developed that seems totally incongruous historically but is none the less appealing to the participating men (and a few women), whether they are playing Moors or Christians, and that is their demonstrative smoking of enormous, fine quality cigars while they march. Some modern accessories like eyeglasses and watches are allowed but, otherwise, everyone is expected to play their part. The event is, of course, a big tourist attraction and the municipalities help defray the cost of the spectacle.

The City of Murcia has even taken the trouble to sponsor an official poem that includes the message of "brotherhood" for their spectacle, lest they be suspected of offending anybody. The introductory stanzas are as follows:

BIENVENIDA A MOROS Y CRISTIANOS 2003
Moros y Cristianos, Murcianos y Murcianas,
Bienvenidos a la casa de todos, la que nunca cierra.
Nuestra Murcia, la más festera, símbolo de fuerza,
es ejemplo de convivencia, de lo noble de esta tierra.
Murcia vive hoy los desfiles,
Que en otro tiempo fueron guerra,
Pero nosotros sabemos cómo darles la vuelta
a los malos momentos, y transformarlos en juerga.
Y ahora convivimos, recordando viejas batallas
de Moros y Cristianos, al ritmo de marcha.
Igual hacemos cada año
Pólvora y arcabuces están revisados, los trajes engalanados ,
espadas en ristre, sables brillando, para pasear la hermosura
de cortejos de antaño.
 ¡¡¡Vivan Moros y Cristianos!!!
¡¡¡Viva la Fiesta!!!
¡¡¡Viva Murcia!!!

WELCOME TO THE MOORS AND CHRISTIANS 2003
Moors and Christians, Men and Women of Murcia,
Welcome to everyone's house, which is never closed.
Our Murcia, the most festive symbol of force,
an example of living together, of all that is noble in our land.
Murcia experiences today the parades
that meant war in another time,
but we know how to reverse the things of bad times
and turn them into a party.
And today we live together, remembering old battles
of Moors and Christians, to the rhythm of marches,
This we do every year.
The gunpowder and old muskets are checked,
The suits decorated, swords at the ready, sabres shining,
To spend a beautiful time of the court retinue of long ago,
Long Live the Moors!!!, Long Live the Christians!!!
Long Live the Festival!!!
Long Live Murcia!!!

265

The participating groups called *comparsas* are often dressed up and equipped to simulate marching armies and they are followed around by bands. Arabs, Berbers, Tuaregs, Afghans, Persians, all the diverse Muslim peoples and their exotic costumes, are portrayed preparing for war. Other groups of Andalusian bandits, Basque soldiers, an army from Asturias, and perhaps a band of Valencian peasants armed with farming implements are shown getting ready for war.

Martial music announces the coming epic battle. The people lining the streets admire and encourage the warriors. Soldiers march, sergeants wave at the crowds and horsemen show off their skills. The two armies march up and down to the delight of the crowds and the encouragement of the harem women.

In several cities, the battles are staged with mock gunpowder that fills the air along with the battle cries of the soldiers. Usually the Moors are allowed to win at first but then have to retreat and surrender before the victorious Christian armies under the banner of St. George.

Preparations for the fiesta go on for 12 months – so that the participants can show off for three or four days. Membership in the many Moorish or Christian armies is much more than a hobby. Members of the associations meet regularly throughout the year to socialize, raise funds, organize banquets, and plan the fiesta's many activities.

Las Tres Culturas festival in Murcia

A very different cultural event has been held in Murcia for the past ten years. It celebrates all three major cultures and religions of Medieval Spain in a more serious format of lectures, dance, music, song and cinema, and often involves the participation of the University of Murcia and the Murcia Symphonic Orchestra. The lectures and artistic performances are a much more serious way of stressing the positive aspects of the coexistence in Medieval Spain of three great civilizations.

The *Encyclopedia de Murcia* makes an important point that Murcia as an independent kingdom never experienced any pogroms – the violent attacks against Jews that were frequent elsewhere in the country. The 2004 programme of the *Festival de las Tres Culturas* below features a depth and variety of entertainment, culture and enlightenment:

Medieval Spanish poetry by Jews, Christians and Muslims.

The ballet and dramatic musical *Zhara, the Favorite of Al-Andalus* by Antonio Buero Vallejo.

The play *Via Dolorosa* by David Hare.

Deb – an Algerian Folk-Rock Group.

The Klezmatics from New York featuring *The Music of Wandering Jews*.
Sirma – Sepharadi Music for voice, percussion and strings.
De Trinitate – Gregorian Chants;
Spanish Medieval Ballads from the 15th and 16th centuries.
Jewish and Christian religious music performed by the Symphonic Orchestra of Murcia.
Gospel music concert by the Georgia Mass Choir.
Sheva – The Israeli Ambassadors of Peace performing Israeli Music.
Romances and songs of the 13th to the 16th centuries.
Al-Andalus with Tarik and Banzi – the traditional Union of West and East.
Rock & Raï of Today – The Transarabian Connection.
Carmen Linares singing *Popular y Jondo*" – a journey of the Arab-Sepharadi memory.
Barrio Chino group performing *Méditerra Nostra*, Sepharadi, Arab and Mediterranean melodies.
Paco Diez performing *The Judeo-Spanish Voice*.
Orfeo music and dance group, Miserere group performing *flamenco* music.
Dalila and Al-Qamar performing Eastern Dance.
The Wafir Quintet performing *Blue Nile.*
Aisha – Arab and Mediterranean music.

The following lectures were also part of the programme, open to the general public and a fitting tribute to the best in Spain's magnificent past and crossroads location:

Isabel the Catholic – perspectives on the 500th anniversary of her death.
Classical and Modern Judaism.
Murcia de Las Tres Culturas – historia, lengua y literatura.
The Three Cultures and Inter-Culturalism.
Culture, Religion and Politics in the Middle Ages.
The Co-existence of the Cultures.
The Roman Empire as a model of "Culture Without Boundaries".
The Meeting Place of the Believers.
Arabism, Aristotelism and Averröes the Dissident.
Murcia, Melting Pot of Cultures.

Hakitía – or the *judeo-español* of Morocco.
Sepharadi Literature in its traditional texts and voices from 1492 to our time."
Past, Present and Future of *Ladino* and the Judeo-Spanish Culture.

Murcia's *Premio de Novela*

In connection with the 2005 festival, a prize will be offered for the best novel on the theme *Murcia de Las Tres Culturas* – to be chosen by a jury consisting of well-known personalities from Spanish literary and cultural life. Authors of whatever nationality are entitled to enter. Their entries have to be written in Castilian Spanish and be between 200 and 500 pages. The subject has to be related to the relations between Christians, Jews and Muslims, but does not have to be set historically. ●

Semana Santa and Spain's National Day

There are many typical pictures and icons for which Spain is known around the world: bullfighting, *flamenco*, Franco, the running of the bulls, *Las Fallas*, and historical images of the Inquisition and the Catholic Church (see vignette 5). Being Spanish was traditionally equated to Catholicism. Of all the Catholic traditions that are celebrated throughout the year, none is more important than the Passion of Christ or Easter Week, which in Spanish is called *Semana Santa* or *Pascua*

There are three places that are considered to be the most important sites for the ritual celebration of Easter which hold the world's attention, these being Jerusalem, Rome and Spain – with special note to the southern region of Andalucía. Easter is present everywhere and there is no escaping it, whereas at Christmas time there were no special signs of the festivity in the streets until recently, due to the growing influence and presence of north Europeans with their Santa Clauses and Christmas trees. They, too, have now become part of the Spanish scene as well.

Both veteran professional and amateur novice Hispanophiles lament that much of the traditional Spain they remember or hoped to find has "gone with the wind" or, more precisely, faded under the mammoth impact of mass tourism, the influx of retirees from Northern Europe and the homogenizing tendencies of the European union with its standard currency, colossal shopping centres and modern motorways. One eloquent testimony to this are the words of author Paul Richardson in his satirical but poignant book *Our Lady of the Sewers and Other Adventures in Deep Spain*, (Abacus, London. 1999).

269

He cites dozens of folk traditions encompassing the "traditional rural life of Spain, the rich confluence of economy and technology and spirituality that had dominated country life for a thousand years" as about to expire. Yet anyone visiting Spain at other times of the year – or even passing by the countless pilgrims wending their way by foot or on bicycle to Santiago de Compostela – will be hard put to cite any comparable occasions or experiences that so vividly recall the medieval past and Spain's intensely Catholic faith as the processions of *Semana Santa*.

Semana Santa celebrations were already widely known in the seventeenth century for their unique blend of the spiritual, artistic, and emotionally compelling scenes of mass ecstasy. The blend of all five senses in the weeklong celebrations involve the whole human experience. Spaniards celebrate the Passion of Christ with the intensity of the secular madness of Carnival in Rio de Janeiro.

Almost every community in Spain puts on some form of Easter procession on Palm Sunday. They often include brotherhoods of "penitents", robed men in their white hoods and sheets, who so eerily resemble the Ku Klux Klan that even American Catholics wince at the sight. Some people carry large crosses and there are even rituals of self-flagellation.

The Passion Play is enacted in many towns and the brotherhoods known as *cofradías* carry aloft enormously heavy floats (*pasos*), bearing sculptures depicting scenes of the Passion, Christ and the Virgin Mary. The *costeros* who carry the floats, train for weeks in advance to march in the slow procession and get used to the enormous weight. For them, it is a kind of penitence.

The air is heavy with burnt wax from torches held aloft at night. The whole scene creates the impression of a resurgent Church anxious to reassert its hold over the masses – yet the love of such imagery, inculcated over a thousand years of tradition, coexists within a society, especially among the younger generation, that is becoming increasingly secular. This is perhaps the greatest irony or paradox in Spain today.

The centre of this activity is, without a doubt, Seville. It acts as a magnet drawing the religious and those from all over Spain who travel to the city. They are overcome with religious emotion in the expectation of a miracle. Emotions are high and singers in the crowd spontaneously burst into song (fragments called *saetas*) in praise of the Christ or the Virgin. Then, there are the curious and those who are there to experience the scene as much as New Year's eve in Trafalgar

Square or Times Square. The "main event" occurs at midnight on the Thursday and the early hours of Friday just before Good Friday.

The cofradías have an important social function. They consist of neighbourhood associations, clubs, and trade unions with links to the Church, and provide a forum for social identification and involvement. Many date their origin from the celebration of some miraculous event in the past, the identification with a patron saint calling upon local loyalties and the provision of an outlet for camaraderie and marking one's social status.

Spain's national day

Spain's National Day is also known as Columbus Day, *Día de la Hispanidad, Día de la Raza* and October Twelfth. Why does this annual holiday have so many names? It used to be celebrated in the United States as well, under the name Columbus Day, for what seemed the obvious reasons then (i.e. a generation ago), that "Columbus discovered America" and, in so doing, led the way for the arrival of the other European discoverers. (The first European settlement in North America is at Saint Augustine, Florida, founded by Ponce de León in 1513, more than 100 years before the first English colony at Plymouth, Massachusetts). The date also coincides with the fiesta day of the Virgin of Pilar, which marks the end of the bullfighting year.

What is less known is why this date has acquired such a profound significance in Spain and all of the Spanish speaking countries of Latin America. In Spain, the date, as everywhere, represents the anniversary of the arrival of the three small Spanish vessels of Columbus's expedition in 1492. This event opened an entirely new dimension in world affairs for mankind by forming a universal perspective to the former political, economic and cultural frameworks that prevailed in the world before that date.

It also signifies the leading role of Spain as the *Madre Patria* (Mother Homeland) of the Spanish speaking community of nations – with their different cultures and characteristics but who share the Spanish language, which is now certain to overtake and out-distance English as the leading language in the world (after Chinese) in terms of native speakers, who now number more than 400 million people.

Spaniards and all Latin Americans alike are proud of this past and cooperate in promoting their common heritage. For several centuries, this community of Spanish speakers also included the Philippines at a time when the Pacific was almost "a Spanish Sea." It is for these reasons that many geographical names like Tampa, Guadalcanal, the Torres Straights, the Philippines (*Filipinas*) and Carolines (*Carolinas*), San Diego, San Francisco and Los Angeles, are relics of a not-so-distant past. Spaniards and other Spanish speakers refer to this sense of community as *Hispanidad* (Spanishness) and to a sense of being part of the same family, hence the term *Dia de la Raza*, although certainly not correct if taken literally. The community of Spanish nations consists of people of all races.

Since 1965, in the United States the celebration of the holiday has become a major cultural and political event. Thousands of New Yorkers of Spanish and Hispanic origin march down New York's Fifth Avenue, and any politician considering local or national office appearing at the parade has certainly brushed up on his or her Spanish to take advantage of the opportunity to reach millions of voters across the country.

In Spain, the National Day has its main focus in Madrid, where a grand military parade takes place. It is attended by the King and royal family, members of the government and outstanding personalities in the cultural life of the country, who appear on the rostrum to salute the passing troops. It is truly impressive, with many of the diverse units marching in their own very distinctive styles, utilising a quick-paced gait and exaggerated arm-swings.

During Franco's time, the occasion of Spain's National Day was one of fervent patriotism, homage to the flag, rousing speeches with references to Spain's glorious imperial past, an impressive military display and not a whimper or hint of opposition to the regime or criticism of its policies. Times have indeed changed.

Over the past decade, there have been occasional demonstrations in the Basque country and in Cataluña, involving indignities to the flag, foreign guests or political figures representing the government. These have resulted in arrests to satisfy a segment of nationalist opinion. In reaction, proposals have been introduced by self-styled "anti-Fascist" organizations to refrain from celebrating the Twelfth of October in several Basque and Catalan areas.

In October 2003, all the flags of the "Coalition" allies in Iraq were carried past an official reviewing stand during the usual military parade through Madrid. As the American flag went past, King Juan Carlos and Jose Maria Aznar, the conservative pro-American prime minister, government ministers, opposition leaders, and the assembled guests rose and stood to attention, but the leader of the opposition at the time, and Spain's current Prime Minister, the Socialist politician Jose Luis Rodríguez Zapatero, remained seated. He will indeed be in the "hot seat" on future Twelfth of October celebrations as the great majority of Spaniards still take this holiday very seriously, and are likely to be deeply offended by any move to water down its traditional patriotic content. ●

Las Fallas in Valencia and the "Buried Sardine" in Murcia

Much of the Middle Ages survives in Spain. There is no doubt of this for anyone arriving in the period from Carnival to Easter, when what used to be the 40-day period of Lent in the Catholic calendar occurs. This was when the faithful abstained from eating meat.

There are festivals and parades that overflow with an irrepressible gaiety and exuberance. It makes you aware that even in the "dark" Middle Ages or during the grim and puritanical regime of General Franco, most Spaniards still were able to create for themselves a festival of light, colour, food and celebration.

Carnival kicks off the season that witnesses the approach of spring. In Valencia on the Levantine coast and in nearby inland Murcia, there is a celebration of gaiety, energy and fireworks which marks the coming of Easter that should not be missed. Valencia's major annual festival, held from 13 to 19 March, is known as *Las Fallas* and is an unmatched combination of the beauties of floral arrangements in a rainbow of colour with the power and energy of fire.

The *fallas* are papier-mache "floats", made with cardboard, wood and wax and decorated with enormous floral arrangements, which the *Valencianos* build in the streets and burn on the night of the feast of St. Joseph. These figures, also called *ninots* in the local dialect, allude to events and personalities of the day.

Moreover, they give their creators an enormous opportunity for the employment of their skill and imagination to ridicule the famous, wealthy, and powerful in the world of politics, sports, society and the arts. The half satirical, half symbolical *ninots* are created in a style somewhere between Disneyworld and Hollywood.

Like the floats in *Mardis Gras*, these enormous figures demand a whole year's work for hundreds of people and are burnt to the ground on a single night (19 March) in a bonfire of towering flames. Each one is a temple devoted to this colossal festival of fire. It is as if pyromaniacs and artists were allowed to combine their passions in a night of a fiery orgy.

Valencianos and their visitors often act as both spectators and participants and the event has become a major tourist attraction. This was not the original intention, but rather something very flamboyant that has no rival anywhere. It presents a spectacle that turns this city into a theatre during the festival.

The primeval power of fire

When man mastered the use of fire, he gained an enormous power over animals, long before the acquisition of human speech. It is as if this festival was conceived to give licence to one of the strongest human impulses that had been constrained for ages. Who has not been semi-hypnotized by staring into the flickering, dancing flames of a bonfire? The same urge found expression throughout much of Northern Europe and especially Scandinavia to celebrate the arrival of mid-summer. There, this festive season is celebrated by huge bonfires and the burning of symbolic witches.

From the first mastery of fire, man has used it to overcome the darkness of night, cook food, defend himself from wild beasts, and communicate. Of course, these impulses had to be approved by the Church, and a connection was invented to relate the homage due to various saints – namely St. Joseph, St. John and St. Anthony – by the burning of huge bonfires in their honour.

There is practically no documentary evidence as to the origin of the *Fallas*. The best evidence seems to date the origin of the festival to sometime during the Middle Ages in Spain, and connect it with the guilds of artisans, particularly carpenters who used to light bonfires in honour of their saint, St. Joseph. They would burn a pole on which they had kept their lamp during the winter, and deposited their wood-shavings there.

Competition between different workshops and guilds added an element of interest – who could stage the biggest bonfire and burn the most interesting effigy? The added motivation to entertain their neighbours and friends made the holiday an expression of joy in an otherwise cruel and dull world.

There is another theory that the bonfires were definitely pagan in origin and were appropriated by Christianity and the Church, as was Christmas – the midwinter solstice was in order to capture the loyalties of converts to Christianity. By adding images of Mohammed and the Moors to the bonfire, the Church fathers hit on a brilliant idea to convert the centuries-long crusade to win back Spain from the infidel Moors into the theme of a popular pageant.

The earliest documentary evidence of the Valencian *Fallas* as an annual festival dates from the middle of the eighteenth century. The festival is divided into no less than seven stages. Public enthusiasm is encouraged by competitions for various Queens of the *Fallas,* just as in Carnival, and people put on their finest and traditional garb. Following the election of the Queens, there is the "Exaltation" with the offering of flowers. In this ceremony, the Valencian townsfolk and the various institutions pay homage to the Queens, who receive their ceremonial sashes and jewels of office.

As they and their entourage approach the stage, baskets of flowers are presented in homage by local organizations and a chairman, representing the world of culture, who makes a poetic speech to all those present. "The Offering of Flowers to Our Lady of the Forsaken" is the ceremony for which the people of the town turn out in their best dress. They pay homage to their patron saint by offering thousands of bouquets of flowers. For 24 hours, the Virgin receives her tribute. The amount of flowers decorating the principal central square of Valencia is estimated at approximately 30 tons!

On 15 March, the *fallas* are assembled in the squares and streets of Valencia. Hundreds of them invade the city. On this day the carpenters, painters, sculptors, designers, etc., get the opportunity to show off their skills. The favourite satirical targets of the *fallero* masters are effigies representing notable Spanish politicians and other renowned personalities.

The *Crema* is the culmination of the *Fallas,* but for many it is also the saddest moment. The *fallas* are lit on the night of March 19. The award-winning *fallas* are lit last. Valencia goes up in flames at about midnight (with the fire department standing by). It is something not to be missed. But if you do miss it, there is a similar festival at mid-summer in Valencia featuring floats, bonfires and fireworks.

The "Burial of the Sardine" in Murcia

A less dramatic and slightly more restrained event characterizes the approach of spring, the Lent season in Murcia. Its origin can be found in the middle of the nineteenth century when a group of students hit on the idea of staging a symbolic "burial of the sardine" to represent the end of the period of abstinence and self-denial associated with Lent.

It was originally based on an old custom to bury the rib-cage of a pig to symbolize the 40 days of Lent. Some scholars believe it goes back further to an old fertility rite to promote an abundance of fish. Carnival in the Latin tradition is a time of liberty to engage in all sorts of activities that are normally forbidden, and to get drunk, poke fun and ridicule authority and irreverently reverse roles.

Although this might seem to refer to a Christian origin, a closer look reveals the affinity of the originators for Classical and pagan symbols. The floats are staged by associations as in the New Orleans *Mardis Gras.* They are known as *grupos sardineras,* whose names come from Greek and Roman Mythology and the Olympic Gods: Apollo, Saturn, Eros, Neptune and Morpheus. These are all male gods and so the leaders of each association participating in the festival are men, usually the most wealthy and prominent in local society.

Their wives belong to female groups and spend a week walking around the city with their typical dress and giving away gifts to infants, young children, teenagers and women. The "King" (named the "Big Sardine") of the parade receives a sardine from a particular village chosen for this honour each year.

The main parade is on the last day of the event. It consists of many farcical elements and skits with men masquerading in "drag" and wigs as widows of the Sardine. They must confess their carnal sins to a priest who accompanies them in the parade. This seems quite sacrilegious but there is more to come.

The Devil appears with the intention of stopping the Sardine on his way to be buried in the river running through the town, all to the accompaniment of music to *merengue* rhythms and raucous merrymaking. He is warded off by the "widows" using palms to frighten him and defend their feminine charms. The festival in somewhat similar form was brought to the Canary Islands and Puerto Rico, but is still considered be the exclusive hallmark of Murcia. ●

ANNEX
The Four "Official Spanish Languages" and English translations of Official EU text

English
Recently, The Spanish authorities have made the design of the state portrait on Spanish euros. The coins of 1 and 2 euros will bear the bust of the King, Juan Carlo I; on the 10, 20 and 50 centimo coins, a bust of Cervantes will appear; and on the 1 2 and 5 centimo coins, the portrait of the Cathedral of Santiago de Compostela will appear. Moreover, all the coins will bear the name of the state written solely in Castillian.

Castilian
Recientemente, las autoridades españolas han dado a conocer el diseño de la cara estatal de los euros españoles. Las monedas de 1 y 2 euros llevarán el busto del rey Juan Carlos I; en las monedas de 10, 20 y 50 centimos aparecerá el busto de Cervantes; y en las monedas de 1, 2 y 5 cents figurará la portada de la catedral de Santiago de Compostela. Además, todas las monedas llevarán el nombre del estado escrito únicamente en castellano.

Catalan
Recentment, les autoritats espanyoles han donat a conèixer el disseny de la cara estatal dels euros espanyols. Les monedes d'1 i 2 euros portaran el bust del rei Joan Carles I; a les monedes de 10, 20 i 50 cents hi haurà el bust de Cervantes; i a les monedes d'1, 2 i 5 cents hi figurarà la portalada de la catedral de Santiago de Compostel·la. A més, totes les monedes portaran el nom de l'estat escrit únicament en castellà.

Galician
Recentemente, as autoridades españolas deron a coñece-lo deseño da cara estatal dos euros españois. As moedas de 1 e de 2 euros levarán a cara do rei Xoán Carlos I; nas moedas de 10, 20 e 50 céntimos aparecerá a cara de Cervantes; e nas moedas de 1, 2 e 5 céntimos figurará a fachada da catedral de Santiago de Compostela. Ademais, tódalas moedas levarán o nome do Estado escrito soamente en castelán.

Basque (Euskera)
Duela gutxi, Espainiako agintariek ezagutzera eman dute euro espainolen alde estatala. 1 eta 2 euroko txanponek Juan Carlos I.a erregearen bustoa eramango dute; 10, 20 eta 50 zentimoko txanponetan Cervantes-en bustoa agertuko da; eta 1, 2 eta 5 zentimokoetan, berriz, Santiagoko katedralaren irudia joango da. Gainera, txanpon guztiek estatuaren izena gaztelaniaz soilik idatzia eramango dute.

For a free catalogue
of all our books on Spain
contact:
Santana Books,
Apartado 422,
29640 Fuengirola (Málaga).
Phone 952 485 838.
Fax 952 485 367.
Email: sales@santanabooks.com
www.santanabooks.com

UK Representatives
Aldington Books Ltd.,
Unit 3(b) Frith Business Centre,
Frith Road, Aldington,
Ashford, Kent TN25 7HJ.
Tel: 01233 720 123. Fax: 01233 721 272
E-mail: sales@aldingtonbooks.co.uk
www.aldingtonbooks.co.uk